WHITE HOUSE DIARY

White House Diary.

White House Diary

BY HENRIETTA NESBITT

F. D. R.'s Housekeeper

"There will be five thousand to tea . . ."

"The President of Iceland will have breakfast at nine in his room."

These are the sort of messages Mrs. Henrietta Nesbitt took in stride during her eleven years in the White House—one of the largest, most complicated, and most fascinating households in America. Her story is a succession of intimate anecdotes of the great and the near-great—Alexander Woollcott, Paderewski, the King and Queen of England, José Iturbi, Winston Churchill, and of course the Roosevelt family itself. It is also a salty and sprightly record of the world's most demanding job of housekeeping.

White House Diary

Chapter One

It was my first view of the White House. For that matter, I'd never been in Washington before. Dad and I—Dad being my husband, Henry F. Nesbitt—got up early the morning before the inauguration and went through the streets straight to the presidential mansion, as if we'd lived in the capital all our lives. This was Mr. Roosevelt's first inaugural, in March 1933.

We went up to the White House and stood looking through the northwest gate, and I felt like the old woman in the ditty, not certain if it were I, or somebody else. To tell the truth I was scared half to death. It was the biggest home I had ever seen.

"Like a big wedding cake," I said to Dad. "The kind with the white mountain frosting."

We walked all around, peeking through the eight gateways and the iron fence to the green lawns and the flower beds, all planted new for the new president, and across the semicircular drive to the big beautiful house with the tall-pillared porte-cochere. Even the trees looked important, with their names set in the bark, like trees in a park.

I didn't know these very trees had been singed when the British soldiers set fire to the White House, in 1812, that Dolly Madison and her James led cotillions under the elms, and that the big magnolias, starting to bud even this early in the spring, were planted by President Jackson because he

1

was homesick for his Tennessee. All the Presidents, it seems, planted trees to add to the beauty of the grounds.

But I didn't learn these facts until later, along with a lot of other patter I memorized to reel off to guests in the White House, such as commenting on the classic architecture and the historic pieces, and the fact that the cornerstone was laid in 1792 and President Washington hadn't been there to see it put down. I never did find out why.

All I knew this morning was that the White House had me awed, and I didn't know how I'd ever get up enough courage to walk in. But we were going to do just that, Dad and I, right after the ceremonies that had the whole city, and the country itself for that matter, all stirred up. We were going through those gates and into the White House as if we belonged there.

I said to Dad, not to show how nervous I was, "It must take a sight of gardeners to keep all the leaves raked up and this place looking right."

Of course I wasn't thinking much of the garden, because it wasn't my business. The White House was my affair. I was trying to count all the windows, but I gave up somewhere around ninety. How were we going to keep them all clean!

But those windows would have to shine. The handsome, dignified building was the most important in the United States, and that meant in the world. As soon as the Roosevelts moved in, I'd have the care of it.

"Care of the White House." I didn't know it that morning, but this would be my job and my address for the next thirteen years. Through three Roosevelt administrations I would have personal charge of the house at 1600 Pennsylvania Avenue, Washington, D.C.

But we didn't know it would be that long, back in '33. So I just hung onto Dad's arm and spoke as pertly as I could.

"Pshaw, it's only four years. I can stand anything for four years." I guess the Roosevelts, back where we'd left them in the Mayflower Hotel getting ready for the inaugural, had the same idea then.

The White House would be a big responsibility, but Mrs. Roosevelt had said I could do it, so I knew I could. Already the newspapers had thought up a lot of fancy titles for me, along with all the publicity about the new President. "Mrs. Nesbitt—first housekeeper of the land." "Our nation's first housekeeper." "The little lady who rules the President." "Keeper of the White House."

The papers had started calling me all these things, and we hadn't even moved in.

I didn't know a soul in Washington outside of Dad and the Roosevelts. I didn't have another friend in the place. I was small-town and a homebody, and up to this time I'd been content in both categories. Now I was being thrust through the White House doors into a new life and a first job, and in a few days I was going to celebrate a birthday in that big mansion. I'd be fifty-nine years old.

I'd start on my White House job pushing sixty, and through those sixties—the sunset years women call them who have the chance to sit down and rest—I was going to work harder and shoulder more responsibility than ever in my life before. I wasn't going to have the chance to sit down. And it would be harder for me than for women who had always worked, because I'd be trying, not only to keep up with the Roosevelts, but to keep a jump ahead of them, for the next thirteen years.

Dad couldn't admire the White House enough.

"They say an Irishman designed it," he said, with the pride of a man born in Dublin.

I laughed and felt better. I was glad Mrs. Roosevelt had asked us both, bless her, when she asked me to be their housekeeper in the White House. "There'll be work enough for you both," she had said, in that wonderful tactful way of hers, as if she hadn't guessed how blue Dad had been, being out on his luck for so long. I was glad he was with me and Dad was as grateful about things as I was.

I like remembering what an adventure Washington was for us, and how happy we were.

Because, if I was scared to my bones that March morning it was for reasons beyond this new job and its responsibilities. I was afraid of everything that was happening in the America that was the only country I knew. It was the start of the panic and the depression years, and everyone we knew seemed to be out of work and everything we'd had faith in seemed to be crumbling away. Something terrible was happening inside the land in which I had been born. A woman like myself was reared in a home, grew to love and tend that home, and left it for another where her married days were spent and her sons and daughters were reared. No matter how little there was in it, for women of my generation there was always the home.

But now all over the country roofs were being snatched from over women's heads, and their men couldn't prevent it. Children weren't getting enough to eat. Nothing was going in the old, narrow, certain ways we had known. At first I had worried for Dad and myself because we were getting along, but since '29 my fears had been for those who were young and strong, and that's the worst of all fears, when young folks don't know what they can do, or who they can trust, or where to turn. We older folks expect to have qualms, but there is something terribly wrong when young people are afraid.

Millions were out of jobs this spring. Breadlines were inching along the wet sidewalks of all America's cities and people who had been rich and held their heads high were selling apples at five cents apiece in the streets. It seemed to me millions of frightened faces were turned toward this big white mansion and the man who would enter it tomorrow as the thirty-third President of the United States.

Tomorrow I'd have to stop thinking of him as Franklin Delano Roosevelt, our neighbor at Hyde Park, and call him

4

"Mr. President." Tomorrow he'd move into this big place with his big lively family, and I'd trail along in my own small fashion to see that he was well cared for so he could attend to the big job of straightening us all out. He was going to have more on his mind than any one human should be asked to bear. He needed an easy-running house and well-chosen meals. I would be a very small cog in the complicated mechanism required to turn such an institution as the big white house behind the tall gates, but to the best of my ability I'd help oil the wheels.

So I told Dad: "It's just keeping house, and I've kept house all my life. Only, instead of seeing that you and the boys are cared for, I'll have the President and his family to worry about. You'll see how simple it will be. I've been keeping house for six. Now I'll just multiply by ten, and keep house for sixty!"

Little did I know of the chits and memoranda that would pour on my shrinking head, signed with Mrs. Roosevelt's scrawled signature.

"Mrs. Nesbitt: There will be five thousand to tea—six thousand—seven thousand——"

If I'd known, back in '33, how it was going to turn out, I'd never have had the courage to go through those doors as housekeeper of the White House.

As I say, I've kept house all my life. It's as natural to me as breathing. I come of stock whose men are proud of their husbandry and the women take pride in housewifery. My people were well to do back in Germany, but the revolution of 1848 left them with a hankering for democracy they felt could be satisfied only in a newer land. They wanted freedom more than comfort, so they sold their nice home and came to America, bringing along a couple of other families who wanted to come but couldn't afford the passage.

Right away my family were taken in by fleecers. There

5

were a lot of Yankee sharpers operating in those days, selling malaria land in Illinois and Minnesota to emigrants who didn't know any better than to buy sight unseen, thinking everyone in America was honest. Well, the emigrants recovered from the blow and turned the poor soil into fine American farmland.

That was frontier in Minnesota where I was born. I can remember how cold the winters used to be in Duluth, and I recall watching the Indians trudging over the ice on the lake, on snowshoes and with dogsleds, to do their trading in the stores. Once when I was a little girl my grandmother took me to spend the day in a house where an old lady sat by the fireplace spinning yarn on a wheel.

But I don't remember learning how to cook.

As soon as I could toddle I was following Mother around the kitchen, mixing the bits of dough and batter she gave me, and watching them bake in the oven of her big wood-burning range. "Dabbling," she called my efforts. They say a kitchen is the heart of a home, but I think it can be the soul. Just the same, I don't believe in spending the whole day in it. I try sidestepping the long methods and save time and effort where I can. Overdoing is being overfussy. A house that is kept too tidy stops being a home.

I've seen young married women make hard work of housekeeping. Some even refuse to learn how to cook. Spoils their figures, they say. Well, I've cooked all my life and I don't think it hurt my figure any. Seems to me a smart girl enters marriage with the job of learning to cook behind her, so she can concentrate on having a happy marriage. And why not learn? Even if she never has to do her own work, it's good for a woman to know how, otherwise she is at the mercy of her household and can't teach her cook or improve her cook's talents with the extra touches that make up an enjoyable home.

I remember making the cake for my eleventh birthday—

6

chocolate, I think it was—and I brought up both my boys to help around the house, and they're big, strapping fellows. We were outdoor people who liked fishing and skating and camping, and outdoor cookery was important in our lives and both the boys learned.

Some women sniff at housewifery, but it's something to fall back on when their other arts and sciences fail. My knowing how to keep house pulled us through the depression and into the White House. At a smart salary, let me add!

As for excitement and glamor, well, there aren't many career women who have found themselves chatting away with a Queen of England. I've known women who left their homes to find romance in travel, but they never met up with the folks I have. They never bumped into Mr. Churchill as he was hurrying into the map rooms with plans to shake the world, or gone shopping for special tidbits for Madame Chiang Kai-chek.

If I sound pretty smug, perhaps it is because I've been happy, and I guess happy people are always a little smug. Looking back, I can see that no matter how much Dad and I had to pull against, we had a happy marriage. It wasn't an easy one, because there were hard work and hard luck all the way, with never quite enough to go around comfortably and leave a little trimming for safety.

Dad was a good-hearted, good-looking, good-natured Irishman and everyone called him "Harry," or "the Colonel," or "the Governor," because of his gallant airs. Through no fault of his, three of the firms he worked for failed. The first was the insurance business he was with in Duluth when we married and set up housekeeping in a small apartment. Then he became salesman for a whaling industry, but whale meat didn't go over. Finally he worked for a cooperage concern in Poughkeepsie, New York and, that shut down and left us stranded.

Meantime Buck and Garven had been born—Buck's real

7

name is Trevanion Nesbitt and he says he may forgive me for it sometime—and I had to do something to help out. As a young girl I'd worked after a fashion. My father had a drugstore in Duluth, with real drugs, let me tell you, that he took pride in selling. When he became ill I went into his office and took over the books, and later I helped keep the books in my brother-in-law's insurance office. Another time I started a Woman's Exchange in Springfield, Massachusetts. Otherwise, I'd never worked outside my own home.

For a while I helped by managing a show place sort of farm at Staatsburg on the Hudson, a few miles above Hyde Park, that belonged to my sister, Mrs. William Schupp. There were two hundred acres for the boys to run wild in, and I looked after the place for four years and then stayed on three more until it was sold, after my sister's death. This gave Buck and Garven wonderful boyhoods to look back to, and I have always been grateful for those years on the farm.

After it was sold we went to Hyde Park to live. This was about 1927. The depression hadn't started for the rest of the United States but it was heading for the Nesbitts. But a person can only do their best, and Dad did his with the whale meat until the business buckled under and left us high and dry in Hyde Park with neither of us getting any younger.

I loved Hyde Park just the same. The neighbors were all friendly, and across the way from us was Mrs. Belle Saltford, whose husband was a florist in Poughkeepsie. We started out as neighbors and ended as friends.

Mrs. Saltford was public-minded and thought I should be. I had spent my life tending to the house and family affairs, and then, for the past seven years, I had been isolated on the farm. I didn't have much idea of what was going on inside the United States, but I suspicioned it was trouble.

My public-mindedness started when I loaned out my chairs. They were heavy mission oak dining-room chairs and could stand a lot of sitting, and people began to borrow them

8

for public meetings in Hyde Park and even in Staatsburg, six miles away: I was tickled when I heard that one of the neighbors, a Mr. Franklin D. Roosevelt, who was running for governor, liked my chairs because he couldn't walk and liked a strong chair he could depend on. I didn't meet him, but I kept on loaning the chairs.

One afternoon Mrs. Saltford asked me over to her house for a neighborhood get-together. It turned out to be the start of the League of Women Voters, non-partisan, of Hyde Park. There were a lot of women sitting around, some I knew and one I didn't know. She was a tall woman with a warm way of meeting folks and the kindest face I'd ever seen. I was drawn to her right away, and while we women had our tea and sandwiches and talked politics, mostly I talked to Mrs. Roosevelt.

"I know about your husband," I told her; "he's the one who likes my chairs."

She told me they lived in a large old house on the Hudson River, that he had been in the Assembly and had been stricken with paralysis, and that she had become interested in politics for his sake. I found it easy to talk with her. Eleanor Roosevelt takes as well as gives, and not many women do. We didn't get a chance to talk much, for the meeting began and the branch of Women Voters began organizing and making up officers, and was I surprised when they elected me to an office, treasurer, I think it was! It was the first office I'd ever held, and I was pleased as punch but a little nervous, because I wasn't certain what politics were, let alone doing anything about them.

But Mrs. Roosevelt said I'd do fine, and looked so sure of it that I stopped worrying and thanked everybody, and I don't remember another word she or anyone else said that day.

After that I saw a lot of her. She took to dropping in pretty nearly every time she passed the little house Dad and I had rented in Hyde Park. As women, we had a lot in common,

9

with children grown and grandchildren coming or hoped for. Most of hers were still away in school, and I don't think she liked that very much, but that was the way children of rich families were brought up, and I've been grateful that mine haven't been given so much and were brought up, so to speak, under my thumb. The boys claim it was a firm thumb, but then they're always teasing about something or other. "Henrietta" they call me, instead of "Mother." No respect for gray hairs, I tell them, but I've never known better sons nor more loving, and if I was strict in spots, it hasn't hurt them or taken the sass out of them. But at this time they were both trying to get ahead of the gathering depression, along with thousands of other young Americans.

Mrs. Roosevelt and I always found a lot to talk about.

We even went to the same church—Episcopalian. She had a lot of irons in the fire apart from wanting her husband to be governor of New York State. She was interested in so many things, she got me interested. We worked together in the League of Affairs and went to Albany with the convention of Women Voters, and then she wanted me to start a Woman's Exchange in Poughkeepsie in connection with Val-Kil, the factory she ran with her friends Miss Dickerman and Nancy Cook, where they made good furniture and pewter work and such. Before we got it started, all sorts of things began happening to Mr. Roosevelt, so the plan fell through But she and I had talked a lot about the Exchange, and I'd told her about the one I'd begun, and how disgusted I had been with the queer messes women offered for sale at such places, and wondered why the cooking standards of some American women were so low.

We talked a lot about cooking, and in a way it was a loaf of bread that sent me to the White House with the Roosevelts.

There is nothing on earth equal to the smell of fresh bread. When I was a little girl the finest treat my mother could give me was a slab of it, crusty, and fresh-baked, smothered over with butter and honey. Since then I've liked making my own, and in Hyde Park I started experimenting with the more nourishing grinds. The son of a friend of mine who had come back from World War I with stomach trouble was told he couldn't eat white bread. I don't approve of white flour, anyway, so I sent away for some specially ground whole-wheat flour and made up a batch for the young man. I gave a loaf to Mrs. Saltford and she gave some to her friend Mrs. Lent, and she gave some to Mrs. Roosevelt.

That's the way things get passed around among neighbors at places like Hyde Park.

Mrs. Roosevelt came right over. She was all excited about the new bread.

"It's given me an idea, Mrs. Nesbitt," she said. "Ever since my husband started running for governor we've had a steady flow of visitors at Hyde Park, and we can't keep up with the baking. Would you mind making up some of the extras for us?"

Would I mind! I'd known for some time something drastic had to be done, but I hadn't known what to do, until she told me. Baking was right up my alley. Best of all, I could do it at home, in my own kitchen. I dug up all the old family recipes and put them to work.

My mother had taught me all her baking tricks. She had come from near Vienna, and her excellent pastry work was all in the Viennese tradition. Bustling around, baking for the Hyde Park table, I kept thinking about Mother and the fun we'd had making apple strudel together on the long extension table back home. We'd flour the tablecloth and then Mother and I on either side would stretch and stretch, until the pastry was like tissue, and then we'd stretch some more. There was nothing in the dough but flour and water, and it was wonderful how much give it had. When it was paper-fine and covered the table, we'd sprinkle it over with sliced apples, bread

11

crumbs fried in butter, sugar, cream, and more butter, bake it brown, and serve it with plain cream, and that's real Hungarian strudel.

My mother, working over the long pastry, could never have guessed she was teaching me a trade that was to help me out when I was years older than she was then.

All the coffeecakes and pies I began baking for Mrs. Roosevelt came from my mother's side—the German side.

I'd learned my piecrust from Mother and worked at it until it suited my own taste. It was either too short or not short enough until I learned to use the puff paste trick of cutting the shortening in with a knife and setting it in the icebox to chill. It took me years to work it out the way I liked it. I take one and a half cups of bread flour with a half teaspoon of salt, cut a half cup of lard into the flour with a knife, and moisten it with about a fourth cup of water. Now comes the puff trick—I roll out the pastry and spread it with an extra fourth cup of creamed lard, dust with flour lightly, fold in three, and roll again, spread with more of the creamed lard, fold in three, and reroll. Each time I put it in the icebox to set, until it has been larded, chilled, and rolled three times. I start with lard then switch to margarine.

Fruit pies are the sort I like best, and I was glad to find out that they were the Roosevelt's favorites too. Mr. Roosevelt's favorite turned out to be apple, and for these I'd try to get the full-flavored early apples, slightly green, and use maybe five large ones to a pie. I line my pan, then pour a half cup of sugar over the lower crust, then the sliced apples which I dot with bits of butter and sprinkle with salt and more sugar. It's the salt that gives it the buttery flavor. Then I dribble a teaspoonful of vanilla over the apples and tuck down the upper crust and bake it for an hour or more.

Pumpkin, cherry, and apple pies were all from Mother's old recipes, and so were the stollen and rolls—I can smell and taste them now.

12

My father's sister had taught me to make the puff paste by using an egg or two, a tablespoon of water for each egg, a little brandy, and enough flour so it can be rolled. I add half lard and half butter creamed, fold the dough over, leave it in the icebox half an hour, and reroll and rebutter it. Three times is about right for that too.

I like this puff paste baked inches high and slit, with homemade jelly put inside. Nothing nicer for a midafternoon snack, with a pot of good coffee!

Mother Nesbitt—my husband's mother—was Irish and not so skilled in cookery, but she had handed down a few wonderful old family recipes brought over from Ireland, and among these were the English plum puddings and fruitcakes that I made by the dozens for the Hyde Park house, and later by the hundreds for the White House. There was a dark fruit cake and a white Scottish fruit cake from Mother Nesbitt and the Roosevelts loved them, and I'd start work on them months before the holidays, even before Thanksgiving. I use a neat trick of hers, too, wrapping the tag ends of the pudding bags into neat handles, so they can be hung like gourds.

I made all these things, and other pies and cakes of all kinds, and all sorts of rolls, cookies, coffeecakes, strudels, and streusels, all the time Mr. Roosevelt was running for governor. I liked thinking my cooking was helping out the campaign. Mrs. Roosevelt had me swamped with orders from the start. I had never cooked on such a large scale before, and in my small kitchen it seemed a terrific undertaking. Dad and I couldn't get over marveling that these recipes that had been our families' treats for so many generations were turning into bread-and-butter and rent money for us now. Dad was working right along with me and loving it, doing all the buying and helping out with the shelling and slicing or whatever, and packing things later—he was a neat packer—ready for the car Mrs. Roosevelt would send over from the big house by the river. Sometimes I went along, and to my notion the Roosevelt house was one of the handsomest in the land, and even after seeing the White House, it still seemed pretty nearly as grand.

One of the odd jobs was the peanut salting.

"My husband loves peanuts," Mrs. Roosevelt told me, and I'd order fifty pounds of the jumbos, shell and skin them, boil them in olive oil and salt them, for Hyde Park.

After Mr. Roosevelt became governor they switched mostly to almonds, but he still liked peanuts, and we kept on fixing them until he'd been President for almost a dozen years and was put on a diet and off everything fried.

By this time I knew pretty much about him, the way he liked things, and how he thought, but I didn't meet Mr. Roosevelt in person until he was nominated for governor and we went over to congratulate him. He had me awed. He was just as charming as she was, and as friendly and kind, but I decided that while I admired him a lot I'd never find much to say to him. He seemed on another plane, pure thought it was and over our heads, and his thinking seemed to be as broad as the world while the rest of us were mulling around in our own little areas. Still, knowing the way he liked peanuts, I wasn't as awed as I might have been.

I went to all the political meetings I could and heard some of his speeches and thought they were wonderful. No matter what he said, I thought it was wonderful.

By this time I was beginning to have some sort of inkling about politics. I hadn't any before I met Mrs. Roosevelt. I'd been brought up in a world that I took for granted was solid Republican. "Only saloonkeepers are Democrats," was a slogan I'd heard as a girl. Suffrage came and went over my head, but I liked the idea of voting, so I voted. Dad being a Republican, I voted Republican.

But way back at the start of the century I'd taken up the study of astrology, and the stars foretold that this was

14

the start of the woman's era, that the man's world was coming to an end and the world of the female was starting. I took it all in and believed it, and I'm still secretly convinced that this is a woman's world, or is starting to be, and that what she makes of it is up to woman, and she'd better work fast. Think of the progress women have made in the last eighty years! Before then a woman couldn't call her second-best bonnet her own.

So I had been for suffrage, but in a cosmic sort of way. In my early days a girl who worked was looked down upon, and I had even been made to feel self-conscious for taking my father's place in the drugstore when he was sick. Few girls went out to work in the early 1900s, and then they could only be nurses and stenographers, and even these jobs were considered "not quite nice." I'd held my tongue and bided my time along with all the other women in America. I didn't see woman's progress from the sociological point of view, but I was firmly convinced that we women were moving into a larger sphere, and I was all in favor of it. My mother and sister and I had talked it over back home, but never before the menfolks. No matter how much they loved us, most of the men seemed dead set against our going anywhere, particularly into a larger sphere.

To show how strictly a girl was brought up in those days, the first time Dad and I went out together we went bicycling and it got to be late in the afternoon and we were hungry so we stopped in at a restaurant. One would think I had been compromised to hear the way the family carried on when we reached home.

Now, thanks to the League of Women Voters and Mrs. Roosevelt, I was branching out for myself in the thinking line. The League held conferences on all sorts of subjects and brought speakers to Hyde Park to talk on both sides. I began forming opinions. They were the first I'd had, and I was proud of them. I saw how much broader the Democrat speakers were, and I liked that. I remembered Teddy Roosevelt, Mrs. Roosevelt's uncle who had been President, had broken up the trusts. I'd shaken hands with him once in Duluth. So I used my thinking cap and made my selection and joined the Roosevelt for Governor Club, and was I surprised to find that Dad was ahead of me, and had already joined up! He'd reached the same conclusion but in a different way, and I think it was because of the chicken breasts.

The chickens belonged to a millionaire Republican who had a Hudson estate close to the Roosevelts. He was one of the many Hyde Parkers who were so dreadfully perturbed at the thought of Mr. Roosevelt being made governor, but I didn't know anything about it at the time, not being used to politics. Anyway, Dad was over at this man's place one day, and he was watching one hundred chickens being dressed for a house party he was giving. The servants were stripping off the breasts and throwing the rest of the meat away. Dad saw all that good chicken going into the garbage cans and thought it was a pity.

"Why don't you give it to the people who work on your place?" he asked the owner.

"What, make beggars of them?" the millionaire answered sternly.

After he went into the house Dad ambled over to the garbage cans and looked in. The men working on the chickens looked at him and grinned. They had lined the cans with clean sheeting and would take the rest of the chicken meat home without the millionaire knowing.

After I began hearing the talk against Franklin Delano Roosevelt I remembered the man with the one hundred chicken breasts who hated Roosevelt. Rich men like that along the Hudson turned him down. One who had been his closest friend never entered his door again after his marriage to a rich girl in the Hudson hierarchy.

16

When he began cutting down their kind of people by trimming the cheap labor field and making it hard for them to get richer, they looked on him as a traitor and were mad as hops at the idea of his holding any sort of political power.

There would be a lot of talk about his being unpopular at Hyde Park. He was, with his own kind, the big estate owners. They were afraid of him even then. But even in that Republican stronghold there were plenty who loved him, and these were the men and women who voted for him and rejoiced when he won and held the torchlight parades to his door.

He signed his letters to them: "Your neighbor, Franklin D. Roosevelt."

They were the kind of people who elected him governor of New York.

We went to Albany to congratulate him. In '32, that was. Mrs. Roosevelt sat beside him. Behind them hung dozens of photographs of the people they liked best and places they had seen. Little did I think, seeing all those framed pictures, that they would hang on even more historic walls and the responsibility of keeping them all dusted was to fall on me.

The higher Mr. Roosevelt went in politics the more involved I became with the Roosevelts. I had thought that their moving into the governor's mansion, way up in Albany, would end my cooking. But now they were entertaining larger groups and serving more food, and I had larger orders than ever before. Mrs. Roosevelt would write or telephone lists of the things she wanted, and we had to get them ready and aboard a certain train.

I was snowed under with orders. One list arrived on a Sunday morning and everything had to reach Albany by Wednesday. It called for twenty-four dozen raised doughnuts, pounds of salted almonds, and all sorts of date bars, cookies, and I don't know how many shortbreads. The doughnuts floored me. I'd never fried so many at one time. How much

17

dough? How much fat? We didn't have enough of anything in the house and no stores were open.

Dad drove to Poughkeepsie and persuaded Mr. Fry to open up his store, and hurried back with supplies. Some neighbors who dropped in to spend a quiet Sunday afternoon were put to work shelling almonds. The house reeked with good smells for two days, and somehow Dad got everything packed and aboard the Poughkeepsie train and they reached Mrs. Roosevelt by Wednesday.

It was all hard work but fun, and Dad enjoyed it too. But baking for the governor wasn't solving all our problems. About this time the owners of our little house returned to Hyde Park and took the house back to live in themselves. The housing shortage was something we began hearing about for the first time. Finally Dad and I had to move in with Garven, our eldest, and his wife Mary, and their firstborn, Bobby. No matter how dear a daughter-in-law may be, and Mary and Midge, who later married Buck, are the dearest girls I know, still there is an old saying that no roof is large enough for two families, and it wasn't fair to Garven and Mary, crowding in on them. But there was nothing else we could do.

It took Mrs. Roosevelt to show me the way out. Her husband was running for the presidency of the United States. I helped get votes. The Roosevelt for President Club gave me a list of fifty people, and I went to see them and talked to them about our candidate. It was all new to me but I had a good time and enjoyed thinking I was helping, and maybe I was.

All the time I knew that what would be wonderful for the Roosevelts and the nation would be fatal to our small affairs, because the baking had been a godsend and it would end if Mr. Roosevelt became president. I couldn't ship a fresh apple pie down to Washington.

This didn't interfere with my excitement over the cam-

18

paign and the election and nobody was happier than I when he won.

But afterward I felt let down and I could see Dad did too. We were losing our best friends in Hyde Park. I knew Dad was feeling he'd lost out in everything, and it made me feel worse than he did, to know he felt that way. There's just no way a woman can let a man know she's just as proud of him for having done his best.

That was a snowy winter, when '32 slid on toward '33. Sometime, between Thanksgiving and December, Mrs. Roosevelt dropped in. I'd been pie-baking to ease my mind. There is nothing like pie to take a woman's thoughts off trouble. These were pumpkin, I recall, only I make them with squash, rich as custard, with plenty of eggs, milk, brown sugar, ginger, and cinnamon. I had the pies in the oven and Bobby in his playpen on a sunny spot on the floor. I peeked out of the window to see if Dad had cleared off the walk, the way I'd asked him to, and I saw Eleanor Roosevelt coming up it, sailing along in her firm way between the drifts as if she liked the snow and the cold. Her cheeks were red and she had a tweed suit on and looked happy. For the life of me I didn't see how she could. I felt low enough about the hard times, both the personal ones and the one hitting all the United States. The depression was on full blast by this time, and her husband was going to be President and in the thick of it. But she was never the kind to avoid trouble and neither was he. I knew that by this time, knowing them the way we did, as neighbors and friends.

She came in, fresh-faced and cheerful, plumped right down, and took Bobby on her lap. I never saw another woman as crazy about babies. She never seems complete without one on her lap. She played with him, and made him "open wide" to see his new teeth, and we talked about the pies. It seemed like any of the other visits. Then she started right in, with Bobby on her lap.

"When we go to Washington in March," she said, "we'll need a housekeeper in the White House. I don't want a professional housekeeper. I want someone I know. I want you, Mrs. Nesbitt."

Then she added, in that kind, warm way she had:

"We'll need Mr. Nesbitt, too, to take care of the White House and take care of us."

I don't know if she ever realized what it meant. I'm not one to talk much. But it was like a rope tossed out to the drowning, and I'll never stop being grateful. The kindest part was her offering the housekeeping of the President's house to us both as one job.

As it turned out, there was a decided place for Dad in the White House. As custodian or steward—he would be called both—his knowledge of accounting was put to good use. He kept the set of books, took charge of all wines and staples, and checked all the packages that went in and out, so that his office was one of the busiest in the building. I know, because later I took over his duties in addition to my own.

But that was much later, and it warms me remembering that she asked for us both, and that we went to the White House together, Henry Nesbitt and I.

I remember one other thing Mrs. Roosevelt said that day. She had put Bobby back in his play pen and was about to go. She stood looking at me, and her rosy face was suddenly serious, as if there were something she wanted to warn me about. I had an idea what she was thinking. There was black trouble all around us and the man who was going to be President would be in it the deepest. I guess she already had inklings of the tide of hate that would rise around the Roosevelts in the White House, and that not even the meekest and mildest marcher in their parade could escape the defiling pitch of that hatred.

Suddenly she spoke up, very seriously, as if she had read my mind, and was explaining for the man who would be

President as well as for herself. Coming from a woman usually serene and cheerful, what Mrs. Roosevelt said that winter day sounded rather sad to me.

"Well, Mrs. Nesbitt," she said, "all we can do is lay the very best plans we can, and stick to them, no matter what happens to us."

Then I was sure she was speaking for them both.

Chapter Two

After all my dreading, we just walked into the White House as if we belonged there. It was run informally in those days before the war, with no police at the gates, so it didn't seem at all formidable. The doorman took my coat with the big fur collar and hung it over a nail in the hall rack and the nail went right through the fur!

It wasn't a young coat by any means, but I was put out.

I made a mental note to get rid of those nails. But I never did. I would succeed in ridding the White House of cuspidors, feather dusters, and corn brooms, but I never did banish the nails. They were traditional, like so many other things. So I ran my neck into tradition my first minute in the White House, and it was the start of struggle that would last thirteen years. Sometimes I won, but tradition won most of the time. I didn't mind too much, because I was still filled to the brim with President Roosevelt's inauguration speech. It had made me feel better about everything, particularly that part about not being afraid.

Inauguration Day had turned out to be blustery and stormy. The seats Mrs. Roosevelt got for Dad and me were in the grandstand in front of the White House, but it rained so hard, and I was so excited, that I didn't see much. We both caught colds, so our first visit inside the White House was to the doctor's office, and I developed a swollen face that lasted a month, until I had a tooth pulled.

Everything happened so fast at the inaugural I didn't realize how much was going on until it was all over. The motorcycles roaring toward the circular drive made an awful lot of noise, and we were all cheering, and it seemed only a moment that I saw him taking the oath on Jimmy's arm, with her beside him, looking tall and proud of him and kind-looking to everyone. But I memorized the words he said and repeated them over a lot in the years that came after this, particularly the part that went:

"The only thing we have to fear is fear itself—nameless, unreasoning, unjustified terror. . . ."

I believed then and I believe still that this is the greatest rule we Americans have had laid down for us in our time, and it was all the majority of us had to cling to then and for a long time after. They can preach all they like about the dignity of poverty, but I've met up with it a lot in my lifetime, and I've never seen it look dignified. People who are afraid lose their human dignity. President Roosevelt seemed to know that, and Mrs. Roosevelt even more, and I never could figure out how she knew, reared as she was in private schools and on the fat of the land. But I always felt a lot of her soul went into those words that were falling like the balm of promise on scared people.

Afterward Dad and I went into the White House to attend the Inaugural Tea, along with the Democratic organization from Duchess County, but I caught only a flying glimpse of it that first visit, and my courage went to my shoes when I saw all those people milling around with cake and tea.

I said to Dad, I thanked my lucky stars. "That's one thing I won't have on my shoulders," I whispered to him in the crowd. "I'll be spared handling an inauguration. I don't think I could survive taking care of as many as this."

The time would come when I'd look back on that performance as a mere handful.

Mrs. Ava Long, the Hoovers' housekeeper, had agreed to

stay on a few days to see the Roosevelts launched, so I didn't take up my housekeeping duties until March 7. By that time the Roosevelts had been in the house three days and had all their stuff unpacked and had issued hundreds of invitations for all sorts of things that would hit me smack in the face when I took over.

In the meantime Dad and I had the chance to look around Washington and find a place to live. There were so many Roosevelts there wasn't room for anyone extra in the White House except Missy LeHand, who was the President's private secretary and truly a right hand to him. Malvina Thompson, Mrs. Roosevelt's secretary and "Tommy" to us all, had found a little apartment near by and the rest of us would scatter as close to the White House as we could, although later Mr. Hopkins and some others would move in with the Roosevelts.

I didn't know that as housekeeper of the White House I was entitled to a car and a driver of my own. Dad and I walked all over Washington trying to find a place to live. At first we were very firm about what we wanted, a little place, not over five rooms, reasonable in rent, and close to the White House. We didn't know Washington was overcrowded and that in spite of the bad times rents were sky-high. Dad and I got into some dreadful places, not knowing the city, and finally we came to earth in a tiny apartment in the Monmouth on G Street, and felt lucky to have landed.

Afterward we had a chance to drive around the city, and saw Washington's tomb and the tomb of the Unknown Soldier. I don't know which moved me more, but we stood longest looking at the tomb of the unknown boy who had died in the last war that was truly to be the last war. Dad and I took comfort in knowing there would never be another. I guess every mother or father who looks at that grave above the city of Washington, lonely in spite of the uniformed lads always on duty there, says a prayer for the unknown and their own son, not certain for a moment which is which.

One nice thing about our apartment, it was within walking distance of the White House. Early on the morning of March 7 we walked over there, and I was praying all the way. I knew we could count on President Roosevelt, but still I was worried. He had proclaimed the bank holiday to stop hoarding. People had created a national emergency by putting their money away in safe-deposit boxes, he said, so right after his inauguration he proclaimed this emergency act to stabilize the banks. It was the first of the changes that were to change all our lives. It was the start of the blue eagle, the NRA, the new deal, the new administration, and what would be talked about for some time as "the first one hundred days."

In a small measure, walking into the White House that morning I was setting out on a one hundred days of my own. Everything I was going to do would be different from anything any other housekeeper in the White House had done before, and I wouldn't have dared try any of it without Mrs. Roosevelt's spurring me on.

The ushers took me right in to her. She was in the Red Room, wearing a dark print dress and looking happy and friendly, as much at home as if she'd been living in this big place all her life. In a way she had, for she had visited there as a girl when her uncle Teddy was President. I had made up my mind to put everything between us on a business basis and keep it there. She was First Lady of the land now and I her housekeeper, and we couldn't be chattering away together as we had in Hyde Park. So I went up to her solemn and businesslike, and we kept it that way pretty nearly always. Only sometimes we broke down. Things made us laugh, or provoked us, and it couldn't help but show.

She was ready for me with a list of papers and a little brown leather book, and we started out together at a trot, the way she always goes about things.

"I'll show you over the house first," she said. Then she gave me a look I recognized. One with a sort of twinkle. "Mrs. Hoover took me around," she said. "In one hour."

25

I made up my mind that if the wife of the departing ex-President had awarded her only one hour, that I would not waste any more of Mrs. Roosevelt's time than I had to. Her hours were certainly as precious as Mrs. Hoover's. I heard afterward that the two of them whisked from one end of the White House to the other while Mrs. Roosevelt scribbled notes. She had an eagle eye for detail, and all she had seen and heard was ready for me: four long legal sheets written solid with White House routine, the list of servants, their names, duties, and schedules, all noted and written down in a single hour.

She had an organizer's mind. She led me all over the White House. There were four floors, each like a house in itself, and every room had a separate life and history of its own, with rules and regulations laid down, all to be observed and kept running Every scrap of furniture, I found, had its own tradition to keep up.

It was so bewildering I didn't know how I'd ever get the rooms straightened out in my mind. I couldn't even sort out the parlors that first day. I didn't see the need for so many. Later I could see how they all had their uses, with so much going on and so many Roosevelts. I would hear of the way other presidential families seemed to rattle around in the big place, but now, wherever Mrs. Roosevelt and I went, we kept on bumping into Roosevelts, and they all seemed full of spirits and happy to see each other, though they might have parted only the minute before in the next room. But they are like that, and you can't help liking them for it. I can't recall now how many Roosevelts were in the White House that day, and they'd keep coming and going and popping in and out for the next thirteen years. They all seemed glad to be there. They're happy-looking people as a rule, except maybe Elliott. He has a broader streak of the Dutch in him than the others, and sometimes it gives him a puzzled look.

The farther we went the more confusing it all seemed. We

zipped through the Blue Parlor, the Red Parlor, and the Green Parlor. The Blue Room is the oval reception room where the President receives diplomatic guests, and the Green Room is the most formal and the farthest away from the dining room, so the ladies can go there to drink coffee while the gentlemen stay on at the table to drink toasts and get business done. There were impressive pictures and hangings and tables and chairs everywhere we went, but the things I noticed first were the chandeliers. The one hanging in the Green Parlor was prismed with Irish Waterford leaded glass, and there was a chandelier with even heavier prisms in the Blue Parlor.

I warned Mrs. Roosevelt right off: "That hand-cut glass is going to be awfully easy to chip."

I found out later what headaches those chandeliers could be. A special schedule had to be worked out just for them. There are twenty-two thousand pieces of glass in those in the East Room alone, and the White House carpenters built trestles under them for the washers to stand on while they dusted the chandeliers, removed the glass prisms, one at a time, washed them with alcohol, polished them, and hung them back in place.

We did this once a year, just before the social season started, and it took six men a day and a half to do the polishing on one and about a week for the whole process, and all the time I was hovering over those crystal prisms as if they were crown jewels.

I guess I groaned out loud when we reached the East Room, for there over our heads hung those three immense crystal chandeliers to be kept glittering, and four big fireplaces to be stoked and cleaned. It was a gold-and-white and curlicued sort of room, with big pictures—I noticed the portraits of the Washingtons first of all—and costly bric-a-brac that would require careful handling on the mantelpieces, and expensive-looking sofas and chairs pushed back against the walls. There was an outsize gold piano, too, and the room looked formal and empty and like a ballroom.

That was the moment I decided I'd never be happy traveling in Europe. I'd get no pleasure out of seeing palaces and museums for worrying about the responsibility of dusting all those treasures.

As for myself, if I was rich as all get out I'd never want more than the smallest sort of house, that doesn't require much tending. Just the same, I don't think any person can go into the East Room without feeling that everything of importance in American history has echoed against its walls. It's the inner heart of the White House, and I lost Mrs. Roosevelt a couple of valuable minutes, just standing stock-still by the gold piano and taking in everything.

I guess it struck me the hardest, in the confusion of the day, because I suddenly remembered that despite its awe-inspiring occasions and stately memories, our illustrious dead always lie in state in the East Room. President Harrison had lain before that white-and-gold wall, I remembered, and President Taylor, after overeating milk and cherries one hot Washington afternoon, which gave rise to the legend that they are poisonous together, but that isn't true. There is nothing nicer on a hot day than a slice of cherry pie and a glass of cold milk.

President McKinley, too, after being shot in Buffalo, was brought to the East Room, and Warren Harding, after his sudden death in San Francisco.

Most of all the room brought back memories of pictures I had seen of President Lincoln, laid out there on a black-shrouded bier in April 1865, and I remembered how he had told before his death of seeing himself there in a dream, and hearing the weeping.

It gave me the shivers for a minute, beautiful as the room was, and with the spring sun pouring through the draped windows and Mrs. Roosevelt beside me. But I'm not super-

28

stitious, and I know there was no looking forward to another April and another war's ending and another President lying dead in the East Room. Almost thirteen years from this day we would draw the curtains of the East Room and still be unable to shut out the sound of American people crying in the streets outside.

There have been a lot of happy goings-on in the East Room, too, and I heard of them later. Some of the daughters of Presidents were married there—Nellie Grant, Maria Monroe, Jessie Wilson, and Alice Roosevelt, who was Mrs. Roosevelt's cousin and married Nicholas Longworth. "Princess Alice" was still queening it over Washington society, and we were going to see a lot of her.

The room had its lighter memories. Abigail Adams, the first of our first ladies, hung her wash in this empty room when it was bare and new, and "Teddy" practiced jujitsu on the floor with a Japanese trainer.

Mrs. Roosevelt and I rushed through the rest of the house. I could see she loved and reverenced every inch of the place, and wanted it to have the best of treatment, outside and in. We hurried through state dining rooms and family dining rooms and servants' dining rooms, and everywhere I caught flying glimpses of dignified furnishings and learned what their treatment was to be. I didn't say so, but I could see a lot of places where the first mansion of the land needed shining up, so to speak, and I didn't know that before doing the shining I had to have a get-together with tradition. Brasswork centuries old shows erosion and the finest rugs will ravel in time and the choicest of brocades fade. There isn't much appeal for me in magnificence frayed at the hem.

But one thing at a time, I told myself, scribbling down notes and wishing to heaven I hadn't forgotten all the shorthand I learned once, because Mrs. Roosevelt talked faster than I could write. Then we reached the kitchen, and I tell you my heart sank. We both stood stock-still and looked all around and then at each other.

I've tried to describe the White House kitchen as it was then. Some newspaper writer did it better than I ever could. "It looks like an old-fashioned German rathskeller, with a great deal of ancient architectural charm."

I can't work up any charm for cockroaches. No matter how you scrub it, old wood isn't clean. This was the "first kitchen in America," and it wasn't even sanitary. Mrs. Roosevelt and I poked around, opening doors and expecting hinges to fall off and things to fly out. It was that sort of place. Dark-looking cupboards, a huge old-fashioned gas range, sinks with time-worn wooden drains, one rusty wooden dumb waiter. The refrigerator was wood inside and bad-smelling. Even the electric wiring was old and dangerous. I was afraid to switch things on.

So far as I could see, the kitchen hadn't seen many improvements since the hour the Adams moved into the brand-new White House in 1800. But Mrs. Roosevelt said it had.

"There are the trivets and iron bars in the walls where the old cooking fireplaces stood," she pointed out. Then she added, just as I was about to say it:

"There is only one solution—we must have a new kitchen!"

I noticed an odd thing. There wasn't a scrap of paper in the kitchen. There wasn't a cookbook in the White House.

"Good thing I brought my recipes along," I said grimly to Mrs. Roosevelt.

As a matter of fact, I'd nearly left them behind in Hyde Park. I'd expected the White House kitchen to have a full library of books on cuisine. My lifetime hobby has been collecting cookbooks and recipes, and I had filing cases filled with old family recipes. At the last minute I'd packed them in among the odds and ends we shipped down on the trucks along with the Roosevelts' things. Only we hadn't brought much. It didn't seem worth while packing and unpacking for only a four-year stay.

I made up my mind right then that when the Roosevelts left the White House I was going to leave behind complete lists and files of everything needed, including our sources of supply, lists of the services we dealt with, the staff and its duties, and every detail that goes into the running of the White House.

There weren't enough utensils left in the kitchen to cook a fair-sized family meal. The kitchen, like the rest of the White House, was depleted. All during our tour of the rooms I'd been peeking into closets—there were only a few in the halls and wardrobes in the bedrooms—and noticed the linen situation was hopeless and I didn't see how I'd manage without enough bed, bath, and kitchen linens. This was a great big wonderful old house, and it was almost empty of the necessities.

And while I don't like a lot of cooking utensils, I do appreciate the minimum, and I saw I'd have to skip around shopping for a few aluminum odds and ends, just enough to get us by.

All this time, between meeting with young Roosevelts, seeing rooms, and catching glimpses of history, Mrs. Roosevelt was introducing me to groups of the staff scattered here and there in charge of the building. "This is the new housekeeper, Mrs. Nesbitt." By the time we were through with the kitchen and the lower regions Mrs. Roosevelt was in a hurry to be off and I was weak in the knees.

I had a hazy view of what lay ahead of me.

There was a staff of thirty-two men and women to be supervised. Later we cut to twenty-four, and went back to thirty. There would be small armies of others, coming in for the day in times of extra stress. Sixty rooms to be kept immaculate. Drapes, linens, curtains, furniture, china, glassware, silver to be replaced or renovated. Upstairs and downstairs,

31

through four flights, the food, tables, linen checking, daily cleaning, beds, bathrooms, closets, and parlors were all my responsibility.

There were the ushers, secretaries, ladies' maids, the President's valet, doormen, butlers, chambermaids, engineers, maintenance men, the Secret Service men under Colonel Starling, and the President's personal, military, and naval aides.

All these had to be looked after and kept track of in their needs, and beyond all was the President's family to be made comfortable, and their visitors and house guests to be tended. And how that circle of friendship grew!

Meals had to be planned, passed upon, ordered, overseen, and served, to two or to two thousand, with not long enough warning at times.

But foremost and beyond all other responsibilities was the health and well-being of that man whose hearty laugh could be heard ringing through the White House halls in these trying times, as if to let us know that everything was going to be all right. No matter what else might happen, it was my duty to see that meals were served on time, well cooked, tempting, and nourishing, to Franklin Delano Roosevelt, thirty-third President of the United States.

My responsibility, as great in a tiny home as in this institution, was the maintenance of a calm and peaceful atmosphere. I would have to struggle to maintain peace and allay friction among the people of so large a staff. Nothing must ever interrupt the smooth-running machinery of a great white shell of a building that housed the hopes of the entire world. A million details to remember. A thousand things to go wrong.

I saw at last, in the White House's depleted kitchen, that the job of housekeeper of the White House was surrounded by tradition, sentiment, and protocol, and by responsibility so vast, I didn't think I could go through with it.

Mrs. Roosevelt was smiling as if she knew. She had appointments and dozens of people to claim her attention but she stood waiting to hear what I had to say as if we had the whole four years in which to talk.

I said weakly, "I'll have to come to you for help."

Up to this time we'd stayed all businesslike. Now she patted my shoulder.

"You're not to worry about anything," she said. "You're going to be all right."

She made everything sound easy.

That was the way she got everyone around her working her way and doing their best.

Chapter Three

I spent the next few days trying to remember everything Mrs. Roosevelt had told me and all I was finding out for myself.

She and I had just about galloped through the White House in that one hour. Later I met Captain Daily of the transport section, who had brought our goods down from Hyde Park along with the Roosevelts' things. He was a friendly Irishman, something on Dad's type, and I asked him to go around the White House with us, and he did, and it took us all day.

Then Mrs. Long, the Hoover housekeeper who was leaving, gave me an hour just as Mrs. Hoover had Mrs. Roosevelt, and told me about the shops they had been buying from, and I was kept hopping, trying to learn and remember it all.

Mrs. Roosevelt had given me a beautiful little brown leather diary, chased with gold, and I'd carried it about that first day scribbling down notes as we went, but it would take a genius to keep up with her. Later I got large black diaries and kept accounts of everybody who came and what they had to eat and so on, and a lot of the notations written in them were so hush-hush it's hard for me to remember now what they meant and why we had to be so secret about them at the time.

But in the first little book there are sentences written on the gallop, and the first page reads, Tuesday, March 7, 1933, and on another is scrawled "Pader," and that is as far as I got for Paderewski when Mrs. Roosevelt told me the Polish Premier was coming to dinner about two nights away.

"It will be your first formal dinner," she said, smiling, and I was so petrified I couldn't finish the "ewski."

My first menu is there, too, and it was for lunch of that first day I kept house for the Roosevelts. It served twelve, just the family and a few close family friends. We always served a good lunch, because there were usually men. It's typical of the way the Roosevelts ate when they weren't being formal, and the dinner that night was also family and simple, the way they liked it.

LUNCH

Tomato Juice Cocktail
(JUST LEMON AND SALT, MRS. ROOSEVELT SAID)
Stuffed Eggs
Cold Cuts
Salad—Hot Corn Bread
Stewed Fruit—Cake
Coffee

DINNER

Clear Soup
Broiled Lamb Chops
Green Peas—Baked Potatoes
Fruit
Coffee
(SANKA FOR THE PRESIDENT AND MRS. R.)

There are thousands of days of menus before me now but none is more representative of the way the Roosevelts lived than this, made up on my first day.

That day after Mrs. Roosevelt left me I had my pretty new notebook and no place to put it. Every room I peeked

35

into had people busy in it, and all the desks and tables were heaped with presents and flowers sent to the new President and his family by people who wished them well. Finally I caught up with Dad, and found him busy as a bird dog in a little office of his own on the lower corridor, with packages piled to the doors, and cupboards of canned goods all around, and all sorts of excitement going on outside. Dad had taken over all the packages, accounting, purchasing of supplies, and the wine cellar. Somehow, in all the confusion of leaving Hyde Park, Mrs. Roosevelt had found time to ask me to make out a long list of staples, and sent it down, and Mrs. Long had ordered them, and there they were heaped up in cases and packages around Dad, ready for me to take over.

"Find yourself a chair," he said, waving his fountain pen at me hospitably, and went right on checking packages. I found a chair, dumped some gifts off it, pulled a little panel out of Dad's desk, and started right in making lists and menus.

Later on I would have my own office, in a room that had been a dining room for the colored help, but that wouldn't be for several months, so all that time I did my paper work next to Dad, and we were happy as only people can be who like working together and like the work they're doing.

Dad shifted things around so I would have more room. He was ingenious about planning, and loved making things over, even at home. He organized the system of records for the packages, typing out a filing system, dates and all. That first day two hundred and forty-seven packages came into his office, and they all had to be recorded. What they were, who sent them, to whom given, what answer was required, and so on.

So many people, he found out, would send things in and then ask for them back or demand payment. For example, a haberdasher might send in two dozen ties that the President hadn't ordered, and didn't like, and didn't keep, and then the man would send in a bill.

36

A lot of people sent in family pictures and heirlooms without a word of explanation, and later, out of a clear sky, demanded them back. So everything had to be checked.

Dad and I were helping each other in everything and I don't know how I could have managed without him.

People kept running in and out, to bring packages, or get acquainted, or just out of curiosity. That first day Dad gave the answer he kept on giving for years.

"We aren't politicians," he would say. "We're just Hyde Park friends of the Roosevelts, come down to look after them."

The corridor outside our door held the inner activity of the White House, and it was like setting up business on the sidewalk of the busiest corner of a new city. Dad was busy, I was busy, everyone was busy. There was so much activity going on out there that I didn't know how I was going to think, but I found out one can concentrate anywhere if one has to.

There were always about half a hundred people out in the hall, milling around waiting for the elevator, dodging in and out of the offices and kitchen, talking and smoking. The kitchen was at one end and the doctor's office across the way, and the china room and help's dining room and library and diplomatic reception room were ranged about, so there were all kinds of activities going on, from culinary to diplomatic. The social bureau was down the hall, and all the place cards and invitations were written there, and waiters were dashing across the hall, getting dishes out of the china room, and adding to the confusion, until I changed things around and found an easier way to get at the dishes.

I was surprised to find a lot of the people were waiting in the hall to see the new housekeeper. The change in administration had raised the hopes of all the Washington tradespeople who had not been selling to the White House, and I was hounded by tradespeople of all kinds, offering samples and price lists on all sorts of things. Mrs. Roosevelt, too, was besieged by trade until we almost had to lock our doors.

37

Now, I knew that on the great estates along the Hudson River the 10 per cent system prevailed. "Kickback" is the slang for it. Superintendent, housekeeper, gardener, butler, or what have you, buy from their favored dealers and get back a commission on all their purchases. That was one of the first things I took up with Mrs. Roosevelt.

"That may work along the Hudson," I told her, "but there won't be any 10-per-centing on the Potomac, not while I'm responsible."

Maybe I cut into tradition there too. But I never heard any complaints.

My position was a queer one. I was in charge of the domestic staff and responsible for all they did, and whatever went wrong in the domestic line would be my fault. I worked directly under Mrs. Roosevelt, and she arbitrated between the ushers and me. Every meal and function that came up was bewildering and likely to present some new problem, and these affairs came along at the start so thick and fast that for months it seemed to me I was serving one single meal.

I say "I served," but of course the housekeeper doesn't actually serve. She watches the comings and goings, tastes, sips, suggests, and bosses the job. Just the same, I sometimes felt as if I'd done the whole meal myself, down to the last wiped spoon.

Before functions I had to check with the ushers, the State Department, the Social Bureau, and the Secret Service. Gradually I began getting everyone sorted out, and there were some lovely people in the White House. Ike Hoover, in charge of the ushers, got me off to a good start and was wonderfully kind, and I felt I'd lost a brother when he died some time later.

Colonel Starling was in charge of the Secret Service, and that gallant Southerner saw me through many a bewildered moment. Naturally I saw a lot of the Secret Service boys because they were underfoot night and day, but that was their job and they couldn't help it. I don't know whether the colonel ever knew how upset I'd get when things went gee-hawed and every which way. If he did, he never let on, and I tried not to. I even tried to dress serene and orderly, in trim cotton wash frocks that looked cool even when hot weather started coming on. The newspaper writers commented a lot on my calm air. One of them wrote that I "looked like somebody's beloved aunt."

Well, I wasn't calm inside. It was all new to me, and everything was working out on a bigger scale than I'd expected, and I found myself being trimmed down in size every day.

But all the staff co-operated. Everyone was kind. I talked a lot over the phone with Missy LeHand and Miss Tully —she had been Missy's assistant in Albany—and Tommy was a comfort. Then there was Mrs. Dennison, who was "Pa Watson's" secretary. It was like a family, and we all worked together. There were two sides to the family. Tommy, Mrs. Helm, and I worked with Mrs. Roosevelt, and Missy and the others were with the President.

Then there was "Hacky," Miss Hackmeister, on the telephone exchange. "If anyone is alive and on earth, Hacky will get them," we used to say. She was a wonderful character, and with German tenacity she would keep on until she got her party. She had the affairs of the world at her fingertips, and nothing escaped her, and nothing could ever be got out of her. She went where the President went, Washington, Hyde Park, Warm Springs.

There was Gus Gennerich, the President's bodyguard, who was devoted to them, a diamond in the rough, if ever a man was. He was East Side New York and some of the things he said startled me and must have surprised the Roosevelts. One of the others I liked was Bill Hasset, who was then under Early and had charge of publicity. He was a bachelor and easy-going.

The engineer, John Heisler, the White House carpenter, Mr. Shepherd, and Ross Edmundson the painter, became my allies.

Yes, there were lots of lovely people.

Sooner or later everyone passed through the corridor. Cordell Hull, Harold Ickes, Frances Perkins, Henry Wallace, Henry Morgenthau, Junior, were familiar faces. I came to know them all, and to like some better than others.

We didn't see much of the President. He'd come and go by elevator on his way to the executive building or to the doctor's office when he went to have his sinus treated. Usually three bells warned us. Three buzzes sounding near the elevator meant the President was coming down and that meant the police would snap on guard at the doorways and everybody else clear out of the way.

Two bells meant Mrs. Roosevelt was coming down. One bell was for any of the others.

Sometimes I was on an errand in the corridor and couldn't clear out, so I saw a lot of people I guess I wasn't supposed to see.

As I say, there were so many affairs right at the start that the whole spring social season seemed to me like one continual meal. I remember the Paderewski dinner, because it was the first of the formals. I knew he was a great man, not only as a pianist, but as Premier of Poland. He was over here asking help for his troubled land.

They were all coming, all asking help. Prime Minister Ramsay MacDonald was coming for England, and when President Roosevelt closed the banks, I heard he made the remark that this canceled the need for his trip, which was to try to help arrange an economic adjustment. Premier Herriot was coming to adjust France's monetary conditions with the United States. Prime Minister Bennett was coming down from Canada. They were all on their way to ask the aid and advice of the big-shouldered smiling man who was whisked out of the elevator and into his office so early these trying mornings, whose laugh we sometimes heard as he spun his wheel chair along with hands that were as strong as if he'd earned his living with them all his life. All these world leaders were swooping down on us from all directions and I couldn't keep track of them for trying to think what they'd like to eat and planning menus for them, as well as keeping up with all the other menus in the White House, dozens of breakfast lunches, dinners, trays, and side snacks, each and every day.

The economic despair seemed familiar to me. I'd gone through it before, back in '93, when banks had also failed left and right, and money seemed to go underground. Now it was '33, and things were just as bad.

Living in the White House was like living on the pinnacle of the world. I could look down on all the troubles but I couldn't understand them. I only knew something was terribly wrong.

It seemed to me there had been some mighty poor managing.

But I remember Mr. Paderewski's dinner, and the menu was just as I scrawled it down, galloping around the White House after Mrs. Roosevelt that first day.

Fruit Cocktail

Cream of Celery Soup

Planked Shad Roe   Swiss Dressing   Sliced Cucumber

Crown Roast   Mint Jelly

Green Peas   Scalloped Corn   Pan-roast Potatoes

Lettuce Hearts   Cream Cheese   Bar-le-duc

Strawberry Cream

Cake   Coffee

And this was for the fanciest sort of dinner! I was going to spend my first year in the White House trying to match the need for saving with the swirl of entertaining. I've seen a copy of the menu card of the dinner Teddy Roosevelt gave in the White House in 1902 in honor of Prince Henry of Prussia, and it took a card three pages long to list all the fancy dishes.

But Mrs. Roosevelt and I had our economy program all mapped out and we were going to stick to it. With so many Americans hungry, it was up to the head house of the nation to serve economy meals and act as an example. I'd been trying to manage the best meals for the least money all my life. And while there is nothing nicer than a good roast of lamb, still it isn't the most stylish dish one could set before a king—or the Polish Premier.

There were about twenty to the dinner, and when it was all set up and being served I lit out for home. I didn't stay, as I didn't know I was supposed to stay. Mrs. Roosevelt sent for me first thing next morning.

"After this," she said, very kindly, "when there are twenty or more, I'd like you to stay."

After that I stayed, and I found out how necessary it was for the housekeeper to be on the job as long as any serving went on in the White House. I had to oversee co-ordination between the service and the pantry, heal breaches, and watch trays up and down. We had one temperamental cook, a wonderful woman with an excitable streak. Captain Lock had her on the carpet more than once, but I wasn't allowed to fire anyone, and the President wouldn't send her away. Mrs. Roosevelt was so forgiving. "We have to treat her like a child," she'd say.

So we did, and many a dish was spoiled, thanks to her having a sulking spell, into the third administration. She played havoc through the first two, but the President was patient, until she began sending up too many dishes she knew

42

he didn't like, and that was the end, even for anyone as for-giving as Mrs. Roosevelt. She was transferred to another department.

Mrs. Roosevelt saw everything without seeming to, and she was a martinet for detail, but she could make excuses for almost anyone.

St. Patrick's Day came right after Mr. Paderewski, and I was looking forward to it because I knew it was the President and Mrs. Roosevelt's wedding anniversary, and the first big family affair since the Roosevelts came in. I really spread myself for the occasion, because I always would like fixing for the family affairs more than for crowned heads and such. The Roosevelts had so much fun together that it was a pleasure to do for them, and it being St. Patrick's Day, of course the table was green as a garden with decorations and favors. There were always favors at Roosevelt parties. Mrs. Roosevelt used to pick them up wherever she found them, and we had doodads and knickknacks for every sort of occasion.

All the time I was planning the dinner I was remembering the accounts I had read at the time of their wedding. Twenty-eight years ago, it had been, and Teddy was President, and came to it, stirring all New York with excitement. It was a different world when they married. I'd seen pictures of them, standing tall and young together, with good, well-intentioned faces even then.

Dad, being Irish, took a little pot of shamrock up to her that morning, to start the day on, he said. She was always delighted with any little attention, as if it were a surprise to her to be remembered. The German word gemütlich describes Mrs. Roosevelt to my mind, and no other word applies both to her spirit and soul. Anyway, she was so tickled that after this Dad always managed to find a little pot of sham-rock for the occasion, even after they stopped bringing it from Ireland and it became scarce. It was a little tradition between them.

43

I chose cream of crab soup as a starter, in Mrs. Roosevelt's honor, and fried chicken with Maryland gravy because Mr. Roosevelt liked it that way. Green peas, asparagus, and endive salad with French dressing contributed to the green effect, and there was baked Virginia ham with candied sweet potatoes, and for dessert, ice cream, angel-food cake, fruitcake, coffee, and cheese. The angel food was her favorite and the fruitcake his, and I always made one for his birthday, but these were fixed specially, anniversary fashion.

All the Roosevelts liked fish and soup, so the crab-meat soup was a special treat, made from an old American recipe that had been a favorite with George Washington. Whenever I wanted to do something especially nice for Mrs. Roosevelt, I'd order this soup, just the way Martha Washington used to have it fixed at Mount Vernon.

It calls for a pound and a half of crab meat in nice chunks, and you can use the claw meat. I take a quart of either milk or light cream, or half and half, depending on how rich the rest of the dinner is going to be, two tablespoons of butter, one of flour, a grated lemon peel, one teaspoon of Worcestershire sauce, one half cup of sherry—don't let anyone try to tell you it doesn't pay to use the best sherry!—salt, pepper, and two hard-boiled eggs.

Blend the butter and flour in a double boiler, add the mashed eggs and lemon peel, then the milk, and stir until it thickens. Add the crab meat, let it simmer five minutes, then the seasoning, and just before serving stir in the sherry and let it get hot clear through again.

Mrs. Roosevelt loved it, and the anniversary dinner was a success. All the family dinners were. I don't remember exactly who was there, but the family alone made quite a crowd, and I know the President's mother, Mrs. James Roosevelt, was down from Hyde Park, and probably a few more of the close relations and the Morgenthaus and Mr. Howe.

It seemed to me there were Roosevelts of all sizes and ages, from the little tykes up to Mrs. James, or Miss Sara, as she was sometimes called. Anna and James were the oldest, then Elliott, then Franklin, Junior—so like the President in looks it gave one a turn sometimes—and John, the youngest and my favorite. He seemed the most serious and quietest, leaning over a little backward, maybe, to the conservative side. There were so many of them, coming and going, it kept a person on his toes trying to keep track of them. Then the grandchildren helped fill up the house, and they were all companionable and seemed to have a grand time. There were cribs, high chairs, and perambulators all over the White House, and kiddie cars, tricycles, and scooters were parked outside under the stately porte-cochere. There was a slide on the lawn and a jungle jim and children racing about and dogs barking.

They were nice children, uninhibited and friendly, and not in the least spoiled. Anna's children, Sistie and Buzzy, were there the most, and people knew them best, but the others were just as sweet. Sistie looked exactly like her grandmother, and was a beauty. She had a birthday along about this time, and it was the first of the birthdays that were always so much fun, because Mrs. Roosevelt made a great fuss over them, and celebrated everybody's as they came along. There was always at least one beautiful cake—the candles left off on the sixteenth birthday and after that there were only sixteen no matter how old you got—and a glass tube in the heart of the cake sprouted flowers, and in between layers were little silver favors that told your fortune. Mrs. Roosevelt kept birthdays in mind all the time, and was always thinking ahead to presents, and ordering cakes baked to send here and there, complete with candles and pretty cards, and beautifully wrapped and boxed. Making people happy, and surprising people, was always on her mind, in spite of all the other things a President's wife had to think about.

Of course she had bigger problems now, and the family celebrations had to be squeezed in, and the time would come

45

when that was even more of a struggle than it was this first season, with the heads of the nations swarming in on us. I had seven-course meals to worry about along with the condition of the world. We had two state dinners right off, one for Herriot and one for Bennett, and I recall the Herriot on March 27 because the next morning Mrs. Roosevelt told me things had gone beautifully and the dinner was delicious. I was pleased and grateful to Fields. He was head butler and a wonder, a good organizer who knew how to get the fullest co-operation out of his men.

But there was no chance of my getting a swelled head. If anything went wrong, the President pinned my ears back. The first dressing down I took was about the coffee cream.

"Mrs. Nesbitt," the President said to me firmly, "I like my cream in lobs and gobs."

I was having trouble with the cream, but it was difficult to explain. I had been flooded by requests from dairies wanting to sell butter and milk and cream to the White House, so I went investigating, from farm to farm, around Virginia and Maryland. Naturally I was on the lookout for the heaviest cream. It wasn't being provided, at least not for Washington, D.C. But I couldn't explain to the President of the United States that he was just a country boy at heart and accustomed to the rich production of the Hyde Park cows. I didn't know how we could get any better unless we brought a cow to the White House, the way President Andrew Jackson had one in the lean-to, so he could have plenty of butter. I often wished we could follow his example, particularly when rationing started, and from buying butter by the keg I was reduced to buying it a pound at a time, and for the executive mansion of the United States!

Dad had his eye on the old space formally used to cool milk in cold running water. He said it would make a fine ham cellar.

I had cause to remember May 24. We were having the

Japanese contingent to dinner, and matters were looking pretty ugly between their nation and the Chinese at that time. Japanese love crab meat, and the specialty was to be the crab-meat soup according to Mrs. Washington's recipe. We had a Chinese cook in to cook it for the dinner, and when I talked to him about the soup and he found out it was for the Japanese affair—well, a look came into his eye that I couldn't blame him for, but just the same it was a ticklish situation. We liked him and trusted him—I knew we could trust him—but I could put myself in his place, and in a world crisis such as we were facing I didn't dare let the soup go on. Ida, the cook in charge, was a dear, she saw the point and hovered over the crab meat to the last claw, and we both heaved a sigh of relief when it was all together.

I wrote a dark comment in my diary that would have mystified anyone who did not know. "Never again! Hereafter Ida does the cooking. No one else!"

It was a silly episode, but it was my first glimpse of the responsibility of overseeing food and drink in the President's house. I was really upset by it, and went out into the garden to see how the trees were getting on. It was so lovely outdoors this springtime I had to make myself stay inside. There was a lot of commotion out there, because the veterans' garden party was the next day, and carpenters were working about putting up marquees and electricians were stringing wires through the trees. Dad was standing under a magnolia chatting with a gentle, grayish man with a soft twangy voice. Dad introduced us. It was Will Rogers. He was spending two or three days in the White House. We stood awhile talking about the veterans' party next day.

This was my first garden party, and I was staggered at first by the amount of food called for. Three thousand two hundred sandwiches was on the list, the way I figured—three to a guest. Well, this was just the first of the veteran affairs, and before long I'd have eight women spreading, and two men with slicers, working a day and a half, all day. For one inauguration we turned out twenty-three thousand sandwiches, with both sides buttered! When I had to stop buttering both sides, I stopped making sandwiches in the White House.

"Have something substantial," Mrs. Roosevelt had urged me, and I planned to do that, and get the garden party business systematized, so I could learn how much was needed and what to count on next time. I wanted to have plenty and still see what I could do about keeping prices down, for this was the first of an endless series of such affairs, I knew, and couldn't appear too opulent.

Just the same, we wanted the best for the veterans. I ordered the cakes from the farm women, sixty-five of them, chocolate, angel, and other kinds, and cookies, mostly honey drops. Mrs. Taylor, who ran a bakery, made a lot of cakes for us too. Ice cream came from the dairies, and we made the lemonade and had five-gallon thermos cans of coffee sent in. How much juice to a crate of lemons? How many gallons to a hundred guests? I had to figure all this out, and wound up squeezing two and a half crates of lemons in the White House kitchen with an antiquated hand squeezer.

"Next year," I vowed, "we'll have an electric."

The grounds looked beautiful. We had two marquees, with tables spread with damask. Each marquee had its service tent, and all the tables looked gay and welcoming under the trees, with big bowls of flowers and big frosted cakes. Veterans began arriving by the hundreds until there were more than a thousand milling around the President's wheel chair under the trees. They were from Walter Reed, Veterans' Bureau, and St. Elizabeth, all veterans of World War I. It seemed terribly sad to me to see the lame and amputees passing first before the President's chair. There were wheel chairs after wheel chairs, and trucks loaded with them. I couldn't help wondering how he felt, knowing how it was with them, as

48

only a man in another wheel chair would know. His smile was wonderful.

They swarmed four deep around the marquees where the sandwiches and cake and coffee and ice cream were being passed out. I tried to steer some of them over to the other tent, but found things just as busy there. I was checking over things in the service tent when one of the veterans came in and edged up to me in a curious way.

"I want a glass of milk," he said.

I knew there were some mental cases in the crowd, and realized he was one. He was looking me over and looking ugly. I didn't want to shout for anyone and upset the party, so I just kept backing away.

"We haven't any milk," I said, as cool as I could.

"I'm a stomach case," he said. "I have to have milk."

He looked threatening.

There was coffee cream. I poured out a glassful for him, on the double. He drank it all down, and seemed satisfied, because he backed out and went away.

I got out of the tent fast. The veterans cleared the food from the tables like magic, and the butlers were kept running to and fro with empty plates and bringing back full ones. Such hungry boys—it made me feel like crying to see how much they were enjoying the food and everything. It was more substantial by far than we served at the social garden affairs, and when I saw supplies running down, I sent out for twenty more gallons of ice cream and seven more cakes. That taught me a lesson, and from then on I learned to keep a dessert backlog on hand of boxed or canned cookies and wafers that the stores could take back if not used.

I also learned that at every big veterans' party like this we had to feed about fifty motorcycle police. It hadn't occurred to me that those handsome fellows in uniform got hungry too.

The next day I figured up all the costs, and I'd managed the affair on a whole lot less than I had expected. Mrs. Roose-

velt had asked me to check the figures, so I carried them upstairs to show her. She was in a huddle with the President,
Louis McHenry Howe, Mr. Early, and Mr. McIntyre. They
were having a confab on the national budget and how to cut
down country-wide expenses. Mr. Early was talking the loud-
est.

"The party cost us thirty and a half cents per head," I told
her.

Her eyes popped. Then she chuckled, and turned to Mr.
Early.

"You ought to get a manager like Mrs. Nesbitt to run the
country for you," she said. "You'd save money."

Chapter Four

Mrs. Roosevelt started writing her column "My Day" around this time, and I often thought privately I was living a "My Day" of my own, and the morning consultation with her was its high light. I liked talking with her because she had a way of keeping your enthusiasm stirred up. Everything I was trying to do was revolutionary. First, there was the problem of trying to cut down.

Americans were hungry. We in the White House were the guinea pigs, and the new system of economics was being tried out on us. Dieticians flooded us with theories calculated to teach people how to manage with cheaper cuts and get the most nutriment for the littlest cash.

I take my hat off to the saving ways and good dishes of the French, Italians, Germans, and Swedes. We can learn from them.

Then there was the overseeing of the actual running of the White House, all of which had to be fitted into my day along with all sorts of meals and festive affairs.

Before the first week was over I'd worked into a routine that didn't vary except by minutes for the next thirteen years.

At first I was in my office by seven each morning, but later I slowed down to half past or a quarter after. I'd get busy right away checking over the day's meals and making certain how many would be there to eat them, although I could never be sure until they were actually sitting at the table.

Then I'd telephone for anything needed for lunch, which would be my first order of the day. Meanwhile our breakfast was brought in, and Dad and I ate on the run, in the office, and I brewed the first coffee of the day. Usually the aroma brought company in from the outer corridor, secretaries and clerks and admirals and Secret Service men or anyone else who happened to be there. Before long I was making coffee at odd times, and some of my nicest friends on the corridor were made that way. They came to depend on it.

I'm fussy about coffee. I'd catch the kitchen dripping more water into leftover grounds, even for the President, and it would make me cross. There was only a big old-fashioned coffeepot in the White House at first but I changed all that. Personally, I like a tricolator, but what is really important is the whole bean, ground fresh for each making. Grinding releases the aroma and oils. Dad found a little wooden grinder for me, to hold in my lap. I use a tablespoonful of coffee to three fourths of boiling water, and keep the coffee hot on a low-heat electric unit or the back of the stove. Don't forget the dash of salt!

Before long the admirals brought us a lot of green coffee from South America and we roasted it quite dark for the President fresh every morning. Like everything else, if I didn't keep an eagle eye out, the White House coffee was likely to lose its flavor, not being done just right. If it wasn't, the President was frank about letting me know.

Meanwhile I was bobbing to and fro keeping an eye on the kitchen and the trays going upstairs. The butlers were carrying up the breakfasts.

Breakfast at the White House is from six to twelve. Maybe a member of the family or a guest had to catch an early train, and the tray would be rushed up early. Some guests liked to combine breakfast with lunch. Brunch, they called it, a word I refuse to use. It doesn't sound tasty. No matter how many guests there were, they all seemed to like different hours, so the trays were going up in the elevator all morning long.

By that time lunch was on the way.

The White House was the center and jumping-off place for all sorts of people, and Mrs. Roosevelt was the perfect hostess and wanted them to do what they liked and have anything they liked to eat. She always asked them, last thing at night, what they wanted for breakfast, and what hour, and last of all she asked the President, and sent the lists downstairs.

No matter what the papers said, he never did have any repetition in meals. She always sent down a note, last thing at night, so it couldn't have happened.

The queerest meal was the one President Prado of Peru ordered. He had for his breakfast beans, cauliflower, boiled ham, fruit juices, hot and cold milk, coffee, and toast.

We had to remember flowers on the trays; and packages of cigarettes.

The President's tray was the one we were most particular with, not to forget the pitcher of hot milk, and a dog biscuit for Fala after the little black Scottie joined the presidential family. Most of the President's breakfasts were served in bed, and his luncheons were also on a tray in his study or office. But dinner was nearly always "family."

The President also liked fresh flowers on his desk mornings. Sometimes he breakfasted with the family, and they talked so long it cut short the rest of their day, and the President and Mrs. Roosevelt would have to rush through things. Once Mrs. Roosevelt and he talked so long she could give me only three minutes. She wrote about it in her column. But in the beginning we had leisurely visits when I went up to her room mornings.

I very seldom saw Mrs. Roosevelt before breakfast. As a rule she had been up for hours and had her morning's horseback ride along the Potomac, or, after the pool was built,

53

gone for a swim. No matter how late she had been up the night before, she was up with the birds, and as filled with life. She always looked fresh and neat, and sometimes she was wearing one of the beautiful negligees she wore for the family breakfasts upstairs when she had time to relax a bit. I suppose they had been given her, because I can't imagine Mrs. Roosevelt spending a lot of money on luxuries for herself, no matter how lovely they made her look, or how much she spent on others. Once when she was ill and ordered to bed I saw her in a bedjacket that was not elaborate at all, and I don't think she ever went to great extravagance in undies or outer clothes unless it was for some big occasion and she had to dress up to her station. But she was forever ordering hand-embroidered undies and handkerchiefs for other people, and she liked monograms on handkerchiefs. She always chose lovely ones for the President and had them specially embroidered FDR.

Tommy, her secretary, might be in the room, or Mrs. Edith Helm, her social secretary, but pretty nearly always there were babies. Busy or not, the babies were brought in by their nurses at this time, and they'd be on her lap or playing about with their toys on the shabby carpet—and how I wished she had a new one. But no, she said firmly, the budget wouldn't yield a carpet, not this year. Otherwise, she gave me full leeway.

We would discuss her day's routine, where she would be, and what she would need, and go together over all the household details, the menus, change in guests, orders for the girls upstairs and for the butlers up and down. Maybe there were furs to be stored in the cedar room, or laundry to be checked, or something that just had to be bought for the house.

She grasped it all and remembered it, to the last detail, quicker than most women would.

"I trust your judgment, Mrs. Nesbitt," she'd say. "Just go ahead."

That made it even more my responsibility. She knew I'd

save penny for penny, for the Roosevelts or the voters, as if it were my own.

We never crossed opinions on anything. One newspaper reporter wrote that Mrs. Roosevelt and I "got along together like pie and ice cream."

She'd dictate letters to Tommy or approve menus for me with a baby on her lap, and perhaps the older children would run in with their problems and questions and she always found time to answer. Sometimes the babies struck her as being too cute, and she'd scoop them up and rush them into the President's bedroom and plump them down on his bed and we'd hear his booming laugh and the babies' squealing. The Roosevelts all had good, strong beds and needed them, because they were a family that did a lot of wrestling and pillow fighting. The babies got into their beds with them mornings, and the boys, big as they were, wrestled with their father, and I've heard them whooping like Indians when the President tackled them all at once. He had a giant's shoulders and was the strongest of them all.

The strong furniture they liked was Val-Kil, brought down from Hyde Park.

Mr. and Mrs. Roosevelt seemed to have more fun than most married people. The children called them pa and ma, and the President called Mrs. Roosevelt ma, and kidded her all the time. Both loved to laugh, and both could take a joke, even on themselves. She would come out of his room chuckling and laughing and I would hear him laughing.

Sometimes she would tell me scraps of their hilarious conversations, either teasing or controversial, and she would laugh again. Their family talk would keep anyone in stitches. All the Roosevelts were vocal. The butlers would come out of the family dining room with their faces split open with grins. Fields would tell me how hard they tried to keep their faces straight, and sometimes couldn't.

As a family they enjoyed one another.

Downstairs in my office again I'd revamp my ordering and start all over. I'd make out my orders for the next day, plan official menus, and order for them at least two weeks ahead. "Put aside six good roasts of beef," I'd say over the phone, "or save six turkeys." As a rule I'd telephone two or three orders a day.

Once I ordered seventy-five turkeys and one hundred and fifty chickens way ahead, and had them frozen. This was in wartime, and they proved to be a godsend.

By planning two weeks ahead of every big affair I got so I could stop my worrying before it started.

Sometimes after seeing Mrs. Roosevelt I'd send out cars for the last-minute extras, or go myself. I had a car and a colored driver named Moore, whose five sisters all had worked in the White House at one time or another.

I'd have to send out cars to meet guests coming on trains or planes, or take house guests to stations, or fetch extra help, or deliver or pick up packages, besides picking up all the groceries.

It seemed funny at first to be co-operating with the Secret Service on fish fillets or sausages for the President's breakfast. But we had to be careful about such things. Each morning after the war started the Secret Service picked up the groceries I had ordered the afternoon before. They didn't even like my phoning the orders, but it seemed to me safe enough, since all the store people were checked, and the Secret Service men were on the trucks. Last-minute checking does no good unless the store people have been checked first.

There was one shop I liked because the fish was fresh and dependable, but Colonel Starling found out the man had relatives in Germany, and when talk started about ugly activities in that country, and reprisals, I had to stop buying from the man. I was sorry, because we knew he was a good citizen, still there is no use taking chances with food as open to suspicion as fish. I had to watch the security angles as well as the dollars and cents.

Sometime, morning or afternoon, I'd get out for a drive around Washington, picking up fresh fruits or vegetables in the farm markets, hunting for extra tidbits, or buying equipment for the house. This was one of my responsibilities until Maintenance took over everything mechanical in the kitchen line, which was a load off my shoulders. We had a lot to do with Maintenance at first, as we were continually constructing. The pool was built the first year. In '34 the executive office moved in on us and took over and the new kitchen was built in '35 and changed to A. C., which seemed historic to us, though it didn't stir up much excitement outside. Then in '36 we had the rewiring, so we lived the first four years in a continual mess.

But one thing at a time.

The Roosevelts were such a big family that I bought wholesale wherever I could. Sometimes after articles began getting scarce I went incognito to stores where I was not known and managed to scare up a few bargains that way. Once, when lemons went up to seventy-five cents or a dollar a dozen, and we needed dozens for a garden party, I drove all around Washington picking up a dozen here and there. First I sent the driver in, but they charged him a dollar, so I went in and came out with a dozen for seventy-five cents. I realized his uniform upped the price, so after that I did a lot of toting myself in big paper bags. I felt like President Harrison, who used to go to market with a basket on his arm.

But I want to say right here that nearly every person we traded with in Washington was fair and square and didn't up their prices when they saw someone from the White House. And they were wonderful about telling us of specials, and sending out extra deliveries, and opening up at odd hours in an emergency. All the stores and hotel kitchens would open for us Sunday or after hours, and I could depend on them if I got caught short.

By the time I'd wound up my morning menus and phoning,

my secretary—after I achieved one—had the mail opened and sorted. Ruth Terry was my first. Then we had letters to answer, because the White House housekeeper gets an awful lot of mail in her own right, and most of it wanting recipes, or asking what the President liked to eat. Then there were all sorts of telephone calls, and people kept coming in.

Before and after my talking with Mrs. Roosevelt, and on through my day, I was busy bobbing in and out and conferring with the butcher and baker and candlestick maker. I interviewed fishmongers and washwomen, the butlers and head cook, and the supervisor responsible for each floor. I talked with Maggie Rogers, who had been thirty years in the White House and had her own staff on the second floor. I checked with the linen girl who counted the laundry out and back. All the housegirls, between tasks, mended linen. In conferring with the storekeeper, I checked the day's supplies.

There wouldn't be a moment when half-a-dozen people wouldn't be waiting in my office to make reports or ask for information.

Meantime I was checking the monthly bills, straightening the records of my various accounts—petty cash made the most work—and checking the supplies on hand once a week with Dad. I was grateful for the days I had kept books in my father's drugstore.

There were always the upsets. Something got lost, or someone forgot an order, or the oven wouldn't bake.

Maybe it would be five o'clock before I left for home, all tuckered out.

There would be time to take a hot bath and a short nap, write my personal letters to the boys or my niece or the old friends I tried to keep up with, and cook my dinner. It was never an elaborate meal, but Dad and I enjoyed it the more for having seen streams of fancier food all day. Sometimes I'd be too tired to eat once it was cooked.

But if an official reception or dinner was on I had to go

back. I'd wear a dark evening dress, so as not to be conspicuous, and mingle with the guests to see that everyone was taken care of, meanwhile keeping a weather eye out for ash trays and spilled glasses. Dad and I would receive the crested cards, just like regular guests: "The President and Mrs. Roosevelt request the pleasure of Mr. and Mrs. Nesbitt——" Sometimes the Social Office made it "Colonel and Mrs. Nesbitt," to tease Dad.

The part of the evening schedule I enjoyed most was serving sandwiches and coffee to the Social Bureau. These people couldn't leave until all the cards were in the right places on the table and all the guests were checked in, so they couldn't get away until maybe eight-thirty and were glad for a snack in my office. But I had to stay on to the end.

After the long dinner was over I'd go up and see if the pantry girl had everything cleared away, and into the kitchen to see if all the cakes and cookies that could be saved were being saved, and the kitchen itself cleared and scrubbed. I felt cross every time I went into the old kitchen, for no amount of cleaning could make it look clean and I felt sorry for the people who had to scrub it. The kitchen staff left once the kitchen was clear, but the butlers stayed on.

Afterward I'd stay until the reception ended, or the concert, or the dancing, that always stopped just before midnight. Sometimes there would be a motion picture, which always started late so all in the house could go. There were newsreels and good pictures, the newest. The President seemed to like the comedies best, particularly the animated kind, like Donald Duck. No matter how bad things were with the world, he could always be heard laughing over Donald Duck.

Once he sent word that a German film was showing and he especially wanted me to see it because I knew German. I went, but it was a dull picture, and I wished I could leave. Mrs. Roosevelt was bored, too, and slipped out. I saw her go, but I

59

couldn't leave, since the President wanted me there. I forget the name of the picture.

Sometimes it was so late before everything ended, and I was so tired I wouldn't go home. I'd go upstairs to a room I knew had no guests in it and plop down into someone's historic bed and sleep the night through in the White House. Sometimes I'd lie there and not be able to sleep.

Fifty people to dinner. Five hundred to lunch. Five thousand to tea.

Lists like this ran through my head night and day.

What if I did keep them in mind? Or know months in advance who the guests would be, how many we would serve, and what dishes? Then, at the last instant, as thirty guests sat down to a carefully worked out meal, word would come down that twelve extra guests were there.

Word would come down that twelve hundred extra guests would join us at a tea planned for three thousand. I had to keep my head.

I couldn't have done any of it without Mrs. Roosevelt's example. I'd think over the way she did things, and marvel. I'd see her dash through crowds, shake hands with every person there, make graceful exits, change her clothes, come back to meet other multitudes, calm as a queen. She'd keep it up, day after day, year by year. Why should I get flurried when she didn't?

No matter how bad my problems were, she'd straighten me out. I could always ask her.

President and Mrs. Roosevelt were also guests in the White House. Their conduct was public. They had no private lives.

This big building had to be kept open to the world. No matter what happened inside, the machine had to run. Other houses can draw their shutters or lock their doors against disaster or death. Not the White House. No matter what happened, to a Roosevelt or to a nation or the world, the White House stayed open. Twenty-four hours a day. Every day in the year.

I'd think of the children, sleeping in their rooms upstairs, on a third floor that was honeycombed with watchers.

I'd think of my own sons' carefree lives on the farm and thank God we'd been poor, and that they had known work, and freedom.

The family of a President has no life of its own in their fishbowl world. The White House children were normal, happy children, but they were always being watched. Each division of the family had its own Secret Service Guard. Wherever they went, Texas, San Diego, Seattle, Virginia, they lived and slept under watch.

These were the years of the dreadful kidnapings. The Lindbergh baby's murder left a terrible fear. No matter how serene they were, the parents of the President's grandchildren were always afraid.

Even the Roosevelt sons, big as they were, were always under guard.

The iron gate at the Grand Staircase was locked at night and the door guards were before it. On the second floor the Secret Service men were trying to make themselves comfortable for all-night duty. Then, too, the ushers didn't leave the floor until the President was safely in his bed.

The Roosevelt dogs were all over the house.

Around the White House the guards were on patrol all through the night. Sometimes the thought made me shiver before I dropped off to sleep. It was a terrible way to live.

Chapter Five

It was wonderful, considering how little she ate herself, how much Mrs. Roosevelt's mind ran on food.

She wanted to please her family and guests, and she was always fitting menus together and thinking up dishes to please them. She wanted plenty, enough for everyone, and some left over. For herself, she was too much interested in talk to care what she ate. She'd eat anything put before her. Only once did I hear her complain.

That was after a wartime trip she made to England.

"Mrs. Nesbitt," she said to me then, almost pathetically, "please don't serve me any more Brussels sprouts or carrots." But she was particular about everyone else's likes and dislikes, and most of all her mind was on the President's meals. If he praised any dish, or complained about it, she came straight to me. She never went anywhere without having his meals figured out way ahead, and most of our consultations were around the things he liked or didn't like. They were democratic in their tastes and liked everything, until the strain began affecting his appetite.

The day I entered the White House she had been ready with that long list of things he liked to eat, and that list was a Bible to me until Congress got to acting up, and the war worsened, and his temper and appetite failed together. But all in all, the President was an easy man to cook for, once you knew what he liked, and he didn't mind letting you know.

No chance for me to get conceited, looking after his meals.

The newspapers took to saying I ruled the President with a rod of iron. Nonsense. I had an awful time getting vegetables down him.

I've come to the conclusion men just don't like vegetables. They're meat-eaters by nature. There was nothing Mrs. Roosevelt liked better than a nicely arranged salad, but the President always looked at anything with lettuce in it with a sort of martyrish eye, as if he knew it was good for him, but that didn't make him like it. Potatoes seem to be the male notion of a vegetable, even if the man is a president. So one of the hardest jobs Mrs. Roosevelt and I shared was trying to coax vegetables down the President of the United States.

I scoured the countryside around for fresh vegetables. President Roosevelt, as with the country cream, was accustomed to vegetables off the vine at Hyde Park. Even in New York the cream of the crops can be found. The finest, freshest vegetables go to New York. But in Washington, where all the diplomatic world was gathered, it was almost a miracle to find tender peas and young carrots. I found out that the Southern people let their vegetables get riper than Northern people do.

Mrs. Roosevelt seemed to have full confidence in my buying, but once or twice she called my attention to the vegetables. I'd explain they were fresh picked and cost more.

The word niggardly was not in her vocabulary, but nothing escaped her. She wanted the best, but within reason. We bought only in season, waiting until the string beans or berries or whatever were really in. First things are not only too costly, but also they don't have the flavor, and I don't believe in getting the first. Sometimes for a treat I would buy a pint of early berries just for him, and Mrs. Roosevelt took to coming back from her country drives with big bags of fresh vegetables in her car.

The Maryland Farm Women had two markets in the Washington suburbs. We'd bought some of our cakes for the

63

big affairs from them since our first week in Washington. Mrs. Roosevelt was greatly interested in the things they were doing. Several made wonderful cakes, and I gave them some of the recipes the Roosevelts liked. Another was selling home-made furniture, and one enterprising woman sold the legs of frogs her son caught in the river. The President loved frog legs, and when he liked anything, he always took a second helping. We kept an eye on the market for anything that might tempt the President.

Mrs. Roosevelt came back from a trip to New York one day with reports of a wonderful vegetable plate she had at a restaurant, one of a chain.

"They have the most marvelous way of cooking vegetables," she said. "I wish you'd take a run up to New York, Mrs. Nesbitt, and find out how it's done."

So I went to New York and spent a couple of days in Schrafft's kitchens, and they were as nice as they could be, and showed me just how they managed to get every bit of vegetable from kitchen to plate, looking as if it were specially cooked. In a way, each bean and sprout and green pea was cooked separately, because they had a trick of keeping the pot boiling and cooking just a handful of vegetables at a time, so each order was fresh-cooked. It was a neat trick, and I brought it back to the White House and we fixed the vegetables that way ever after.

Cooking the vegetable water down to a broth afterward, to make it tastier, was a trick of my own. Especially for peas.

The President would eat salads if they were dressed up and had a tang to the dressing, and for that I leaned on the White House herb garden, using all sorts of herbs for spicing vinegars and changing the taste of salads, vegetables, soups, and all sorts of things. I don't see how people keep house without a bed of chives near the kitchen.

Even the herbs were historic. For lamb and peas I'd make a trip to the mint bed started by Theodore Roosevelt. But I guess the garlic was my innovation. I can't cook for people who don't like garlic. I don't think they're normal.

All through '33 and '34 we were setting an example to the nation. We used the Cornell economy methods, based on the scientific studies of balanced diet, in the hope of interesting the rest of the nation's housekeepers in getting the most nourishment for the least money. Economic departments all over the country sent me tomes of recipes. My cookbook library and files grew by the yard, until I had the carpenter put up special shelves for them. I learned to keep recipes under lock and key and have copies typed out for the cooks, because people never gave them back.

Mrs. Roosevelt was interested, not only in American cookery, but its history, and she wanted to get American women interested and proud of our traditions. She invited Mrs. Sheila Hibbens, the authority on American menus, to come to the White House and spend several days conferring with me. Mrs. Hibbens gave me, among the other unusual recipes, the one for the George Washington soup the Roosevelts liked so much.

Anna began writing for *Liberty* magazine about this time, and came to me for sample recipes to print in her column.

"Give me one that will really save money," she'd say in that breezy way of hers.

I'd been specializing in that type of recipe for years.

We didn't preach anything that wasn't being practiced right in the White House. We cut the rims off all the sandwiches, and that was an item. We always kept sandwich makings in the White House, where people seemed to get hungry at the queerest hours, particularly after the war started. Then there were the thousands of sandwiches for the big affairs, twenty thousand or more, in a day sometimes. At first I saved the crusts for some of the White House policemen who kept chickens, but later I used them for bread crumbs and puddings, and after the food shortage started we didn't cut off the crusts.

Yes, the Commander in Chief ate leftovers—hash and bread puddings. Relished them too.

Except for special occasions, the White House family was eating like any other American family. Some of the dishes I served regularly were corned-beef hash, poached eggs, and creamed chipped beef. I didn't serve hamburgers, in spite of all the newspaper talk about the President liking them, along with hot dogs, which were mostly for Hyde Park affairs and out of doors. I figured hamburgers were a bit too plebeian for the White House, but the time came when we served them, during the meat shortage. Sometimes, if the food was too simple, the President made wisecracks, and I'd have to stir myself and think up something fancy to even up. The family loved fried corn mush with maple syrup, and we sometimes served it for dessert at lunchtime. Wheat cakes and syrup were Sunday-breakfast standbys. Sunday evening was merry and informal, just for family and friends, and I'd send the eggs up unbroken to the table and Mrs. Roosevelt or Anna would scramble them in the big silver chafing dish by the fire, and they'd have bacon or sausage, salad, coffee, and dessert.

Mrs. Roosevelt sent me a note once:

"The President says that Sunday night when he and Miss Le Hand were alone they had enough bacon and scrambled eggs for six people. I imagine that what happened was that you ordered sufficient in case there were a number of people and then, of course, they did not use their judgment in the kitchen when there were only two people." What she imagined was right. White House cooks had to be omniscient.

I don't think I ever found her irritable. She'd correct people, but so gently, it wasn't like a reprimand. If she did get angry she never took it out on anyone else. Once there was wild duck for dinner.

"The President," the cook Ida used to say, "likes his duck just chased under the flame."

The President told Mrs. Roosevelt later that the duck was overdone.

66

She asked me about it, and I asked the game cook.

I got a meaning look with the answer:

"She took advantage again."

I knew who he meant. No need mentioning names. Mrs. Roosevelt had a guest who had ideas about her importance none of us on the White House staff shared.

Everyone knows duck has to be timed to the split second. Dinner had to be at a certain minute. Just as the party was about to go down to the dining room this guest stopped everything.

"Let's have cocktails," she demanded, as imperiously as if it were her party. It was a fatal interruption. The butlers had to scurry about mixing and serving.

I explained, and Mrs. Roosevelt said it was all right. She kept on inviting the guest, who kept right on acting up.

No matter who came to dinner at the last minute Mrs. Roosevelt never changed the menu. Guests had to take the Roosevelts as they found them. She might order an extra platter of salad and cold cuts, to fill out, but if creamed chipped beef was the entrée that day, creamed chipped beef it was, and no excuses.

Even when guests were leaving, driving back to New York maybe, Mrs. Roosevelt was still urging something nice on them. "Wouldn't you like a picnic lunch to eat along the way?" she'd ask. Then we'd pack a basket with sandwiches and stuffed eggs and cake and maybe salad, and always a thermos of coffee and fruit. We'd make it as nice as we could on short notice. She would have fed the whole world if she could.

I finally reached the point where I was making up two menus daily, one for the President and one for the rest of the family. I ordered the help's food and they fashioned their own menus. Sometimes the dogs had menus too. They need vegetables with their meat like anyone else. Anna usually fed her own dogs. She was thoughtful in little ways, like her mother.

67

All my menus are saved, and Mrs. Roosevelt's scribbled notations are on most of them. Thousands of them were checked over, added to or improved upon, by Mrs. Roosevelt. If they went any place to visit she would ask me to make out their menus ahead, whether it were for a day or for six weeks.

Sometimes I wrote the menus in a criss-cross. No one could ever have made them out. That was when Mrs. Roosevelt told me the President was going some place, and I was supposed not to tell.

There was a sort of unwritten law that a President never dines outside of the White House. But President Roosevelt did. He liked going to the Joseph Kennedys', our Ambassador to England, who had a big family and a place in the country. He liked to visit Pa Watson's lovely place, you could see Monticello from his front porch, and the President would visit Charlottesville when Franklin lived there, and Princess Martha's.

No other President ever did that that I know about, but no other President left this country in wartime, either.

When he went to South America on the *Houston*, I made up a list of his favorite dishes for the ship's mess, and it was practically a copy of the list Mrs. Roosevelt had made out and had ready for me my first day in the White House:

FOODS FOR THE PRESIDENT

Roast beef pink juice running

Steak either with mushrooms, fried onions, or Spanish sauce

Corned-beef hash with poached eggs

Cold corned beef and cole slaw

Lamb legs, filet mignon, or beef

Pork loin or crown, only once in a great while, veal legs the same

68

Chickens braised

Broilers plain or Maryland

Scrambled eggs, fried ham, bacon, or sausage for Sunday nights

Baked Virginia ham

Is fond of calf's liver, calf's kidneys, lamb kidneys, calf's brains, sweetbreads and mushrooms. All kinds of game and guinea fowl, squab, wild ducks, tame ducks, quail, and pheasants

Sunday-morning breakfast usually consists of pancakes and breakfast sausages

Vegetables—No cabbage or kale. We use no canned meats or vegetables—fresh vegetables always or frozen vegetables. I have found that frozen vegetables come up to a very high standard and have used them when the others were poor. I prefer the frozen peas, baby Limas, asparagus, which do not compare with the fresh, but can be used. Also frozen strawberries, raspberries, and cherries for desserts

All kinds of cold cereals. Wheatena served hot

All sorts of salads, especially fond of artichokes, grapefruit, and pineapple

Fond of all cheeses and especially fond of Swiss with mustard and common Gruyère

Uses condiments or sauces very little. Especially fond of caviar and pâté de foi gras. Prefers to eat them with saltines and not on bread.

We use salt or sweet butter

Uses Sanka coffee at night.

Large pint coffee cups for breakfast

Is especially fond of chocolate desserts and is fond of blueberry and other berry pies

We serve fruit and cake most of the time for luncheon desserts

We use whole-wheat bread and unbleached flours. Ceresota is one of the unbleached flours

Whole-wheat flour ground on old-fashioned stone mill can be had from W. R. Crump, R.F.D., #3, Middletown, Maryland. We also get our whole-wheat bread from them. (Taylor's Bakery.)

We vary our rolls and toast with bran muffins made with Kellogg's all-bran and also the different types of hot breads for breakfast

We serve fruit and other ice creams, but the President is especially fond of chocolate

The President does not indulge in many desserts but prefers cheese and crackers

He does not care for either Coconut or Anise flavoring

He had simple American tastes, as a rule, but just the same he was a cosmopolitan and a connoisseur in foods, and if there were special things on the menu, he wanted them just so. He liked things he could dig into. There was a special pâté de fois pastry we used to get for him, and he'd eat it down to the shell and we'd save the shell, put it in the oven next day to heat through, and he'd eat it to the last crumb. But he was a gourmet, not a gourmand.

Mrs. Roosevelt, on the other hand, would be likely to order crackers and milk, or soup and fruit, for her own meal, especially if she were going to catch a train.

One of my small jobs every morning was reading the market news for the best buys. I checked the grocery ads and the market reports before telephoning in orders.

We had the same amount of money to spend that the

other Presidents had, but we managed to entertain a lot more people, because we were thriftier.

The prize foods of many states were sent in as gifts to the President's table, and these helped out the budget. In their season we would receive mangoes from Florida, persimmons from California, frog legs from Florida, cantaloupes from the Middle West, prize beef, ducks, quail, mountain sheep, moose, caribou, quail, venison, brook trout, grouse, oysters, clams, smoked wild turkey, terrapin, and among the first gifts to arrive, was that special delicacy, a beautiful Nova Scotia salmon that weighed forty pounds.

Now salmon was President Roosevelt's favorite dish, and after that any gift of salmon called for it planked or with boiled white sauce, the way my mother-in-law taught me to cook the Lake Superior fish back in Duluth.

Fish, like everything else, is mostly a matter of timing. A four-pound saddle of salmon, cleaned and wrapped in a cloth and tied with string, should boil forty minutes or longer in a kettle of water to which a half cup of vinegar and two tablespoons of salt have been added. The sauce I served with this is simple egg sauce:

Two tablespoons flour and two of butter. Salt and pepper. Two cups of thin cream, or milk, and two hard-boiled eggs mashed with a fork.

I blend the butter and flour in a double boiler, let it simmer a few minutes, add the milk or cream slowly, and stir until smooth and thick, then add the mashed eggs.

For planked whitefish I have the bones removed and place it on a thick oak plank with a ring of salt around to prevent its burning. I brush melted butter over the fish, place it under the broiler to brown slowly, and brush it with more melted butter. It's done when it flakes and the flakes aren't transparent. A delicious sauce for this, if you like chives, is made by

71

adding two tablespoonfuls of chopped chives to a cupful of mayonnaise, with enough paprika to make the sauce pink.

Dad had charge of all the gifts that came in, and he and the President had an argument about hanging the game. Dad believed in hanging birds from the head, the way the English do, because they think in that way the insides can't get a chance to flavor the breast. But the President said, "No, they have to hang by their feet." So of course they did.

Dad built the "ham house" for "the Boss," as he called the President, out of the century-old milk cooler. The hams sent in as gifts hung there, wrapped up in brown paper, and the game was hung there to season.

Dad fixed a lot of things. He built a wine cellar, and set all the bottles on racks, tipped, so the corks stayed wet. When repeal went into effect he typed out a list of everything in the cellar for the President, and at the bottom of the list he put "Nesbitt's home-brew." The President, just as seriously, ordered it.

Lots of wine was sent in for samples, and much of it was not good enough to serve at the table, so Fields made it into punch. I collected punch recipes for the big garden parties. One woman wrote in after eleven years to ask the recipe for a certain punch that had served seven thousand people.

"It was pale green and had a most wonderful flavor," she wrote. "We remember it yet, after eleven years."

I remembered it too. We had mixed gallons of frozen raspberry sherbet with lemon juice and added lemon or orange ice in big bricks, instead of ice. That was Fields's idea. He had good judgment.

The only accident I remember was with a punch bowl at a garden party, when a butler was carrying a big silver bowl with a big cake of ice in it. It was a new bowl, filled to the brim with punch, and the handles broke off.

The different fruit festivals provoked me, but they saved on the grocery bills. The President was showered with prize

cherries, pears, apples, peaches, and every imaginable sort of
fruit. Once a large cherry pie came in that weighed more than
fifty pounds. After its first serving Mrs. Roosevelt dropped
into my office.

"John doesn't want any more cherry pie," she said with
emphasis.

John had loved cherry pie up to then. He must have out-
done himself. So we sent the rest to one of the hospitals, and
got word back that a woman sat up in bed for the first time in
weeks when her slice came in.

"I've just been a-hankering for cherry pie," she said.

Oh, the queens! I was sick of them—the Peach Queen, the
Potato Queen, the Cherry Queen, the Cherry Blossom
Queen. Every festival has to have a queen, I suppose, to come
bearing gifts, but they certainly got in our hair. Once, just as
I was in the thick of affairs on a Saturday afternoon, trying to
get home and back with a diplomatic reception ahead, Mr.
Early's office phoned that a Peach Queen was on her way in
with a basket, and the President's office couldn't see her and
would I pinch hit. I would, gritting my teeth, and a little girl
all made up, about sixteen years old, came in, with an agent,
a chaperon, a manager, and a photographer, and a little basket
of green peaches.

The office filled with smoke and exploded flash bulbs, and
it all seemed such a vacuous affair.

It seemed a pity that the head of a nation, busy with affairs
of government, was supposed to stop and receive these agents
of trick advertising. I suppose, in a way, it's also a form of
diplomacy, but it doesn't seem right. Maybe I don't take a
broad enough view, but a whole lot that went on didn't make
much sense to me.

My cookbook shelves lengthened by leaps and bounds. It
turned out I had to learn the religious and racial customs of

73

our guests who represented other countries and their taste in foods as well. Before long I was collecting cookbooks from every country in the world.

One of the first diplomatic dinners was for the Chinese representatives, and for Chinese people I'd always try for a bland menu. Then for the Mexican dinner I'd have something hot, like Spanish sauce with the chicken. The State Department warned me early in the game to be careful of such matters.

My first lesson came when Ras Desta Demtu, the Abyssinian Ambassador and son-in-law of Emperor Haile Selassie, of Ethiopia, dined at the White House on July 2, 1933. It was one of my first meals for foreign people.

I was going ahead as I would for anyone else when the State Department telephoned to explain that the Ambassador and his retinue were Coptic Christians, and I must act accordingly.

I had to look them up in the encyclopedia. Coptic Christians, it turned out, are members of the native Christian Church of Egypt and eat no meat, butter, cheese, or any product of animal food. That barred my favorite standby, ice cream. Nearly everyone can be counted on to like ice cream.

Finally I worked it all out, using peanut oil for baking, even to the rolls, and olive oil for frying, and a sherbet dessert, which eliminated the use of cow's milk. The Abyssinians sat down to melon, clam cocktail, saltines, stuffed olives, ripe olives, prime fillet of bluefish, grilled tomatoes, Mexican corn, molded potatoes, cucumber and cress salad, beaten biscuit, pineapple ice, stuffed dates, ripe figs, and coffee.

Another thing I learned—Abyssinians always bring gifts to their hosts. The Ambassador brought the President a photograph of Emperor Selassie in a beautiful silver frame and a lion skin rug that turned out to be the bane of my life for fear of moths.

I used this same menu plan for all the Hindu and Moham-

74

medan affairs that came afterward, although the Mohamme-
dans could be served lamb.

But from this time on, when any foreign names popped up
on the lists, I'd telephone the State Department at once,
usually Mr. Sumerlin.

At diplomatic dinners we always tried to give each foreign
representative a dish of his native land, but mostly it was
American cookery.

Dad and I were terribly impressed by one diplomatic reception. I thought the most distinguished were the Hungar-
ians, with their astrakhan turbans under their arms and their
coats fastened behind on their shoulders. There were capes
and swords clanking and lots of gold braid, and Lady Lindsay,
who was so sweet and a great friend of the Roosevelts, and her
tall husband, representing England, six feet four inches of
gold braid. He stood talking to Mr. Sze, the Chinese Ambassador, who was a sizable man but not up to Lord Lindsay.
They looked impressive together.

Then in came little Japanese Ambassador Saito. This was
after the Mulden incident and Japan had started misbehav-
ing, but Mr. Saito was much loved in Washington. He was
very small, and friendly.

England and China were angry with Japan.

I don't know how he felt, but he walked past the two, Mr.
Sze and Lord Lindsay, walking ever so slowly, and looking up
appealingly. But they didn't see him. They didn't speak. He
was so diminutive. He walked past again, but they didn't see
him. They looked straight ahead, a yard over his head, and
went on talking together. I felt as though two great Danes
were ignoring the appeal of a Chihuahua.

Of course I don't pretend to know anything about diplomacy, but it seems to me if I had been one of those two big
men I would have tried to talk things over.

75

Chapter Six

I was like a cat in a strange garret that first summer. Caring for the White House hit me so hard I didn't come out of the fog for months, and not knowing a soul in the city didn't help make it any more real. Mrs. Roosevelt and Mrs. Helm of the Social Bureau saw to it that we had tickets to the White House concerts, and we went to those.

Then there was always Tommy. I couldn't have lived through things if it weren't for Tommy, and I think Mrs. Roosevelt felt the same way. She kept us all cheered up.

Isolated as I was inside the big house on Pennsylvania Avenue, I didn't hear any of the bad talk at first. But it was already starting. It began with the WPA. It began with joking and a lot of sour talk about people falling asleep on their shovels and being made lazy by government support. Those who laughed didn't stop to think it was a matter of life, to say nothing of pride and morale. And they didn't stop to consider that it wasn't the idea that was bad, but that among so many administrators, trying out so vast a new scheme for keeping Americans alive, a lot was bound to be in error. Better a meal by unskilled cooks than folks going hungry!

Then the joking and mean talk started on the CCC, and again it didn't seem amusing to me that six hundred thousand homeless boys were being given work that would help them and help their native land.

President Roosevelt had pointed out that one third of our

great rich wonderful United States—one American in every three—was ill-housed, ill-clad, and ill-fed. He was trying to help the third American.

I had a chance to see some of the Civilian Conservation Corps at close range, for our eldest, Garven, became a supervisor in mechanical maintenance and went from there into the rolling stock, bulldozers, and other engines. He traveled from one camp to another, from Maine to the Carolinas, and talked with thousands of youngsters, and once I had the chance to drive with him to the Carmel camp in New York State Park. The boys looked wonderful, tanned, and as if they were eating, and I thought of the freight trains that had inched across America with thousands of our American youth aboard, wandering and scared and homeless. Lost tribes, whose crime was being young.

These lads at Carmel had put up a bridge and built a lake where none had been before, and it seemed like progress to me. Looking at it in dollars and cents, instead of human salvage, it still seemed a good investment for the nation.

Now it was a queer fact that the first anti-Roosevelt talk I heard came from the inside.

Right away, after he went into office, Washington wages were cut and all government workers' salaries were trimmed 15 per cent. I began hearing ugly comments all about. The criticism and complaining and resentment came from people in government employ and I couldn't help but be disgusted. They knew it was important that the nation try to save, and it wasn't as though they weren't getting enough to live on. Everything was cheap in those days. Food was cheap, clothing was cheap, and even human life itself, with so many banks having failed and people jumping out of windows. Government employees with steady incomes and prices down had not felt the depression.

It seemed to me that people who lived by the government should be willing to live for it.

But this was the first ugly talk I heard, and it came from within the government and inside the White House. The President wasn't working for the job holders but for the people, and this, it seems, was the first charge against him. He was trying something different. From then on all he did was criticized.

Mrs. Roosevelt got the barbs, alongside of him. She would be used, abused and misused, from the start. To my surprise, I would find I was in for a drubbing along with the President and First Lady, small cog though I was, and trying to run my own small affairs in a quiet way. But the first criticism I heard against our housekeeping was when Mrs. Roosevelt brought in all colored help, instead of the mixed staff the Hoovers had in the kitchen, until it was solid Negro.

We retained many who were already there, and brought down two colored butlers, the President's valet, and the two cooks, Ida and Elizabeth, from the governor's mansion in Albany. Ida was temperamental, but she could rise to an emergency better than anyone I ever knew, and Elizabeth was easier-going and even-tempered and later became head cook with the Trumans.

Well, this started the to-do about our way of running the White House, and it kept up for the next thirteen years.

We had our reasons for making this change. Mrs. Roosevelt and I agreed that a staff solid in any one color works in better understanding and maintains a smoother-running establishment.

I had seen this work when I ran three households on the Staatsburg farm, and Mrs. Roosevelt had found it out over a lifetime of running large houses. Personalities have to mesh like gears in a successful household. We finally achieved a wonderful staff of fine people who worked well together. But that didn't stop the talk.

Even the food was under fire. If we pinched the budget to give the guests something extra nice we were extravagant. If we tried to be an example and live economically we were not living up to White House standards and traditions. There was no in-between.

It was turning out as Mrs. Roosevelt had warned that winter day at Hyde Park when she asked me to be housekeeper in the White House. "All we can do is make a plan," she had said. We had our plan and were sticking to it, and the chips were flying all around.

One of the later charges, I remember, was that the Roosevelts owed money to some tradesman in Hyde Park and didn't pay. Fiddlesticks! I know that never happened, and no presented bill was ever ignored, because I paid the bills. I made out the checks and Mrs. Roosevelt signed them.

Budgeting fell on me like the weight of doom, and I couldn't sleep nights for thinking of the awful responsibility of spending money. I'd pinched pennies all my life and now I was pinching thousands of dollars and trying to spread them around. I had three accounts to keep straight. This is the way the funds were distributed.

First, the entertainment fund.

This was given the President by, I think, the State Department, and was to cover his traveling expenses and all the formal entertaining and other expenses his office as President demanded. For this he was given $25,000 a year, later raised to $35,000. I kept the entertaining expenses inside the entertainment fund, and while all official and foreign affairs were supposed to be charged to the state, the Roosevelts entertained many an official guest whose expenses were never charged to the official account.

Every month the President turned $2,000 of his salary over to Mrs. Roosevelt for the White House food, and she turned this over to me. Out of this Mrs. Roosevelt laid aside a certain amount for Christmas expenses, which she had on deposit in another bank. These were usually made out for several consecutive months during the summer, when she did most

79

of her Christmas buying. Sometimes on trips she'd send back asking me for a check, and I'd know it was for gifts that she was picking up here and there all year round.

After the heavier war taxes were imposed the President cut her household account to $1,800.

This money came from the President's office, out of his own salary check.

Each new President is given $50,000 for repairs, refurnishing, extra maintenance, and so on, and he gets this every four years if re-elected. President Roosevelt refused this once that I'm sure of, and I think, too, the last time. The third and worst account was the maintenance, for the upkeep of the White House, given us by the Office of the Interior. This was planned and figured out by the maintenance officer—an army engineer until war turned all engineers back to the Army—and he put in his estimate each year against the coming year, and our budget for it was around $125,000 to $135,000.

This covered all the running expenses for the White House, such as gas, water, upkeep of the building, painting, salaries of gardeners, housekeeper, servants, replacement of household furnishings, kitchen utensils, glass, silver, linen, laundry, the force kept on to maintain the house such as the engineer, electrician, carpenter, painter, and their helpers, and per diems brought in extra to help out with the official entertaining. Soap, wax, plumbing, and electric bills all came out of this. The wages of the White House staff totaled about $100,000. Our electric bill was nearly a thousand a month. Laundry was between three and five thousand a year.

Curtains, draperies, carpets, rugs, and so on were squeezed out of maintenance, in this way—if there was a surplus at the end of the fiscal year it was usually turned over to me for these replacements.

There wasn't enough left over at first to allow for the new rugs I longed for, especially in Mrs. Roosevelt's bedroom, where the blue carpet was so historic it caught your heels. I brooded over that carpet all through the first administration, but Mrs. Roosevelt insisted it didn't matter and we needed other things more, such as the new kitchen, so we could entertain properly. The Roosevelts entertained more than any other presidential family, traveled more, had more friends and more enemies.

Also I was kept busy completing the maintenance lists Dad had started and classified: dairy, candy, nuts, groceries, meats, fish, wines, bakery goods, and such, so when anyone wanted to know how much coffee or anything else was being used, I could put my finger on it in our large cash journal. I knew to a penny what was being spent.

All these and a hundred other headaches came under the heading of maintenance. I dreamed about it nights.

Still, I knew what a small task it was, compared with all the President was trying to do. He was trying to balance the world's budget these trying times, and keeping a lot more cheerful about it than I did, wrestling with White House checkbooks and trying to find out how much was spent for shoe polish for the upstairs valets.

He was trying to persuade the countries of the world to lay down their arms, and as a result all sorts of mysterious emissaries from foreign lands were coming to the White House, and we were supposed not to talk about some of them. "Hush-hush dinner," I'd write in my diary, or "Mr. B in the Rose Room," about some of them. Things were beginning to look bad over in Europe this summer, for Hitler was given supreme power over Germany, and the ugly reports showed that country heading straight back to the Dark Ages and worse. The stories coming out of Germany made me sick at heart, because we knew they were true.

One of the never-ending jobs was the effort to keep the White House tidy. In these prewar days more than a million people came each year to see the White House and had to be shown all over the grounds and through the rooms. You know how you feel when your house is clean and somebody's feet track in mud. Well, multiply those footprints by a million.

The ground floor was in a perpetual state of being cleaned. The floor was scrubbed early in the morning and mopped up in sections through the day when needed. The linen covers on all the chairs had to be changed each day and the stair railing of the Grand Staircase was dusted three or four times daily. A man kept on wiping his way to the bottom and starting up again.

No old house stays clean very long, especially in the heart of a busy city, and with all those people coming and going we dusted the entire house two and three times a day.

Sometimes we served beer at press parties from barrels in the lobby, and the next morning we would have to go over it with the electric brush and mop and marble dust, and the stairs, too, and all before ten. The President's office had to be dusted before breakfast. Then there were cigarette stubs to deal with. Smoking was allowed in the lobby but not in the dining room at these crush affairs, for fear of fire and the President.

We always had a fire chief and his aides watching in every crowd.

There were sixty rooms to be cared for and twenty baths. Every floor had to be polished, and every rug vacuumed each day. The linoleum on the kitchen floor had to be hand-washed with soap and water and waxed and polished at the end of each day.

The White House leaked a lot. Rain came through the soft stone and stained the guest-rooms walls. So we had to have them done over all the time. We painted, washed twice, then painted again. Mr. Edmundson, head of the painting department, could match a dirty paint as exact as if

82

it were fresh. He could patch a wall so it wouldn't show. Painters, carpenters, electricians, plumbing forces, formed a parade that never ended.

All of the kitchen end of the White House was cut up and difficult to operate in before we remodeled. We had the storage space that had been a dairy cooler in early days, with cement troughs to set the milk cans in, so water could run through to cool the milk. Trouble was, the rats ran through them too. We were warring on rats day and night.

Dad winked at the cement trenches. "Let's make a little fix," he said, and he had the engineer fit tin roofs over the trenches and they kept the rats out of the storage at least.

I'd known at the start all those White House windows would be a pain, and they were, and I'm not trying to be funny. They caused a great deal of tension. There were one hundred and sixty windows, I think, five to each corner suite, plus the fan windows. The floor men were expected to clean them along with their other work, and no one seemed to understand that our floor boys were busy all the time. There were six boys and girls to each of the four floors, responsible for the cleanliness of the rooms.

The floor boys also served as valets to the guests, and many of our guests were demanding, giving suits and shoes to be cleaned, and issuing orders as if they were in a hotel. The boys had to defer their schedules to the guests, and if a guest felt like sleeping late, they had to work around his room.

Of course the living-room floor, where the Roosevelts lived and the guests stayed, was my main concern. The second floor it was called. Mine was called the basement floor, though it wasn't a basement.

The boys were supposed to do the windows there when the Roosevelts were gone. But the Roosevelts weren't gone very often, not all at once anyway. Washing the windows there, two stories up, was dangerous. The carpenter told me the fastenings were loose in the soft stone, and the boys told

83

me they were afraid. Finally I got hooks put in, and stretched the maintenance fund to bring in professional window washers.

I worked up an efficient corps on the principle, "Put a person in charge, leave him in charge, and hold him responsible." And of course everyone who worked in the White House had been thoroughly checked by the Secret Service. Interviewers wanted to know whether I preferred men cleaners or cooks to women, and I'd never say. Some do one thing best and some another but we got everything to a working system after a while.

The women were to empty wastebaskets, dust the rooms and all low pictures they were able to reach, clean and wash stands, medicine cabinets, closets, dresser silver, mops, and dusters, and see that ice water was in all the thermos bottles. The maids were to help repair and put away linen, put things where they belonged, and keep them there in their free time.

The floor men had the windows, skylights, and stairs, the large mirrors, high furniture, high pictures, and the care of all desks and floors, the study and Rose Parlor, offices and halls, steps, woodwork, banisters, brasswork, floor silver, hall silver and water trays, bookcases and books, and washing up the hearths.

The valets had the cleaning and care of the gentlemen's boots and shoes, packing, unpacking, and pressing.

One of the petty officials heckled me about one of the hearths. He came up to me during a reception, whispering:

"Mrs. Nesbitt, you must go to the East Room, some newspaper is showing in the fireplace."

I hurried into the East Room, where the four fireplaces were all carefully laid, according to tradition. It was one of my more interesting duties to see they were laid out like studies in still life, with paper under, kindling, heavier woods, and on top, ready for the firing, big chunks of wood with knots that I loved to hear popping away in the fire. I looked, and they were all in apple-pie order, but in one a little edge of paper was sticking out. It took me a second to tuck it under the kindling, thinking how easily he could have done it, but no, he was an officer and gentleman, it seemed.

I thought of the dozens of times I'd seen Mrs. Roosevelt poke up a fire or move a chair around or pass plates, even when there were butlers about to do it for her. She didn't take time to fuss. The President didn't care for formality · either. We'd send up snacks when he was in conference, plates of cheese and crackers or bread, and he loved scooping out cheese for the others. Pâté de foie gras, too, when we had it.

We had a set of rules printed for the house so each one could tell exactly what he was supposed to do.

RULES GOVERNING HOUSEMAIDS
AND HOUSEMEN

1.   In the morning, the maids make up the beds using the same linen, if the guests are staying more than the night. They put fresh water in the rooms, clean the ash trays and silver, so the men can follow immediately to do their work. After the men are through, the maids dust the rooms and finish all the little extra things such as pins, stationery, soap, towels, etc., seeing everything is in perfect order. As soon as the rooms are completed, the maids are to retire to the third floor, leaving the second floor for guests only. The maids should be ready to answer any bells when they are rung. All spare time is to be spent in helping with the mending.

2.   When the house is being put in order for special occasions, no one is supposed to leave until everything is in order and ready, regardless of time.

3.   The men and maids must come upstairs when their lunch hour is over, while the family and guests are at

their meals, and have everything tidied up by the time the people return to their rooms.

4. The men must keep the closet clean next Miss Thompson's office, being sure it is left clean every day.

5. The men must help each other to take up and down the laundry.

6. The help must not engage guests in conversation. Only speak when spoken to, unless it is regarding the guests' clothes.

7. When the guests and family go to dinner, the maids put the fruit in the rooms and take out the flowers, tidy up the ash trays, and dust.

8. Maids must not put linen with holes, or torn linen, in the bathrooms or on the beds.

9. Each one should let the head man know when he is leaving the building for an errand, or wants to get off.

10. After the cleaning up after lunch, maids dress for the P.M. The maids must be dressed and at their posts when the guests arrive, if there are ladies coming.

11. The men must look out for the luggage. The men and the maids both unpack if the people wish it.

12. The third-floor man must help to clean the brass from the second floor.

13. The maids are to give assistance when inventory is taken of linen for the second and third floors.

The holidays for the help, turn and turn about, were a problem.

I've just come across a note Mrs. Roosevelt sent to me regarding their time off:

"They may have to arrange amongst themselves in order to

get the time off on a co-operative basis because of the changes." That was when help got scarce.

One of my first moves was the auto-da-fé of the feather dusters and corn brooms. "They just lift up the dust and throw it around," I'd tell the girls. "The dust settles right down again." But the help loved them, so I confiscated them all and burned them.

There was a light well on the top floor that they vowed could be reached only with a feather duster, so I showed them how much easier and cleaner the long-handled vacuum brush did it, and they followed orders, but weren't convinced.

Maggie Rogers, who tended Mrs. Roosevelt's room, begged to keep a little bright-feathered duster she used on all the little jade and ivory knickknacks Mrs. Roosevelt kept on her mantel, so I let her have it. Thirteen years later, just before I left the White House, I caught one of the maids using another big feather duster! Those Southern girls are set on tradition. I couldn't say I blamed them much, considering the Roosevelts' passion for collecting objects.

They loved *things*. Gadgets, mementos, souvenirs, pictures, books. They loved these the way they did people, children, dogs, horses, trees, and flowers. I think they loved everything and everybody and all the world.

Mrs. Roosevelt had her walls covered with pictures, and so did he, and everyone knows what dust-catchers pictures are. All the Roosevelts were addicted to pictures. In their New York apartment he had one hundred and eight pictures in the hall alone. Currier and Ives prints mostly. The President had one of the biggest collections in the country. She had pictures on the doors that held linens, and one wall in her White House sitting room was solid with photos of family and friends, all collecting dust.

We had one room we called the Gift Room, where the President put all the gifts sent him. That was a mess! There were three cabinets of quartz, crystal, jade, and ivory carvings alone, and an oriental rug woven in his likeness, and paintings, mosaics, things made out of cigar boxes and fantastic roots and seashells, and caricatures of him, or maybe good paintings, on paper or wood, and in china and bronze. Some of the things were real art and some gave y the shivers. There were beautiful gifts, and touching one d some that were plain crazy.

There was his collection of wooden 1 , his stamp collection, and all sorts of bowls, vases m and goblets. All to be dusted. A gruesome job.

There was also Mrs. Roosevelt's gift room, where things were ranged alphabetically, on shelves.

Dad used to shake his head at all the things.

"When the Roosevelts decide to go home," he'd say, "it will take a fleet of trucks to move the presentation gifts alone."

There was the storeroom, too, where we kept things a certain length of time in case people might send along a bill for their "gift." There was one "gift" that made us more trouble, and kept our corridor stirred up through one summer. It was a miniature someone sent to Mrs. Roosevelt, and then sent a letter demanding it be paid for. Mrs. Roosevelt hadn't seen the picture, and referred the matter to Tommy, who referred it to Mr. McGee of the Social Bureau, who referred it to me. Dad brought out his records, which showed that the little picture had been sent to the Social Bureau.

By this time the corridor was in a tizzy and the Secret Service came in on the investigation. Mr. McGee finally found the miniature tucked in the back of a drawer of a desk in the Social Bureau which had been moved a number of times, where it had been placed and forgotten, and I hate to think of the time and money wasted because of a picture somebody sent to a President's wife who didn't want it in the first place.

But there was no wonder it was lost. There were sixteen

desks in the Social Bureau, all crammed together in a tiny office that was even smaller than ours.

Dad, as custodian, was bonded, and so was I, later. Among other things we were in charge of all household equipment. For instance, when Judge Rosenman came to visit, which he often did, and was given a nook to work in. He would take pieces of furniture to work with, a desk and chair maybe. The ushers would borrow other chairs and things, and we had to keep all these things located, and put back.

Silver, dishes, and linen were watched, but things vanished from the White House just the same. I hate to say it, but so many pieces of silver were missing after teas and other affairs that I stopped having the spoons and things monogrammed. When guests commented—guests of the White House are frank in commenting on almost everything—about our silver not being the finest, I'd shut my lips and say nothing.

For the very large convention teas we used plated spoons and picnic china, often borrowed or rented from a government cafeteria.

How did they manage to get those big silver trays out under their coats? After one big function we missed two large trays, and one of four big silver colonial bowls I'd had made up special, and a lot of spoons.

We couldn't keep the twelve-inch trays. I'd send them over to the executive office with things the President wanted, milk or beer and crackers and cheese, and they just didn't come back. Everyone was busy. "What happened to them?" I'd ask. Nobody knew.

They were not sterling, but they did have the presidential crest and the smallest cost five or six dollars. As for the little silver salt spoons for the formal dinners—they just melted. I often wished we could trust the White House guests as we did the help.

Fields reported losses to me after every affair.

Once, after a colored people's tea, he reported to me that a pair of sugar tongs were missing. As head butler he knew things were always missing after any sort of White House affair, usually two or three trays at least, but he seemed terribly put out by the tongs. But Fields's pride was hurt. He knew White House guests took things, but these colored guests were his own people, and he expected better of them.

The silver and the dishes all had to be kept track of. One set of dishes had more than a thousand pieces. Think of keeping track of one hundred bouillon cups! So things had to be watched, as well as kept clean.

The archives, capitol, and executive offices, all had their corps of night cleaners, and I wanted the same for the White House. You can't shoo people out of the White House and clean, as in other houses. The White House keeps open all the time, with no time for a spring or fall housecleaning and we had to work whenever a room was empty. I wanted the extra corps to come in on occasion and give the house a special going over, but I never managed to put this over. The maintenance fund wouldn't stretch.

We watched for departures. If Mrs. Roosevelt went on a trip we rushed the cleaners in for a good "going over" that was impossible while she was in it. The walls were washed, floors cleaned and waxed, and if there was time, the draperies were cleaned. Even if Anna Boettiger and the children left for the afternoon, it gave us a chance to get at their rooms.

Sometimes I longed for a good old-fashioned housecleaning with everything done up at once. But no, we had to work around the Roosevelts and their activities.

I didn't have my diary-keeping regularized this summer of '33, but I did get down some scratches, and most of them were about the Press Party on June 1, and the Abyssinian prince, and Mrs. Roosevelt asking all my family to visit the

White House, with the use of the cars. It was the first of many happy visits the boys and their families made, and while Bobby was the only grandchild we had at the time, the others would come along in turn and have their earliest memories of the big white home that was the heart of their republic, and the tall, kind-faced woman who made them as welcome there as if they were her own. Sometimes Midge, my daughter-in-law, left Lynn with me when she went shopping, and my little granddaughter would go upstairs for her afternoon nap as if the White House were her second home.

The Press Party was the first of that kind for me, and this annual affair became one of my principal dreads year after year. There would be maybe fifteen hundred newspaper people, and dancing and a hot buffet supper. It made a lot of work because of the food served and the coffee and fruit punch. The floor was always a mess after any of these pass-it-around affairs. There would be bits of frosting and stuff in the carpets, and all in all, I dreaded anything buffet.

People bump into each other and spill at teas and buffets. When I knew a meal would be messy I'd have eight men roll back the big dining-room carpet and put it away or we would have to clean it after every party. Just the same, that sort of party always seemed more fun, and more relaxed, then any other kind, which is perhaps why it makes so much work afterward.

I remember on July 20 Ike Hoover came along the corridor and poked his head in our door.

"Balbo is in the East Room," he said. "Want to go up and see him?"

We said we did, so Ike took us in, and I felt embarrassed, because it was the first time Dad and I had done anything like that, and it seemed queer to be going in to stare at guests. But a lot of others of the staff had come in, too, and Balbo and his party stared right back at us, and seemed as interested as we were. Something had gone wrong with the schedule and the President didn't get over from the office as soon as planned, so the Italian hero was being kept waiting. It was terribly hot, and he sat hunched up, with that patch over his eye.

Somehow he looked unhappy and weary, but that was understandable, because he had completed the first flight around the world.

He was supposed later to have been murdered in Abyssinia by the orders of Mussolini. We didn't know then how bad things were. But I remembered his face, when I heard of his death, and he did look haunted.

After that I made a point of going up to peek at celebrities. I saw Marconi that way, and lots of others.

I think it was this sizzling summer that the affair of the music box came up. Mrs. Roosevelt was leaving town for Hyde Park, and she delegated an errand to me. A woman and her daughter were trying to sell Mrs. Roosevelt a music box.

"They seem to be on their uppers," she said. "Perhaps you can call on them and see if they need help."

I'd never had any social-service experience, but I went to see them. They were cooped up in a hot little second-floor hall bedroom, without any food, and without a cent. They wanted one hundred dollars for the box. I could see it wasn't worth much, and Mrs. Roosevelt didn't need it anyway, but I thought at least we could see they had something to eat. They stressed the fact there was nothing to eat in the place.

It was Sunday and the stores were closed, so I went back to the White House and got cooked meat and butter and such, and they were so incensed when they saw it, I had to carry it all back. They wanted money, and nothing else.

On my way back I dropped in on their clergyman, but he just threw up his hands. They'd been bothering him for months, but he hadn't found any way to help them.

They needed care, so I sent a social worker, but that didn't help. They didn't stop trying to reach Mrs. Roosevelt for two years. They kept on writing and trying to see her, to get money.

If she had given to all who asked, she would not have been able to live.

Tommy fought off the pests, but she was hounded. People from all over the United States were trying to get to her. Tommy had to say "no." Tommy would sit talking to me, sorting over letters and tossing them into baskets. She was never through.

They took the typewriter on the train or wherever they went, and started right at work answering letters.

Mrs. Roosevelt didn't believe in wasting anything, even time. Once I drove up from New York with them in the car, and she asked me to please excuse her as she had to write a speech. So Tommy and I sat without talking, and she sat thinking and jotting down notes, and her speech was done by the time we reached Hyde Park.

That awed me, because once in Hyde Park I'd taught a Sunday-school class of high-school age, and I rashly told the minister I'd like to go through the Old Testament from cover to cover, and he told me to go ahead, and I managed to keep just one jump ahead of the class.

By fall of '33 Washington had cooled off and we had the working routine of the White House in order and all the Roosevelts were back and the winter season started off, and what a season that was to be. Mrs. Roosevelt's birthday was October 11, and I had Elizabeth make an angel-food cake, knowing it was her favorite, and we had duckling, too, because she liked that.

Right after that we started planning for our first holidays in the White House. We began working on Thanksgiving months ahead, and on Christmas even before Thanksgiving.

Maxim Litvinoff was in and out of the White House about this time. He was the Commissar from Russia. He and President Roosevelt were fixing up diplomatic relations again between Russia and the United States, which was important, because we hadn't been friendly for some reason since Russia revolted against the Czars. President Roosevelt announced it, this November '33. It was all terribly hush hush, and I never did catch a glimpse of Mr. Litvinoff, but then I didn't try. I was too busy with the fruitcakes to pay much attention to what was going on outside my door. I wasn't supposed to peek, so I didn't.

Maybe if I'd been more curious, I'd have more to say.

Chapter Seven

Before Thanksgiving I was deep in the Christmas dark fruitcakes, the white, and the nut cakes. The plum puddings were made up then and hung in the storeroom, getting darker and richer-smelling by the hour. Mince and pumpkin pies were the favorite desserts up until New Year.

"Mrs. Roosevelt is so pleased," I wrote in my diary. I took my hands out of the fruit-slicing and nut-chopping for Thanksgiving.

Thanksgiving in the White House is almost as important as Christmas. Mrs. Roosevelt sent out hundreds of boxes of homemade things for the tables of friends. Then there were all the turkeys she ordered for people. They had to be checked and packed and delivered.

To show the way she remembered things, I gave her a letter from a woman who raised turkeys, and the next year I brought her another letter from the same woman, and the minute she saw the handwriting on the envelope she said quickly:

"Oh, that's about turkeys."

The President loved the sight of a turkey. It had to come onto the table whole, so he could have the pleasure of carving, and the whole dinner was spoiled for him unless a necklace of little sausages was smoking all around the bird. They had to be a certain kind of sausage.

Chestnut was their favorite stuffing. For this I use two-day-old white or whole-wheat bread, never the crusts, cover them

95

with water, let stand five minutes, and squeeze it out. Chop the giblets fine, add two thirds of a cup of chopped onions cooked until transparent in five tablespoons of fat, and thyme, parsley, savory, nutmeg, and salt. I stir the bread crumbs in with a two-tined fork, to keep the dressing light, then add the chestnuts that have been cooked and mashed through a sieve.

I roast turkey in a hot oven, basting every ten minutes, so it's brown and moist and sweet.

There were always a lot of gay affairs in between the two holidays. December 10 was the Gridiron Widows. This is held while the newspapermen have the President at the Gridiron affair at the big hotel and everyone is put on the pan. Meanwhile, the ladies are asked to the White House, and these yearly affairs were always lots of fun. The ladies had skits that were take-offs on current affairs and people in the news, and once we had a fancy-dress party. Along with the secretaries, I was asked to this affair, and ever after.

The press girls wrote the skits and a lot of them lampooned Mrs. Roosevelt and she'd laugh harder than anyone. She seemed at her best at informal affairs. Mrs. Morgenthau was one of the best actors and always got a lot of applause. Dorothy Thompson often came, and Fannie Hurst. I remember Miss Hurst in a white satin dress so tight it made me uneasy, and Lady Lindsay always came if she was in Washington, and once she got up and gave a humorous talk that was the hit of the evening.

I remember there were three or four hundred at this first Gridiron Widows' affair, and we had supper at little tables in the big dining room and spread over into the parlors. There was chicken salad, angel-food cake, ice cream, and coffee—fifty chickens, forty angel-food cakes, eighteen or twenty gallons of ice cream, and twenty gallons of coffee, I wrote down in my little book. I learned to plan chicken salad at eight people to a hen, if the guests were ladies.

That night I sat next to Mrs. Warren Robbins, from South

America, and related to the President. She was tall and good-looking and the first person I had ever seen with hair tinted lavender. I couldn't take my eyes off her. She turned out to be as smart as she looked, and later on she interior-decorated some of the foreign embassies.

We had the Gridiron Widows, a Todhunter dinner, and a diplomatic reception all in the same week. That week we had the Todhunter senior students as house guests. This was the graduating class from the Todhunter School in New York. Both Mrs. Roosevelt and Tommy had worked in the school, and I used to marvel at the way Mrs. Roosevelt had kept up with her teaching and everything else back in the days when she lived in Hyde Park. Those were the times I was kept hopping keeping up with my Sunday-school lessons, and I asked her once how she managed.

"Oh, I prepare my lessons on the train," she answered. "Going up and down."

She brought the Todhunter girls to Washington to show them the city and the workings of government administration as part of their education. Sixteen or eighteen came every year. We'd put cots up, and the second floor would be like a girls' dormitory, full of laughter and girls running around. These girls were shown a lot that daughters of wealth in other schools never see. They were taken to sweatshops, and told about the way they were run, and into the slums of New York, to see how others lived. It was her purpose to bring up wealthy children so that their minds should be open to suffering. She wanted to give the rich girls a purpose in life that wasn't all butterfly.

Everything she worked for had its purpose. Val-Kil was a purpose. The factory was trying to give people of ability and talent a chance. I think her sympathy came from her own hurt, lonely childhood. In her life, she told how happy she was as a child when she could run errands for anyone, and how happy she was when they noticed her. That, and

97

the charitable training she had had with that teacher in England. I think she felt sorry for all young people, for the under privileged, and for the over privileged, neglected rich children left to servants.

That last kind of neglect is hard to prevent, no matter how much care is taken.

It was during this Christmas season, with the place running over with rich foods and rich smells, that I heard in the kitchen that one of the Roosevelt grandchildren was on a diet, and went up to the nursery floor to see for myself. The simple milk puddings and milk soups we usually sent up to the children had been forbidden, and I found out why. His nurse was on a diet, and was cutting out these foods, which were favorites with the children.

I tried to protest in behalf of the little fellow, who wasn't looking any too well.

"At least he can have his milk pudding," I said.

"He doesn't like pudding," the nurse snapped.

"I do like it," the little fellow protested, but we were both overridden, and he didn't get his pudding, or soup either.

If ever a child looked as if he needed nourishment, that one did. But I was helpless. I had no authority over the nurses. All I could do was feel sorry for a little boy who was the pet of the White House and whose name was famous all over the world.

Standing where I did in the White House, between the back stairs and the grand staircase, I had a chance to see both sides.

December found me still up to my ears in fruitcake. The process from chopping to packing is all joy to me, and part of Christmas. I guess the White House favorite was the dark fruitcake that I made for the household and their friends, and a big one, special, for the President's birthday every year. No matter how many cooks we had, the cake was my work, and baking more than two hundred pounds of cake is a long ,job. The kitchen help got the fruit ready.

Six pounds of cut dates. Six pounds of raisins. One and a half pounds of almonds, blanched and sliced lengthwise. Two and a fourth pounds of citron in long slivers. Three cups of orange peel also slivered.

I defy any woman to chop up fruits like these, all pungent and sugary, and keep up any personal brooding. Fruitcake mixing can be heartily recommended as a cure-all for grouches and blues. For me, it always seems romantic, and reminds me of lines in poetry. "Dates and figs of Samarkand," and "lucent syrops, tinct with cinnamon."

I take my time with the fruit fixing, and enjoy it. Then I pour a pint of brandy or rum over the mixed fruit and let it stand all night or longer.

The batter I mix like a pound cake:

One and a half pounds brown sugar. One and a half pounds butter. One and a half pounds flour. Eighteen eggs.

To this mixture I add one and a half cups of honey, two grated lemon rinds, one and a half teaspoons each of mace, nutmeg, and salt, a fourth teaspoon of cloves, and three teaspoons of cinnamon.

Then I mix in the fruit, and bake it in lined pans at a low oven temperature with a pan of water in the oven to keep the cake moist. The cooks did the baking and watching. The President wrote me a note once, after I'd made one for his birthday. "Perfectly delicious! FDR."

All sorts of things come into my diary this December, along with the accounts of the cakes. A note for December 14 says, "Cardozo and Chief Justice Hughes to dinner." It makes me laugh, seeing this, and remembering how terrified I was, up till then, of Supreme Court Justice Cardozo. I had seen him on the bench, wearing the black gown, looking serious and profound, but with his hair wild. I thought he was as frightening as Napoleon must have seemed in his day.

This evening I was in the corridor when he came trotting in on his way to dinner, and recognized me and stopped to speak. I was so surprised I can't recall what he said. He was all prinked up, dapper and neat, and with his hair combed so, it looked like a halo and made him appear as innocent as an angel. Seeing him close, I realized those snapping eyes that looked so awful in court held a glint of the pixie.

I decided he was real human and after that I loved watching Justice Cardozo come in, always looking like a good little angel prinked up for the party.

Nobody seems awesome when you meet them face to face like that. Put a slice of good apple pie before any human, and he'll melt. Maybe that's why greatness doesn't awe me so much as it does some.

When Christmas came, all the five-ring-circus excitement of the past year seemed to gather to a point in the White House and explode in a lather of tinsel stars. I never saw so much excitement and so much affection shown. I never knew people that loved Christmas the way the Roosevelts did. And to think I'd survive a round dozen more with the Roosevelts, getting more exciting, and sweeping in wider circles, year after year! Even toward the last Christmas was risen to, like a hymn, and no matter how busy Mrs. Roosevelt was, she remembered us all.

This was the day she had been fixing for all the year. It was her day. She never did think of herself. Maybe that was why.

I don't think she ever went on a trip or a shopping tour that she didn't bring home something. "That's for Christmas," she'd say, happy as a child. "Just put it away."

She'd sent big cartons down from New York filled with

gifts to be kept in the storeroom. The last months of the year she sent in carloads of candy and toys, all to be packed and dressed in pretty ways for Christmas.

She bought specific gifts for specific people when she could. She liked handmade things, woven, or beaten out of metal, because she loved anything that people had joy in making. She tried to share her experiences so she did it with gifts, bringing back things from her trips to all of us, to let us know how other places were. She brought me a pin from Guatemala with silver fruits, a knitted suit from Canada, a set of hand-woven doilies from the Tennessee mountains. She always remembered the little things.

She tried to have something for everyone, because she had a place for everyone. She saw something in everybody that made them worth-while—something of value, not to her, but to them. She tried to bring that out by giving them a feeling of self-respect and worth. She believed each person ought to stand alone, in his own right as a human being.

That was the spirit that came out strongest at Christmastime. The President felt the same way, so everyone around the Roosevelts felt their happiness, and there never was a Christmas in the White House while they were there that wasn't joyous. Once Franklin was sick and away in school, and Mrs. Roosevelt went to see him, but she was back in time for the tree.

Everyone in America knew what went on in the White House at Christmastime, because the Roosevelts wanted everyone to know and share in it, but only those inside knew the work that led up to it.

Things started popping about a week before. By this time the storerooms were stuffed, and the pressing room too. Gifts were on tables and shelves, and we set a big table upstairs, and Mrs. Roosevelt's secretaries and the maids would start wrapping, and she'd wrap, sometimes until two in the morning.

"The box is half the gift," she'd say, and she always did gifts beautifully, getting the prettiest boxes to be found, and tying them up with white tissue and the bright ribbons I bought from the five-and-ten. She wrote the messages herself, on their personal cards.

The Roosevelts' Christmas cards were pictures of the White House at various angles, or a photo of them both, or of the children, or maybe one of the dogs. The first Christmas card, in '33, was a scene of the South Portico. Tolly, the White House engraver, did the scenes by hand, and had them copied. He made the pretty shipping tags we used, too, with the steel engraving of the White House.

Meantime the rest of us were whooping it up downstairs. All those cakes and things had to be wrapped. First we worked on the boxes that were to go outside of Washington. There were the fruitcakes I'd mixed and supervised, and all sorts of jars of jams we'd been putting up in the different fruit seasons. We packed carloads of Christmas boxes in my office—a cake to a box, with some jams, jellies, nuts, Christmas cookies, and candies. Mrs. Roosevelt liked the fruitcake wrapped by itself in cellophane, with outer tissue and ribbons, and the other things tucked around, and a tray of candies and nuts on top. And this box might be just one of several we sent to a person.

Any friend of the Roosevelts was likely to get two boxes, one with things to eat and another with something pretty or useful.

Turkeys and fixings were sent out, too, as at Thanksgiving.

I had a long list of people to send boxes to each year. There were always a lot of older people she remembered. There was a vagrant she'd picked up in her car once, and got a job for, and his name was on her list of friends. There was Leo Casey, the New York State policeman who had been thrown from his motorcycle while guarding the President, and often came to see her in his wheel chair. Special boxes were made up for him Christmas and Thanksgiving, too, and I'd put in cheeses and fancy tidbits and ransack the storeroom for things he would like.

There were some names I would have given a lot to have scratched off the list. Even Christmas had its parasites. One man begged of her regularly, when he wasn't in need at all. Another Christmas recipient wrote Mrs. Roosevelt that I had sent him a capon when he expected a turkey. He complained to her!

She didn't get cross, but I did.

Once Dad and I packed forty-seven cakes in one night, to get clear. Captain Lock came in and read us the riot act for overworking.

"You're here to direct, not work," he said. "Let the help do the packing."

But we were in full Christmas swing by this time and couldn't stop. Carloads of boxes were going out of the shipping room, and carloads more coming in.

It was all fun. Dad had two men checking lists, and was still way behind. My stenographer was making lists, and upstairs and downstairs secretaries were trotting around with long lists and mysterious expressions.

The children, of course, were in the usual Christmas dither. There wasn't a trick in old-fashioned Christmas feeling that wasn't poured out for the benefit of the Roosevelt babies.

I suppose world history was being made in the President's office, but I was too busy to think much about it.

Added to the general hullabaloo was the session of affairs that burst out this week before Christmas. December was the start of the winter social season, and there were dinners and luncheons, and one concert with an artists' supper at midnight that consisted of chicken, consommé, fillet of lamb, peas, romaine and grapefruit salad, orange blossom parfait, angel cake, and coffee.

Music seems to make people hungry. That day was solid party from dawn till night. The day before Christmas found us spinning. The trucks came around early to take the pretty boxes to those who lived in the city, and big pots of flaming poinsettia were sent from the greenhouse. The heads and help received one of these plants every Christmas, just as at Easter we were all remembered with Easter lilies. By this time Dad and I had the last of the big pound cakes wrapped and boxed, one hundred and fifty of them, one for each of the Treasury Police detailed to the White House.

These cakes I'd ordered from the outside, and we'd wrapped them in cellophane and pretty tissue, and they were in boxes tied with gay ribbon, and we piled them on our two house trucks and rolled them into the East Room.

The big tree was there, all dressed and lighted for the day. At three the policemen came with their children up to twelve years, and their wives, and the President and Mrs. Roosevelt came in and the policemen and their families passed in line. The President and the First Lady had a Christmas greeting for each one that they managed to make sound special, and the cakes were passed out, and each child was given a paper cornucopia of candy and a toy Mrs. Roosevelt had chosen just for him—a doll or automobile perhaps, or a stuffed animal if he were a baby.

One Christmas my grandson Bobby was spending the day with me, and he wanted to see the Christmas tree so I took him in, and he helped Tommy hand out the candy to the little children, looking so serious and sweet. Mrs. Roosevelt thanked him gravely for his help, and at the very end pretended she had found a fuzzy Teddy bear just for him on the tree. He slept with it for years, and wore off all the fuzz.

After the police families the servants came, thirty or more, with their children, and went through the line before the glowing tree. There was Christmas money for the grownups and a toy Mrs. Roosevelt had selected for each little colored child.

She was having the time of her life. All day long she was racing from party to party, charity organizations, and community affairs, and extending the President's greetings as well as her own. There was a day-long in-between series of parties for children—children in need.

At one-fifteen she presided over one given in the White House by the Volunteers of America, and the minute this big staff affair was over she was off to another party for some very poor children in a dark alley.

The President's own big party was held in the morning in his office. The clerical staff came, and there was always some cute little trinket to commemorate our White House Christmas. I've treasured a White House paperweight and a pewter coin made at Val-Kil with the President's profile and a key ring with a little silver Scottie charm for the President's little dog Fala.

Five o'clock was sundown, Christmas Eve, 1933. I took Bobby by the hand and we went outdoors to the south lawn. All the presidential family was out there to see the President turn the lights on the big Christmas tree that was set on the lawn for all Washington to enjoy. There was a band and Christmas carol singing, and the President looked radiant and yet somehow sad with the lights of the big tree on his face.

I suppose he was thinking of other countries where lights were going out and people were living underground like scared rabbits. Dad and I looked at each other, and I know we were both glad that we had a grandson big enough to be there to see that Christmas tree shining on the kind face of a man who was head of the United States. It wouldn't be long until there were no more shining trees, not even in our country, and there would be none until our Bobby was tall.

The family dinner quieted down the day's excitement. They must have been tired by that time. Christmas Eve in the White House found all the Roosevelts together as a family and out of the public glare. Mrs. Roosevelt decorated their own tree on the family floor in white and silver, and late in the evening they'd all troop off to hang their stockings from the mantel in the President's bedroom.

They used big special Christmas stockings Mrs. Roosevelt's maid stitched up, and every one in the family had one, from Mrs. James down to the newest grandchild.

Festivities started early on the family floor on Christmas morning. The children opened their stockings on the President's bed, and there was a lot of shouting and whoops of surprise. Then breakfast, with sausage and tradition, and the family tree, where each Roosevelt had his own space under the tree, piled with gifts, and later a visit across the way to Christmas services in St. John's, and the President reading the abridged version of Charles Dickens's *Christmas Carol* to the family before the fire.

Christmas dinner was on Christmas night, with all the relations gathered around the table, Mrs. James Roosevelt, the President's mother, and Mrs. James R. Roosevelt, the President's half-brother's wife, and the children down to the littlest. On this first Chrsitmas menu I see there were twenty-three to dinner and four trays, for nurses probably. Plain American it was, the way the Roosevelts wanted it:

1933

CHRISTMAS DINNER

Clam Cocktail   Saltines

Clear Soup

Beaten Biscuit

Curled Celery   Stuffed Olives

Filet of Fish
Sauce Maréchale

Sliced Cucumbers

Rolls

Roast Turkey

Chestnut Dressing

Deerfoot Sausages

Cranberry Jelly

Creamed Onions   Green Beans

Candied Sweet Potatoes

Grape and Rubyette Salad

Cheese Straws

Plum Pudding

Hard Sauce

Ice Cream

Small Cakes   Cookies

Coffee

Candy

Roast turkey and plum pudding were traditional, and the Roosevelts didn't want it any other way.

A lot of plum puddings were sent in as gifts, but they always wanted the two big ones I'd made, brought steaming in wreaths of holly, and blazing all over with brandy.

They were happy people. Apart from all they were trying to do for the world at large, they had given hundreds of individuals a joyous Christmas.

The day after Christmas was the Children's Party, with Sister and Buzzie as hosts, and not a guest over four. The Christmas tree was enjoyed all over again, and there were little gifts, and a collation of cereal and milk, scrambled eggs, brown bread and butter, peas, ice cream, cookies, and milk. I never missed a children's party, because the little ones were so cute and Mrs. Roosevelt so sweet with them. No matter what sort of party it was, there were always gifts and little favors, and nearly always a puppet show, and the babies' faces were wonderful to watch. Their mothers were served cake and tea in the Red Room. That was the only drawback to the children's parties. Sometimes we'd have as many as twenty-five children to fifty-five mamas!

This party and the Young Folk's Dance always came between Christmas and the new year. The latter was for Anna's set and the friends of the Roosevelt boys home from college. December 27 four hundred and fifty-six young people came to dance in the East Room and sit down to supper at midnight—creamed oysters on snowflake crackers, chicken salad, ice cream, candy, candied grapefruit peel, coffee, and punch.

Even the Roosevelt friends were traditional. Habitual guests came to share New Year's Eve—Mr. Endicott Peabody who had been the President's headmaster at Groton, and Bishop Atwood. They would have dinner, and a movie maybe, and then go into the President's study to wait the new year. The young folks came in just before midnight, in time to lift glasses of the eggnog that was also tradition.

White House eggnog has to be made a special way:

Twelve eggs. One pound sugar. Beat the egg yolks and sugar until yellow. Three quarts heavy cream. Coffee cream can be used. One half pint rum, a quart of bourbon whisky, brandy, and nutmeg to taste.

The President always gave the same toast.
"To the United States!"

So our first year in the White House was over, and if I had known the March before what it would be like, I doubt if I'd lived through it.

I hadn't had time to catch my breath.

But we had all come through, and, according to my diary, 1934 started out for us with a bang.

Chapter Eight

"Official entertaining." I came to dread the phrase. That meant large-scale entertaining, state and official dinners and receptions for the cabinet members and administrators, speakers of houses, officials of the Army and Navy, foreign ambassadors and ministers, American legislators and jurists, governors, mayors, visitors and resident Washingtonians—and their wives.

The world and his wife and his children and second cousins came to the White House. It was a wonderful place to see your friends. Sooner or later everyone you ever knew showed up.

I didn't have time for any social life of my own, but I didn't miss it, swept along as I was in the White House torrent.

Almost all the entertaining was political. Official affairs were musts, and we had to fit in all these dinners and receptions to get them out of the way by Lent. That was why, in our first year '33, we started them early in November, but in January '34 we started right in with a reception for more than a thousand on the second day of the year, and all during January we averaged one large formal dinner a week, with big receptions sprinkled in between.

I'd told Dad at first, "I've kept house for six. Now I'll just keep cool and multiply by ten."

Well, we had two or three thousand dinner guests each

year in the White House, and about twenty thousand guests for tea, and every manjack of them to be served in a manner befitting the first household of the land.

They had to be invited, with special invitations delivered by hand, fed, and entertained.

The number of acceptances or regrets had to be recorded, menus planned, flowers provided, music arranged for, food purchased, prepared, and served. Guests moved about from the dining room to the East Room or various parlors for the after-dinner entertainment. It was a full-staff, full-time job, with emergency help for special occasions.

There were so many repeaters! Some people came again and again when, according to courtesy standards, once a year was enough. The same people, the same groups, the same societies, over and over. I wondered why, and was told. They asked to come, or they knew somebody who would ask for them.

When we were doing so much anyway, I couldn't see the need of so much repetition. Besides, these repeaters all lived in Washington, and Washington can't vote!

I was trying to be utilitarian about it. I thanked my stars I wasn't responsible for the protocol end. I wouldn't have the patience.

Oh, the rules, the mixups, the strivings!

It didn't seem important to me, in a world where we were praying for the economic and spiritual future of our sons, whether Dolly Gann or Alice Roosevelt Longworth was seated ahead. But that rocked Washington, I can tell you. Mrs. Dolly was sister and official hostess to the late Vice-President Charles Curtis, and Alice being the wife of the late Speaker Nicholas Longworth it was a question which out-ranked who. Mrs. Dolly was given precedence, and it was reported that Princess Alice refused to attend any more parties where Mrs. Dolly was invited.

A teapot tempest, the papers called it.

It seems you can do a great deal of damage by putting people in the wrong chairs, even international complications can result.

Political factions could blow apart on the question as to who sits the higher—the congresswoman or the senator's wife. The squabble went on for years, and I never did care how it came out, though come to think of it I think the congresswoman comes first.

Dad pretended to take it all seriously. "I sit to the right of our desk," he'd say, or some such nonsense, "because I'm the purtiest!"

Who calls first on who is another hair-splitting subject. I learned that a senator must call on an ambassador, but a minister must call on a senator. A cabinet member calls on a senator and a foreign minister, but precedes them at social functions. A cabinet member's wife ranked ahead of Secretary of Labor Frances Perkins. Or is it all the other way around? I was surprised to find out it was so vital.

The woman guest of honor sits on the President's right, and the woman second in rank to his left. The ranking man is at Mrs. Roosevelt's right and the second at her left. Or is it the other way around? Both ends to the middle, and the least shall be last, at the end. Sometimes it seemed to me a lot of mighty good people sat below the salt.

It's the women who keep it up. I've read that "Old Hickory," Andrew Jackson, tried to break these hidebound sitdown rules that had grown up in our democracy, but the ladies overpowered him. Most women like fuss and feathers.

Mrs. Roosevelt hated fuss, and it was always a marvel to me the way she did everything the correct way, and yet she herself was the most informal of women.

Mrs. Roosevelt took the Dolly-Alice matter quietly. "We'd better not put them too close together," was all she said once when they were both asked to the same dinner.

The whole business had me nauseated. It made me cross

because a good man and woman who were trying to do their best for their country had to get mixed up in such things. Intrigue, it was called in the days of the Henrys and Richelieu, but now it's called politics. Well, I have no patience with social form, but I suppose it's necessary to impress and protect. Anyway, it wasn't in my department.

The official seating was a headache, but not mine, and I was glad the matter of rank in Washington was up to the Social Bureau, the State Department, and the White House Protocol Office, and I had nothing to say about it, though I heard a lot.

Edith Helm decided who was who. Mrs. Helm was a wonder. She was the social secretary for Mrs. Roosevelt, an admiral's daughter and an admiral's wife, and her card list was the Bible of Washington protocol. They'd start with the card lists and work from there.

Visitors left cards at the White House, and sooner or later they'd be asked to something.

My plan for a formal dinner began with contacting the Social Bureau for the number asked and who they were, and then the State Department, to pick up any information that might be necessary about the food. Then I had to arrange for the checkers, extra help for the kitchen and pantry, trays to be served to those in the White House not on the table lists—such as the children and their nurses—and check the rooms, band refreshments, aides ditto, social office ditto.

After that I could concentrate on the table. It's woman's nature to love prinking up tables. My arrangements for the dinner were always finished the day before, so the morning of the dinner the carpenters would set up the trestles and the horseshoe table placed just so in the Green state dining room, and then put on the silence cloths. Then the butlers would lay the long tablecloths that were my pride, and a story in themselves. All our tables were treated with about twenty applications of hot linseed oil so they could stand hot plates. Nothing annoyed the President like a tepid dish.

It took us about an hour to get the tablecloths so they hung just so.

Then I was running up and down, in and out of the kitchen, where cooking had started the day before and was in full blast by this time, and into my office where dozens of people would be waiting, and then lunch had to be hustled out of the way because no matter what was going on in the White House regular meals must be served.

After lunch the extra people came in. Per diems, we called them, because they came by the day. We'd start setting the table soon after lunch, and before we built the new kitchen the per diems would be rushing in and out of the kitchen and across the corridor and into—of all places—the doctor's office.

Poor Dr. McIntyre's clinic was there, where he took care of everyone in the White House from the President down, and to show you how things were cut up at our end, the dishes and silver were kept in a vault in a section of his office, so we had to send a trail of men through the clinic, no matter what was going on in there, and out again, toting armfuls of dishes and silver. Then, in the hall, all the cabinet members coming in and out of the elevator could see us bringing out the dishes.

It was a comfort when we got that reorganized, with all the silver, service plates, and dishes on the mezzanine, even to the wineglasses.

Finally the table was set for formal, with service plates, napkins, and wineglasses, and all the silver, save for dessert, water glasses, the little colonial salt cellars of cut glass in the diamond design—and never any pepper shakers. For official affairs the nut dishes were decorative gold china; there were little silver ones for the family meals. The centerpiece for the family was always a bowl of flowers. A big silver ship in full sail was for teas. But for the formal affairs we used the Monroe gold service. There was always a lot of to-do about this service, which was purchased by President Monroe in France, but to tell the truth it was brass, and plated, with the gold

114

worn off. There was a big centerpiece and candelabra and I had them redipped, and they looked beautiful.

There were probably twelve bowls of flowers on the horseshoe table. We had flowers from our own hothouses until the war, when a road was cut right through twenty-seven hothouses. Mr. Will Reeves, in charge of the grounds and flowers, kept us supplied. Yellow roses were Mrs. Roosevelt's favorites, and we always tried to get them for her.

After the table was set there was a lull. Just before the guests came in the Social Bureau came up with its card plat, with slots in it to show the seating, which Mrs. Roosevelt had approved, and which observed the protocol.

Up to the last minute I'd be pussyfooting around seeing the rolls were put on the plates, on napkins, and the water glasses were full, and all the last-minute details were attended to.

Diplomatic affairs were always dramatic, with the marine band playing, the group of staff watching, and the Social Bureau checking every guest to see they were all there before the President and Mrs. Roosevelt were brought down. There was a lot of checking and a lot of watching to do. We always had policemen, and the checkers I had brought in as extras, for we were responsible for the guests' wraps, and checking the wraps at these big affairs was a job in itself. Once a guest took the wrong wrap, and we had to replace it, and a black velvet coat, the one that was left, is still hanging in the White House, or was, when I left. There were three entrances used for formal affairs, so we had to have checkers in all three places.

The diplomatic reception room would be one of the three oval rooms, closer official friends came through the front door, and the concert people used the east entrance.

When the guests were assembled in the East Room, all holding their little cards, having been introduced to their dinner partners, the Social Bureau would report to Raymond

Muir, the chief usher, that all present were invited guests, and the usher would go upstairs and bring down the President and his wife. One of the naval aides would call out the names, and the guests would come up to be introduced. For some years the President met them standing, then the doctor stopped this and made him sit. Then the President and the lady of honor led the way into the dining room.

Dinner was supposed to be plump at eight, but sometimes it was as late as twenty minutes, and everyone who cooks—or eats—knows how close to fatal that can be. We tried to move some of the bigger dinners up ahead, to allow for the loss, but that didn't work. They were seldom held on time. President and Mrs. Roosevelt were always on time. But some of their house guests weren't.

Every nook and cranny in the White House was starting to fill up with house guests, and of course they always came to the big dinners. Tommy and I held powwows—we were fed to the teeth with some. Mrs. Roosevelt was clever about shifting rooms and placing people and moving beds around. Once a friend came and she gave up her own bed and slept on the couch and got the flu, and in the midst of this, on the same day, we had ninety to the cabinet dinner, Lady Lindsay and the Anthony Edens to tea, and three hundred to a concert plus the artists' supper.

Kings and queens, when we started having them, didn't make any extra fuss, though their servants did, and so did some of our house guests, though none of them demanded much extra in the way of service, except Mr. Churchill and Alexander Woollcott.

At a formal dinner the President and his lady sat broadside, so as to distribute themselves more evenly among their guests. Fields, the head butler, would wait until all were seated, and then give the signal. The pantry boys standing at the dumb-waiters in the service pantry would signal the kitchen below, and up would come the big double boiler of

116

soup. Three or four girls would ladle the soup into the hot plates, and each butler had a plate on a napkin. Serving was done from the smaller dining room adjoining. We had a big table covered with oilcloth, and I took up my position there to check all needs, see the soup plates were hot, phone below if anything was wanted, watch plates, check progress, taste, criticize, and praise.

Two butlers serve eight people for a formal dinner. Each man had to balance a soup plate in and out four times. I used to watch them at their work and marvel at their skill. There is a tradition that no woman is to serve in the White House dining room. She might be up to the mental strain but the physical strain would tear any woman down.

It takes an intelligent man, and a strong man, to be a good butler. He has to have physical co-ordination and apt hands. He has to remember every detail, how to serve, where his silver goes, know every piece of it, every plate and glass, every dish on his tray. He has to have a memory for people and their idiosyncrasies.

Fields, our head, had been the protégé of the president of M. I. T. and graduated from the Boston Conservatory of Music. He had a beautiful baritone that might have carried him to great heights. He knew music, as a musician and the son of a musician.

Serving in that dining room were men who had matriculated in accounting and law. Some had been there before me, some are still there.

To add to their problems, an eight-o'clock dinner always called for trays. Sometimes we had as many as ten to go upstairs to the babies and their nurses. With only one elevator, dishes and food going up, dishes and garbage coming down, the butlers had a traffic problem all their own. Later I worked out a wagonette for the trays, but this came later, with the electrified kitchen.

They had one easement in their terrific task—seconds are

never passed at a formal dinner. The guest has his first and only serving, and if he wants more, he takes it then.

I'd whip down to the kitchen ahead of the main entrée. The old kitchen was a wonderful place to see with a state dinner on, with twenty gallons of soup simmering at once, dozens of ducks and fowl in the ovens, bushels of new shelled peas and other vegetables in big pots, and gallons of ice cream waiting in their frosty containers. I always thought of Dolly Madison, who had been the first to serve that daring new dessert, ice cream, to official Washington, from this same frowzy kitchen.

Ida was in charge here. A good cook must be a first-class executive, and Ida was a born leader. She had eight people always to handle and fifty in an emergency. Sometimes we had as many as twenty extras helping out in the kitchen.

I had a list of about one hundred and sixty-five people to draw from for kitchen and pantry and checking. I was besieged by people wanting work. The depression had struck hardest at the colored Americans, and those in Washington were badly off. I hired collegians, all carefully investigated and approved by the Secret Service.

I'd stand by the staircase a few minutes, admiring the way the waiters swept past carrying the heavy roasts on the heavy silver trays, and while it seemed like a miracle to me, there was never a single accident all the time I kept house there.

Then I was back in the little dining room, and it seemed to me generations went by, and they were still eating. All this time the salad man was in his corner, working away until the last minute that preceded the salad course with the intensity of an artist born. Brooks, the salad man, had a knack for making salad platters look like pictures, and he fixed all the decorative salads for our official dinners. The dressing was poured over just before the platters left for the table, and each guest took what he liked. I'm old-fashioned about salad. I like mine tossed.

At last everything was cleared for dessert.

There was always a rich dessert for these big affairs. There was cake or rich cookies, maybe both, and ice cream or gelatine mousse, and candy in beautiful compotes. Even when the Roosevelts were alone we had candy on the table, a mixture I sent especially for, all the way to Swampscott. Usually sherry and sauterne were served with these dinners. Champagne was special. Coffee was served later in the Green Room, with cigars and cigarettes, and sometimes liqueurs were passed with the coffee.

We had a lot of whipped-cream desserts at first, until cream got scarce. One of our specialties was strawberries Romanoff, with the cream piled over strawberries dipped in port. Even the ice cream was made with real whipped cream.

Ten o'clock brought the concert guests. Maybe two hundred or more. They were kept downstairs until dinner was over. Mrs. Roosevelt led the ladies out of the Green Room at ten, and dinner and concert guests met together in the East Room, and everybody found chairs, and the concert started.

Most people think artists are asked to the White House, but as a rule they or their managers ask to come, and they have to be approved by various people, especially Mr. Henry Junge of Steinway, the impresario who personally brought them into the White House. One pianist who is famous now, and wasn't then, wanted to come, but nobody had heard of him. Then he was asked, and played wonderfully. He was José Iturbi.

Mr. Junge took a great deal of interest in what was being served his artists, and Mrs. Roosevelt was anxious too. As I said before, she usually ordered a soup and creamed oysters and a jellied salad and cake and ice cream and coffee just for them. After they had played or sung they were brought before the President and Mrs. Roosevelt to be introduced, and then taken to the little dining room, where the table had been set for them. Meanwhile the crowd in the East Room had cookies and punch.

Mrs. Roosevelt asked the artists in advance what they liked to eat, she was so anxious to please them, and so appreciative. She loved music and singing, and she loved to dance, and she showed her admiration of people who could do these things.

Before Leopold Stokowski came to the White House, Mrs. Roosevelt was told in advance what he wanted. A mutual friend wrote her that the great musician never ate before a concert, but liked supper afterward.

"His idea of supper," she explained, "is a tureen of pot-au-feu, mostly vegetables, lots of carrots, and not thickened. He doesn't seem to eat bread or drink coffee, but if Mrs. Nesbitt could have this one thing for him, he would be pleased."

Mrs. Nesbitt did.

There was a rule that no "tote" be permitted from the White House kitchen. Nothing could be carried out as in other homes in Washington, where the Southern influence showed in letting the help "tote" home the leftover food.

Mrs. Roosevelt and I had an understanding that red-letter day ice cream and cake should go to the charitable organizations, but we were overruled in this by an older, established White House tradition that decreed all the leftover specially made cakes, the specially made ice cream, and all the food left on the platters, or on the table, belonged to the help. They had to eat it then and there, since nothing could be carried out.

I'd glance into the crowded narrow pantry, where the food came up on the dumb-waiter and the plates were scraped, and see fifteen or twenty men eating turkey or whatever it was, and many had had their dinners before. Waste always upsets me. There were hungry families in Washington. These men would know people who needed this food which they did not need, but which they ate because it was left over. It seemed to me there must be a way we could manage to send it out. But there was no way. No servant must be seen leaving the White House with a package.

I'd go down to the kitchen right after dinner and lock up the non-perishables, or they would vanish with the rest. We had so many extra workers in for these big affairs, and they were all hearty eaters.

Not until the last cookie was hoarded, the last wrap donned, and the last guest bidden good night, could I feel the affair of state was over.

The White House entertaining would have been easier if we had known how many were coming. Before the Roosevelts, an invitation to the White House was a command. But they were lenient, and let it be known that those invited might come or not, as they liked.

So if twelve hundred were invited I learned to figure on nine hundred. Conditions would arise, among so many, that made some stay away. We could never count on how many. We might plan a formal dinner for twelve, only to have it increased to twenty-two.

Now for twelve, we'd plan two services, with four butlers, and prepare food for each service, each platter with, let's say, a crown roast to serve eight. But if twenty-two guests came, that called for three crown roasts, and you can't prepare these in a minute. We had a lot of last-minute squeaks.

There was one Sunday in particular that gives me the chills to remember.

The night before I planned for thirty guests, and at the last minute fifty came. Twenty were coming the next day, but at the last minute forty came, and we didn't even have eggs in the White House because an enormous crowd had dropped in for Sunday breakfast. I phoned one of the hotels, and within half an hour four roasts done to a turn and pots of freshly cooked vegetables arrived in the White House kitchen.

Mrs. Roosevelt had wonderful understanding, but she had never done the actual work herself, and you never know until you do. One who doesn't know will think a handful of extra potatoes in the pot will cover any emergency. Well, it won't cover twenty extras, or prevent shifting and redividing the service, and slowing up the meal.

Adding or taking away, it all took time.

Sometimes the Social Bureau would phone at the last minute that somebody couldn't come, and we'd have to reset a table set for maybe sixty, and the Social Bureau would have to dash up and rearrange the seating and make all the required changes, according to protocol.

Ida the cook could rise to any emergency. In fact, she was at her best in an emergency. When we ran short of help at the big functions she'd turn over her whole kitchen staff.

Once the tea tables were set for three hundred and we waited and waited and nobody came. So I called the Social Bureau. Somebody had forgotten to send out the invitations. They were ready to collapse with chagrin, so Mrs. Roosevelt went in to see them and pass it off lightly and say it was all right, and we sent all the food that couldn't be saved to the orphanage.

I used to complain to Dad sometimes: "I can't even plan for a picnic and know the plans will stick." We'd pack baskets for six, because Mrs. Roosevelt felt like a picnic, and at ten the President would decide to go along, and this meant food for nine more people, because his aides and guards had to go. And all this had to be ready by ten-thirty.

One day in this year '34 I packed· a big lunch with fried chicken and stuffed eggs and everything people like to eat out of doors, and one of the Secret Service men came back and said they hadn't had enough food and half a dozen of the boys had gone hungry. I marched him out to the garage and opened the trunk door of the car they'd ridden in. There was a big market basket stuffed with good picnic food that hadn't been touched.

"Humph!" I told him. "Fine detectives!"

Chapter Nine

A note in my diary for January 12 in '34 says "the President pinned my ears back."

I remember it well. The big January dinner crush was on and the night before we'd had one in honor of Chief Justice Hughes and somebody sent in some terrapin, and I served it as soup. President Roosevelt was indignant.

"Mrs. Nesbitt," he said to me the next morning, "there is no such thing as terrapin soup."

He said it should be a stew.

After that, when terrapin came, he had a chef come in from one of the hotels to cook it, and I'd watch. The only trick was the cream, far as I could see, and the pound of sweet butter that is the base of the sauce. Salt, pepper, and thicken with arrowroot, and just at the last add the very best sherry. There are seven different kinds of meat in a terrapin and it is cooked in its shell. We always served it with corn sticks.

I learned later the gold-standard problem was heavy on his mind, and he had a lot to think about. But he landed on me right after Mrs. Roosevelt had told me everything about the dinner had been grand, and I felt real set up. I learned not to be, in time.

I didn't speak to him often. Usually when I telephoned him it was about game and things that had been sent in to ask what he wanted done with them, so I usually talked with Missy, or Tully, or Steve Early or "Pa" Watson or Marvin McIntyre. I tried not to bother them unless events arose, or there was a change in lunch, but they were all nice to deal with. I felt I could be excused in this case, because I never have seen such people for soup. The Roosevelts had it nearly every day for lunch, and the fishy kind seemed to be their favorites. "President's soup" was our name for cap'n's clam chowder that we served over and over, and he never tired of it. It's easy to make and filling, and yet doesn't make folks so full they can't think for the rest of the afternoon.

White House luncheons had to be chosen for filling, because they were mostly men's lunches, and yet not heavy enough to deaden the minds.

For the cap'n's chowder I take a dozen large-size clams—chowder clams, they call them—two ounces of diced bacon, a small onion chopped up, and a medium potato ditto. I strain the clams, save the juice, and grind the clams. Then I set the diced potato on to boil in a little water, but keep an eye on it, not to burn.

Then I put a quart of milk in the double boiler and let it come to the boiling point, and meantime I've fried the diced bacon slowly to a golden brown in a frying pan, and added it to the milk, saving about two tablespoons of the bacon fat to simmer the onions until they're transparent, then I add them to the milk. Stir two tablespoons of flour to the fat in the pan, adding some of the cold milk I've saved from the quart, and when this is thickened, add it to the double boiler, and lastly add the clams and their juice, season with pepper and salt, and simmer about ten minutes. Philadelphia pepper pot was another of the President's favorites, but it takes a long time to cook and tell about.

Leftover fish of any white kind, cod, halibut, rock, whitefish or such, was saved for kedgeree, and that was Mrs. Roosevelt's favorite.

Two cups of cooked rice. Two cups of the fish, flaked. Four chopped hard-boiled eggs. Three tablespoons chopped parsley. One half cup of cream or the broth in which the fish has been boiled. Salt and pepper to taste.

You toss this all up in an open pan or skillet until it's hot clear through, and serve it heaped on a platter. The President loved it too. Even when the President was being firm about things, like the terrapin, he sounded pleasant.

Two days after this Mr. Howe had a birthday, and the Roosevelts gave him a party and a repeating clock. I haven't said much about Mr. Howe because I don't know how to begin. He was the oddest person, who sat doubled up and peevish, and he and Mrs. Howe came to the White House soon after the Roosevelts did. They thought the world of him. It seems it was he who got Mrs. Roosevelt interested in politics, after the President lost the power to walk, so that she could get him interested. So in a way their being in the White House was all because of Howe.

Mrs. Roosevelt gave him a cape, just like the President's. It was easy to slip off and on, and he'd sit wrapped up in it even in his room. He was a sick man. After his party he sent down word to me that he didn't want anything to eat for a week. "Just cornflakes and bran." He had the queerest notions, but we had to work around them, because he was sick, and lovable despite everything. No matter how odd his notions were, everyone in the house respected them, and did their best to carry them out.

He had a secretary, Margaret Durand, that everybody called "Rabbit," I guess because she got around so fast. She was little, redheaded, and wise, and knew him like a book. She contracted tuberculosis later, poor girl, and was married under an oxygen tent to Aubrey Mills. Rabbit came down to see me soon after the bran and cornflakes edict, and said Mr. Howe had to see me right away. I went up to his room, and he was sitting all doubled up and sharp-eyed, like a little gnome.

"I don't like the cheese," he started in right away.

He wasn't supposed to have cheese at all, but I humored him.

"What kind do you want?" I asked, thinking over quickly all the fancy shops where they sold imported cheese.

"I want some plain rat cheese," he said.

He knew what he wanted, all right. I got into my car and drove all over Washington and brought back, among other kinds, some plain cheddar. "Sharp cheese," it's called.

He pounced on it.

"That's what I want! The kind they set traps with."

Another time he was supposed to be on a milk diet, and summoned me upstairs again.

"You don't know how to cook a steak," he said.

"I'm sorry," I said. "How should I cook a steak?"

He told me.

"Get one two inches thick. Cover it with coarse salt and broil it under a hot fire. You can't get a fire too hot for a steak. The salt keeps it from burning. Then scrape the salt off the steak, slap on some hot butter, and bring it to me." That was the way I cooked steak ever after. Sometimes, for a small thin steak, I use sugar.

There was an awful commotion going on in the children's floor one evening. I ran up, and Buzzie was howling, and Tina, Sistie's little cocker spaniel, was pulling off his pajamas.

"Puppy won't let me put on my pants," he was howling.

Right after this January Mrs. Roosevelt left on a tour of the Southern prisons, because the President wanted to hear how they were being run from someone he could trust. I asked her about the trip when she got home. She looked sad. "It was terrible."

Somehow she found time to make these trips he asked her to, although things were going full blast. Outdoors and in affairs were going on, until I came to hate the mention of the words "tea" and "conferences."

126

I kept charts of the food served at these annual affairs that started in January, so as not to repeat. I made a list of some of the different kinds of yearly affairs too:

Young People's Dance. Press Dance. Diplomatic Receptions. Veterans' Garden Parties. Handicapped Persons' Parties. Senate Ladies' Garden Lunch. Movie Star Luncheons. Cause and Cure of War Luncheons. Colonial Dames. Round Table. School Children's Buffet. Small Children's Parties. Birthday Parties. National League of Women Voters. American Psychiatrists' Tea. Informal Conferences with Snacks. Executive Tea. Official Dinners. Red Cross Tea. Royal Dinners (these were later). Todhunter School Dinner. Conference Luncheons or Buffet Suppers. Reformatory Girls' Party. Page Boys' Picnic. Garden Parties. Teas.

Mrs. Roosevelt had everybody in for refreshments except the Daughters of the American Revolution, and there were too many of them.

Social doings kept mounting in volume into May, which was my biggest month. In May of '34 I listed teas through the month for three hundred, fourteen hundred, thirty-five hundred guests, and so on. On May 28 sixty-three hundred people came. This was when we made twenty-three hundred sandwiches in a single day and I kept women baking cakes until they nearly fell in their tracks. When three to four thousand guests make up two garden parties, totaling seven thousand guests, in one afternoon, with refreshments if you please, Mrs. Nesbitt had to scramble. Everything had to be ready at a certain time, even to the handshaking.

I found out about conventions—people ate hugely. They'd been rushed about and shown things and hadn't found time to eat, so they made up for it. Streusel cake, baked in sheets, and fruit punch turned out to be nice for the Country Women of the World that met around this time in the garden—nearly six thousand of them.

The day we had two conventions converge on us at the same time Mrs. Roosevelt had to speak in Laurel on the Baltimore Pike. The first group of women came, about thirty-five hundred strong, and milled about on the lawn for about an hour waiting to meet her. The ushers wouldn't let me serve without her, so they were kept waiting until the next contingent was due. When she came, she didn't have time to shake hands, and we had only about ten minutes' time in which to serve punch and cake to thirty-five hundred people and then the police had to shoo them out to make room for the next group—women, too, about three thousand, and they had to have their refreshments. I was so embarrassed. It seemed a pity, when they had waited an hour, that all they saw was Mrs. Roosevelt being rushed through the crowd.

The weatherman was another ally in these big affairs and not always dependable. That was one bureau that wouldn't co-operate. I don't know how many orders for fifteen hundred had to be given away to charity when garden parties were called off on account of rain. I ordered three times for one Veterans' Garden Party, and had to give away two complete orders because the weather went wrong. One hundred cakes wasted!

No, they weren't wasted. I sent a cake home to each of the help, and had the rest delivered to the hospitals, the children's home, and the Little Sisters of the Poor, and even the big thermos tanks of hot coffee went to the Mission and the Salvation Army.

All the time we were having big dinners, maybe to a hundred guests or more. This May, while all this was going on, we had the Prime Minister of Belgium and Admiral Byrd, and I don't recall how many others, besides starting preparations for the big conventions to be held in June. And this sort of thing went on every year! I had my fill of social doings. I didn't see how the Roosevelts stood it.

Every year the cabinet ladies gave a picnic lunch on the lawn to the senate ladies, and sometimes there were hard feelings. These ladies were the leaders of political Washington and had rules and observances all their own.

One of the queer Washington customs was that the cabinet ladies had their days at home, and the wives of the congressmen got a general invitation to these parties and drove about from one to the other. Mrs. Homer Cummings was the most talked about, because she served thick ham sandwiches at her open house, and everyone loved them. We served them at conferences in the White House, because we had so many men coming and going, and I had to shelve a lifetime belief that dainty sandwiches were the rule. I liked Mrs. Cummings a lot. She was fun, and clever, and the life of the Gridiron parties. Her husband was attorney general.

Well, all these parties between the ladies culminated in the two big affairs of the year at the White House, when the cabinet ladies gave their luncheon in honor of the senate ladies. The cabinet ladies brought their own food. Mrs. Stettinius brought a couple of big cooked hams on their platters, all fixed up beautifully with decorations. Mrs. Swanson, wife of the Secretary of the Navy, brought the biggest silver punch bowl I'd ever seen, filled with salad, that she mixed with her own tiny hands, looking so serious, as if it were a rite. Mrs. Morgenthau brought great platters of fancy aspic. Mrs. Wallace came with cakes and homemade rolls, and Mrs. Forrestal brought the same. Mrs. Ickes contributed the chickens for the chicken salad, and I forget what Mrs. Stimson and Mrs. Wickard brought, but there were carloads of beautifully prepared foods covering the picnic tables on the lawn that were fixed up with flowers and silver as prettily as if they were inside. It was a beautiful spread. Mrs. Roosevelt had filled in with all the in-betweens, coffee, ice cream, green salads, fruit cup, and soup. One lady sent twelve deviled hard-boiled eggs as her contribution. And there were nearly one hundred guests. I gave a lot of thought to this problem and finally made a suggestion to Mrs. Roosevelt.

"Next year let me buy the food and keep track of the costs, and charge all the ladies pro rata."

Mrs. Roosevelt's face seemed to clear.

"That will save a lot of trouble," she said tactfully. That was how we got around the problem of the dozen eggs.

Some of the affairs were the President's only, such as the Harvard Club affairs, or when he entertained the Hasty Pudding. Then we had Mrs. James's Fortnightly Club every so often—about fourteen ladies who were close friends of the President's mother. She came down for special occasions, and I always popped up to pay my respects to her. Even she didn't approve of a lot of things the President was doing. She was the matriarch, and representative of the Hudson hierarchy. But while she might not always approve, she never stopped being proud of him.

Once she said, "Franklin is better equipped than anyone for the job."

But Eleanor Roosevelt was with him all the way in everything.

I admired and respected the President's mother. We had a lot of ideas in common. Mrs. James hated waste, and she lifted her hands at extravagance. "When I was a girl," she told me, "we made paper spills with our own hands."

I could just see those daughters of the well-to-do Delano family sitting in their parlor rolling paper lighters to start the fires.

Much as I disliked the big tea parties, I loved seeing things fixed for the family teas. Mrs. James always made her own tea and Eleanor Roosevelt too. Maybe there would be a tea to three hundred in the afternoon about four, and an odd tea going on upstairs at five-thirty, and a small tea on the front porch, with Mrs. Roosevelt pouring, or Anna, or Mrs. James. There was always tea.

Mrs. James sent the tea down from Hyde Park, and Mrs. Roosevelt kept it in a silver canister and let Mrs. James know when it was running low. It was a special kind from China, like the tea Mrs. James's father, Captain Delano, had imported a century before. The Roosevelt ladies observed a ritual in teamaking, putting in two or three teaspoonfuls of the loose leaves and being sure the water was at a high boil in the teakettle over the alcohol lamp.

Teas were always sit-down, with a beautiful lace cloth on a small drop-leaf table, a small nosegay of flowers, cinnamon toast, tiny sandwiches, cookies, little cakes, candies, and nuts —nothing that couldn't be eaten with the fingers.

Mrs. Roosevelt would order extra sweet tidbits for certain guests and never touch them herself. She and the President were both disciplined. Mentally and physically they had trained their wills to obey. When the President dieted, nothing could tempt him off his diet list.

Neither the President nor Mrs. Roosevelt ever complained of lack of sleep. Everyone around them did, but not the Roosevelts. They just willed themselves to relax, I guess, no matter how much of a strain was being put upon them.

Honey drops were a favorite accompaniment to White House tea parties, big or small, and they are fun to make.

I make them with one cup each of honey, sugar, and butter, a teaspoon of salt, an egg, a half teaspoon each of cinnamon and almond flavoring, a half cup of chopped walnuts, and a fourth cup of chopped orange peel. This takes about three cups of flour, enough so the batter won't run. I roll a teaspoon of the mixture into a ball in my palm and bake in a moderate oven.

When butter began getting short I went through all the macaroon recipes. We still had to have cookies for the veterans and hospital groups, so I made macaroons of every possible kind, with coconut, chocolate, and cornflakes, dates, nuts, and crumbs. It's remarkable how things can be made to taste rich and sweet when they aren't much of either.

It was like a five-ring circus in the White House, and no matter how high politics and diplomacy soared, it all seemed to come down to something to eat in the end. I heard that the Hoovers had eaten every meal in the State dining room, even if there were only two of them, one at each end of the large table. But Mrs. Roosevelt took over the little red dining room and he and she often sat down alone to dinner there, shooing the butlers out until rung for, so they could have more freedom. Dignity was for state occasions. There was no display for the family.

The President ate most of his luncheons in his office or in the sun porch that jutted out on the roof. It was all over glass, and she lunched with him often there, and they liked it because it was bright and they could talk freely. Finally they took to eating breakfast up there, too, so I brought in a beautiful drop-leaf mahogany table that would seat eight, and Mary cooked up there, and it was simple.

Often Mrs. Roosevelt and Tommy took people away to another room to lunch, so he could be with those he had to see, and sometimes he was peevish about people and wanted to be alone, though usually he liked them.

The President might have one group in his office and Mrs. Roosevelt another and the Boettigers might choose to eat alone, in the West Hall or East Hall or even in their bedroom, so they would all separate. Mrs. Roosevelt liked eating on the porch, or under a magnolia tree in the garden, or in her room, on trays. As a result, meals were being served at all hours, and all over the house, on trays or small or large tables, and this was difficult. I, who had been so impressed at our having butlers, took to regretting we had only six!

At first the family were all served together, but the household confusion developed with the confusion of the times. Political complications knocked the most careful household plans awry.

Of all the homes in the land, this was the first to feel the shock of any political upheaval.

May 3 was Anna's birthday. I was in Mrs. Roosevelt's room when Anna came in, and her mother spanked her, and then kissed her, in honor of the day. They seemed to have a lot of fun together. Anna liked trying to shock her mother. But her mother never let on if she was!

We were talking away when the door opened again and Sistie came sidling in. She was about four years old, and looked like a little angel, only she had a black eye. They tried their best to get her to tell how she got it. Anna had a wonderful way with her children, she didn't baby them, but talked to them man to man. But Sistie either couldn't, or wouldn't, tell how she blacked her eye. "I got a bump," she said evasively. Anna looked at her mother, and they both laughed.

"I think she got in a fight," Anna said, "and somebody bopped her."

As I look back, all of '34 was a mixed-up sort of year, with a lot of dread in it, and some nice things to remember. We had the egg rolling in April—that's one of the annual affairs I forgot to mention—the Easter affair for the children on the White House lawn! This is another tradition that goes back to goodness knows when, and every child in Washington can come, bringing a little basket of colored eggs, and roll them on the lawn, and eat them afterward.

Grownups without children are not allowed inside the grounds. I saw some little boys that looked familiar, and I kept on seeing them.

"See here, don't you sell papers down the street?" I asked one.

He said he did, and told me that lots of little newsboys

133

made a good profit on egg-rolling day, renting themselves out at so much an hour to "parents" who wanted to see the White House grounds.

"I've already made ten dollars," he said, and the party wasn't over.

Then the President managed to get away to rest on the Sequoia. He loved the water, and he could go aboard the Sequoia, on the Potomac River, and hold conferences there, and get a full week end of rest now and then.

In July he went South on the *Houston*, but we didn't talk about it until he was well on his way.

Dad made friends with one of the house guests, who was a friendly man with a patch over one eye. He liked walking about with Dad asking questions and learning about the White House and the way it was run. He was Floyd Gibbons the newspaper correspondent, very nice, and with insatiable curiosity, which is something I guess all newspaper people have to be born with.

A lot of things were going on, wonderful and terrifying. President Roosevelt came home by way of the dust-bowl area, and saw at firsthand the horror of Americans driven out of their lands, and this same July Chancellor Dollfuss was murdered in Austria by the Nazis, and a few weeks later President von Hindenburg died in Germany, and Hitler made himself President and Chancellor too. In September a million textile workers struck in our own country, and the terrible news came that in some places strikers and members of the National Guard met in personal battle, and Americans were killed. President Roosevelt pleaded with the union heads to call off the strike until it could be settled by arbitration, and they listened to him, and did.

Troubles in Spain. Troubles in France. In Yugoslavia. Ethiopia. Italy. Worst of all, troubles in America.

The entire world seemed to be losing its mind.

I'd listen to that man Hitler spouting his bad German over

the radio, and couldn't believe German people were swallowing all that evil and looking at him as if he were a goose-stepping god. But I never heard a speech clear through. I'd get too mad.

Of course none of this appears in my White House diary, nothing except its household affairs.

There wasn't much else to this year, except that the routine kept spinning, and more things happening, all the time, and people seemed to get queerer. The general tension seemed to affect Mr. Howe, whose preoccupation with food got stranger by the minute.

I did my best to tempt him to eat sensibly. He had a relapse and we wanted to build him up. On November 16, according to my diary, I offered him oysters, crab meat, filet of beef, lamb chops, veal loaf, and corned-beef hash. He would have none of them.

The minute I was back in my office Mr. Howe phoned down. By this time I was deep in plans for the Belgium Delegation Dinner. I could hardly hear him, his voice was so weak.

"Mrs. Nesbitt," he said querulously, "I want two hot and two cold codfish balls, and after that I want some corned-beef hash, with a poached egg and chowchow."

Chapter Ten

We would look back to the building of the new kitchen the way people in Bible times did to the flood.

"When we changed from DC to AC," we'd say.

That was in 1935, and it started out like any other year, with the usual pother of young people's dances, and sausages and scrambled eggs and three half barrels of beer in the lobby, and tea the next day, and dinner for sixty the next night, and so on. All through January we lived in a lather of sociability. But a lot of politics was bubbling through the lather, and while I didn't indulge in them personally, some of it shows in the diary I had started keeping regularly.

January 31, 1935, I wrote:

"Tonight we have twenty-four to dinner; it is stag and political, I guess. There has been so much of the campaign talk going on, we here have been right in the midst of it all and feeling is running high. I think it will be a bitter fight in November. We think Al Smith committed suicide with the speech he made at the Liberty League Dinner, that is, political suicide."

From then I went on to consider the cost of eggs, which was rising.

January always brought politics to the fore, along with the bigger functions, and black ants in the White House kitchen. They always showed up around cold weather.

Dad and I were getting engraved invitations to all the

official receptions, and sending stately acceptances back to the Social Bureau just down the hall. "Mr. and Mrs. Henry Nesbitt accept with pleasure . . ." I went to them all as a duty, and Dad went when he felt up to it. No matter how many I saw, I never got over the thrill of seeing the President appear in the doorway of the Blue Parlor, when they received guests, with the color bearers on either side, stiff as ramrods, a soldier on one and a sailor on the other. I didn't see how they stood so still, but there were twelve of these fine-looking youngsters, so they could change guard every twenty minutes.

The President always looked wonderful, but then he was looking wonderful all the time these days.

Mr. Howe, on the other hand, was getting more irascible by the hour. He had always been a free soul, and sickness seemed to bring it out. We were upstairs and downstairs at all hours trying to please him, but nobody could, not even the President, whom he dearly loved.

McDuffie, the President's valet, who had been with him since he was governor, was a proper soul, and one day this February the President sent him into Mr. Howe's room with a message, and Mr. Howe snapped back, "Tell the President to go to hell."

McDuffie was terribly shocked. "I can't tell that to the President of the United States," he said to his wife Lizzie, once he was outside Mr. Howe's room.

Lizzie was the maid who looked after the children and Anna's things.

"I'll fix it up," she said, and she went into the President's room. "Mr. President," she said, "Mr. Howe says that is a hell of a thing to do."

The President, she said later, flung himself back in his chair and roared with laughter.

"That isn't what Howe said, Lizzie," he chuckled. "He told me to go to hell."

On March 6 I wrote in my diary, "Mr. Howe eats too many

137

funny combinations for his good," and on March 16, "Mr. Howe ill. Near call." He nearly died. The Congressional Party Tea was on for the newly elected congressmen, and the President had to carry on, but Dr. McIntyre was upstairs with Mr. Howe all the time, and specialists were called in. We called off all the other teas because of his illness and canceled all affairs. Mrs. Roosevelt was in New York, but she flew back to be with him.

Mr. Howe was just like a member of their family.

I'd go up to see him. He was under an oxygen tent in his Green Room, apparently dying, but that snapping electrical mind of his was as rapid as ever. So much was going on, and he wanted to be in on it. Mr. Early warned us all not to mention how ill he was.

Within the month Mr. Howe was calling me up and giving me queer orders again. He telephoned down on April 4: "I want corn-meal mush, clear tomato soup, scalloped oysters, pork tenderloin, and potato salad." I was worried, and went to see the doctor.

"We let him order to ease his mind," he said. "Mr. Howe is being fed orange juice, eggnogs, and soups."

After that I took all his orders as if they were gospel. The day after the potato salad he asked for cream puffs. I had to drive around to seven bakeries before I found cream puffs. I guess he just liked looking at things by this time, because he'd poke them around with a fork and they'd come down untouched.

Little Bobbie Baker, Mr. Howe's grandson, was about four and the cutest youngster. He asked one of the policemen to make him a bow and arrow, so he could "catch a bird." The policeman made it, and we nabbed Bobbie just as he was going into the President's sun porch where the canaries were.

All this time I was adding up my three complicated accounts and figuring them out in every direction.

"If we could only get funds for a new kitchen," I'd say.

That had been the first idea Mrs. Roosevelt and I had when we entered the White House kitchen. Two years had gone by, and the ovens were still smoking and the refrigeration was worse than before.

Captain Lock shook his head for two years at all my kitchen comments. Then, this March, the situation cleared. He, Dad, and I were invited to visit the General Electric in Cleveland and look over their new electric kitchens with the idea of converting over the White House.

In the end only Captain Lock and I could go. Dad had his first heart attack that summer. When he was about again he was apparently spry as ever, but the fear started that wasn't to leave me. After that it was a fight not to let him do too much.

Well, we went to Cleveland, and the new kitchens were enough to make any housekeeper's mouth water, and we wound up all the usual May mess of garden parties, climaxing with one for five thousand souls, and planned to clear the White House slate for the new kitchen. The Roosevelts would be off for the summer, I thought, either to Hyde Park or Campobello, and the carpenters and electricians and plumbers could operate in a nice big empty White House.

Those were part of the plans I made, not one of which came about as planned.

By June 6 the kitchen equipments, plans and specifications, had all been drawn up and decided upon, and work of excavating had already started under the driveway of the North Portico. The President was not leaving until July, I learned, and meantime everybody else would get out, so it seemed safe enough to start work on the upper kitchen. This was a storeroom on the top floor that we planned to make over into a modern kitchen that would do for the Roosevelts when they dined en famille, and for the children.

The old downstairs kitchen was to be completely done over.

In any other house, even as big as this one, the work would

go swiftly enough. Families move out for big renovation jobs and come back to a place slicked up and new.

Not in a President's home!

Our first setback came when we learned that the President couldn't get away until July.

Excavation had started under the kitchen, and still he stayed on and so did Mr. Howe. Mr. Howe was a sick man and wouldn't move, so we had to keep open all summer. On June 27 we gave an official dinner to the Prime Minister of Australia.

"Thank goodness," I wrote impolitely in my diary, "they are making it a small dinner of thirty-six. He would come when we're practically closed. What a mess he'll find, a big excavation in front and the remodeling starting."

There were tunnels in the kitchen. We put boards over and trotted over the boards to serve this *official* dinner, and it's a wonder some of us didn't break our necks.

To add to the confusion, this was the hottest summer anyone ever lived through outside of Tophet. I felt sorry for the guests in their formal clothes. I felt sorrier for the staff. I never have become accustomed to Washington summers, although the city has been my home for many years and I wouldn't live anywhere else. But this was the sort of summer when people go around gasping for air, and the air-conditioning we had put into the White House wasn't working and had to be taken out, and after conferences the leaders of the land came out dripping and changed their shirts four and five times a day.

The throngs of summer visitors were bigger than ever. People picked their way past the dirt heaps and wanted to be shown over the White House, and no matter how busy we were, they had to be shown.

Mrs. Roosevelt went off for ten days to Hyde Park, which gave us a rest, but the President stayed on.

I wrote with premature optimism, "But no house guests. Mrs. Roosevelt promised."

She sent them anyway. She was too kindhearted to resist. "You're visiting Washington? Why, stay over at the White House!"

Even when both were away, we had house guests.

Elizabeth Moore, the second cook that Mrs. Roosevelt had brought down from Albany, had a baby this month, and Mrs. Roosevelt sent me to the hospital to see that everything was all right. It was a darling baby, the first new born colored child I had ever seen, and I loved him at sight. It was the first-born of the White House household so the entire staff was interested.

Mrs. Roosevelt asked me to look after people for her if they were sick or in trouble and she couldn't go herself. One of my duties when she was away summers was to look after an old colored laundress and see everything was right with her while Mrs. Roosevelt was away. She seemed to have endless faith and interest in everybody.

We had our first and only White House theft this summer, when a maid's purse with three dollars in it disappeared. While the search was on one of the young clerks went up to Mrs. Roosevelt's room and told the maid there to open her bureau drawers. I went in, and he was looking through them, and all her jewelry was spread out in one of the drawers—her nice pearls and diamond necklace. They were not even in boxes. I was horrified. Dad got a small safe and after that her maid locked up the jewelry.

One of the boys was suspected of taking the purse, but Mrs. Roosevelt held to her rule of never letting anyone be dismissed.

"We'll transfer him," she said, "to a place where he won't be tempted."

So they sent him to one of the office buildings.

Her patience was so wonderful, sometimes it put me out.

There was one friend of hers who wrote down from his country estate to ask her to get him a houseman for general housework. It isn't easy to get someone to work in the country, but we got hold of a good man and sent him up to Mrs. Roosevelt's friend. Then the friend wrote down that the man was homesick for his lady love in Washington, and wanted to leave, and would we get him another? He used the White House like an employment agency. She would put so much effort and correspondence into doing a favor like this for a friend, but this one kept putting it up to us: "When do I get a houseman?"

Affairs of the world going on, and remodeling in the White House, and he nagged on all through the summer!

July came, the thermometer kept rising, and the President stayed on. It was nearly one hundred degrees, and my fresh house dresses wilted like lettuce leaves. I didn't see how the President stood it. He was working six and seven days a week. So much was happening to him, deciding whether or not to run for a second term, and the Supreme Court and Congress arguing, and over in Europe Hitler signing a treaty with England promising not to build too big a navy.

July 10 I wrote: "President still here, working like mad. Congress isn't through. We are in an awful mess, hot, and the iceboxes are going to pieces."

Mrs. Roosevelt said while the kitchen was being renovated the family would just picnic, and they did, all over the house. They ate on the south porch, sometimes even having dinner out there, and once the Roosevelts dined alone in her sitting room. With the kitchen dug up with cross tunnels, and the corridor in eruption, I tried to arrange the easiest sort of snacks. Sausages were a lifesaver, and they must run in the Roosevelt family as a favorite, for they tell me Teddy Roosevelt loved them with fried apples. We used hot dogs, too, though the President didn't like them so much as was said, and for a late snack he liked a dish of kippered herring and a glass of beer.

Yes, the Roosevelts were simple enough. If only the house guests would get out! It was difficult taking proper care of the President with so many extra people around. Every nook and cranny was filled with them.

July 18 we gave a luncheon to Lord and Lady Baden-Powell, and had honeydew melon.

Mrs. Roosevelt went to Campobello in July, and the President expected to join her, but couldn't. He stayed on. So did the house guests. To add to our general difficulty, the President couldn't stand the paint, it affected his sinuses, so we couldn't paint unless he got out of the White House, so we'd get things fixed and then couldn't paint. We couldn't get at the White House.

We kept on giving big dinners with trying conditions in the kitchen and the heat getting worse. August found us still digging on wholesale scale, new pipes being laid, and the kitchen still undermined, so that we expected the cupboards to crash. Ida the cook was up in arms, and I didn't blame her. I was having troubles with those two music-box women Mrs. Roosevelt had asked me to look after, and Buck, our younger, was getting married. I made the cakes for his wedding and set flower wreaths around them, just as we fixed the White House cakes. Private and public problems weighed me down, and the thermometer soared to 98—boiling point.

Finally I had to scrap the menus and get in things that required just heating through. I had to co-operate with Ida by changing the menus that took too much trouble. She would be over the cooking, surrounded by a dozen men with wheelbarrows full of dirt. You couldn't tell if the place was the White House kitchen or a quarry. The world and its work kept pouring through the White House, and we balanced on boards over a bottomless pit.

So we served cold cuts and salad, and the guests stayed on.

143

I'd get home, sink my feet into a tub of cold water, and just sit looking at them. I couldn't believe they belonged to me. One Sunday I was stretched out trying to rest and Mr. Howe called me from his bed in the White House.

"I haven't any handkerchiefs!" he complained. And Mrs. Howe sitting right beside him in the room! I talk about Mr. Howe a lot, because the things he did might have been funny if they hadn't been sad, but he was not a trial, not once, to any one of us. We loved him and admired him, and his being sick and unreasonable only made us love him more. Everyone in the White House did all they could to please him, and disturbed as things were, we knew that for this wonderful little man it wouldn't be very long, and we did our best to smooth out the bad hours.

When I get peevish about house guests, I don't mean Mr. Howe.

Mrs. Roosevelt knew what we were going through. She'd drop little notes.

She wrote me from Campobello, Maine, August 11:

"I imagine you must be having a bad time with all the mess, and I do hope they get the other kitchen without too much delay. . . . We have had a grand time—peace and quiet and cool weather. I shall hate to leave here."

A little later she wrote again from Campobello, asking me to send her the two small silver pots she used on her breakfast tray. They were for coffee and hot milk, so you could pour left and right at the same time and make café-au-lait. Anna had given them to her for her birthday one year. She wanted them for the Val-Kil factory, where they made the pewter salad sets and things she liked to give as wedding gifts.

"Miss Cook is going to copy them in pewter," she wrote. "Also in the cabinet in my bathroom is a tube of Elizabeth Arden's sun oil—ask them to send it to me here."

She was always sending for odds and ends. Messages kept coming, later from Hyde Park, where the President was able

144

to join her for a short time. "A birthday cake for the President's mother goes with him to Hyde Park." "Please send up a bathing suit for the President." "I forgot to ask you to send a cake with twenty-one candles over to Mr. Howe on Tuesday morning. This card to go with it."

Mr. Howe was back in the hospital.

Soiled clothes were shipped down from Hyde Park and sent back. The dispatch bags shuttled to and fro with odds and ends of food and clothing and important papers. The President went to Hyde Park, we thought, for the rest of the summer, but no, he had to come back. It seemed we didn't get a chance to turn around before they were all on their way back. There was no rest for the President nor for us. The kitchen was a worse mess than before, of tunnels and pipes, with sometimes the water turned off and sometimes the gas. I couldn't help it. I wrote up to Hyde Park saying I didn't see how we could manage to cook for them.

Tommy wrote back: "Mrs. Roosevelt would much prefer to stay in the White House if possible and the President says he would, too, if only it doesn't cause too much trouble. . . ."

Then they wrote that they would stay on his boat the *Sequoia*, out on the Potomac, and eat on that, so of course I had to write back saying we'd manage, and they came home.

They came back and gave dinners. All those tunnels and we gave dinners.

But every sweltering second of that summer was worth while, because it was during this summer that President Roosevelt signed the Social Security Bill, one of the biggest forward steps, to my notion, since the Declaration of Independence. I knew the way those millions were feeling who had looked with such desperate hope to a man being helped into the White House that first inauguration day. I knew, because I had been one of them.

There would be a lot of talk about that warm smile and friendly voice being phony, turned on and off like an electric light to charm votes. I saw them, before breakfast and late nights, through exaltation and the depths of trouble, for thirteen years. I've seen the President of the United States peevish as a boy because his breakfast didn't suit, and in the moments when he was facing history, quiet and grave and as great as any history has known. The warm looks and friendly ways were real.

Standing where I stood, halfway between the back stairs and the grand staircase, I had a chance to see all the sides our President was facing, and knew for a fact how hard he was trying to bring them all together and get matters, once and for all, to an even simmer.

All these hot months the blueprint of the new kitchen was never far from my hands. I wore the edges thin, studying it. It was the last word in kitchen planning.

The old kitchen was the heart of a labyrinth, where passageways led to cupboards, refrigerators, locker rooms, storerooms, vaults, the package room, the canned-goods room, and the wine cellar.

The new one was ample enough to provide a full-course meal for a thousand people, with seven spacious windows, an electric fan to draw off the odors of cooking, rounded corners to prevent dust, stainless shining metal, electric ranges with red handles—the electric stove cost $5,000 and was sixteen feet long—six electric roasting ovens—you could roast a dozen massive roasts at the same time or bake forty loaves of bread and two dozen pies, and a broiling oven that would hold a covey of quail, thermostat controlled. We had eight electric refrigerators and new dumb-waiters, electrically operated, instead of the old wooden one that went by a rope.

Since entering the White House we had bought very little for the kitchen. I'd purchased just enough aluminum utensils to get us by. Now we had them so shining new they looked like a display window in Tiffany's, and we had an electric meat grinder, all sorts of electric mixers, warming ovens, five dishwashers, waffle irons, an electric soup kettle, a thirty-gallon ice-cream pack, and an enormous oblong pancake griddle. Someone said we could bake enough cakes on it for the entire House of Representatives.

One deep fry pan could hold five gallons of fat. There were so much glittering metal and gadgets the place looked like a laboratory.

One of the innovations we liked best was the new electric wagon for the President's meals. It had three compartments, two for hot dishes and one for cold. It was tricked out with pilot lights and rheostats and thermostats and the President had as much fun with it as he did with one of his boats, and loved turning things on and off and seeing dishes come out smoking hot or dewy cold.

These were the plans, as I hugged them to me in blueprint all these sizzling months, and thought they never would come true. A kitchen fit for a President, dreamed up by Mrs. Roosevelt and myself, and approved and cut down to practical terms by the architect and engineers of the National Parks Service.

These experts from the Bureau of Plans and Designs had also installed the new swimming pool.

We even had trouble with that while the President was away.

We always drained the pool as soon as he left, repaired and scoured it, and let it stand empty until he came back. One young miss in the executive office ordered it filled just for her benefit. She enjoyed her swim, but her ears were pinned back properly when they heard of it.

In September the President got away for a brief trip, taking along big bottles of table water as the doctor didn't want a change, and by October the Roosevelts were back bringing more guests. Meanwhile we had run into all sorts of complications in the remodeling.

We got the house cleared up just in time for their coming, when we found two wires had fused and were a fire hazard, so we had to cut through the walls to get at them. There was plaster dust all over the place by the time that was finished, and a wonderful old Aubusson rug the workmen had neglected to turn back was pounded in with dust. Destruction comes more naturally to folks than construction, I suppose.

I was ready to howl. The Grays were arriving at four, and it was two-thirty and not even the bathrooms were clean. For some reason there never is anything so dirty as a brand-new bathroom, and we had seven, and all in a mess of newness. And Mr. and Mrs. David Gray were such nice people, and relatives of the Roosevelts. I wanted things perfect for them.

We had to work like fiends.

I stood over fourteen men and women until the baths were cleaned with marble dust, the furniture wiped and put back, and even the floors waxed.

We made it!

It was pretty nearly Thanksgiving time, and we were still in a mess.

As always happens, one thing led to another. Our simple plans for changing from DC to AC had led to the discovery that all the White House plumbing was rusted, and rotted pipes had been taken out while more and more flooring and walls were ripped out. The heating pipes leading up from the furnace were all broken, and dust seeped in, which was distributed through the rooms. No wonder we spent so much time dusting.

When practically everything was finished below we decided to put new faucets in the seven bathrooms on the second floor, and they didn't fit, so we had to put in the seven new bathrooms, and found out that in Mrs. Roosevelt's the sewage pipe was no pipe but a trough, and a menace to health.

The radiator in my office had no return pipe in the new cement floor so it would hammer like the dickens when on, and the engineer had to crawl under the White House where the valves were to drain off the water from the pipes.

Things like that were part of the "new kitchen" we put in in '35.

The New Deal Kitchen, we called it.

The Roosevelts thought it wonderful. But we had a funny situation with the help. They wouldn't use the new electric equipment. Our kitchen was a dream come true with its stainless steel and tinted walls, but the help used dishrags and towels when they could, ignoring the new dishwashers, and did their slicing and chopping by hand although the electric company sent a man in to show them how to work things.

Even Ida wasn't reconciled to the "new-fangled" kitchen until the President himself came down, inspected, and praised. Then she changed her mind.

Mrs. Roosevelt often went down after our cooks had left the kitchen. She wanted it left immaculate. Dr. McIntyre went, too, and his chief pharmacist, and I always went.

It didn't stop being a miracle to me. I'd struggled too long with sagging doors and suspicious dark corners. It hurt my feelings to see a fingerprint left on one of the bright red stove handles. Our kitchen was perfect—to the minute. It was a 1935 and New Deal Kitchen and a far cry from the spits and cranes of Jackson's and Madison's day!

All we did was an excavation into the past, and a lot came to light. When we got into the plaster of the walls we found old laths split by hand. Dad dug into the archives for facts to fit the discoveries we made. He found a paper that told how George Washington had been interested in the building of the White House, and when the workmen chopped the plaster off the brick portico and saw the Masonic Emblem embedded there, Dad was so excited I had to calm him down. Dad, being a Mason, was almost as pleased as he had been to

149

discover the White House was designed by an architect born in Ireland.

There were other improvements.

The preserve closet was my pride. It was kept locked, and dark, as preserves should be kept, and the shelves were lined with jams, jellies, and pickles. There were jars and pots that shone like jewels, of Bar-le-Duc, wild strawberry and beach plum jams, cranberry jelly from Cape Cod, and honey cream, a specialty made and sent to us by a group of nuns in an Illinois convent.

I liked to serve these with formal dinners. After all, a formal dinner is formal and doesn't allow much scope—filet mignon, crown roast, roast chicken, or something else stereotyped. The only way you can make it different is by serving some unusual relish.

I liked the canned-goods room where the shelves were stocked with dozens of cans of soup and vegetables and tidbits of all kinds. However, we made all our own soups.

Dad's glory was the ginger-ale closet, where bottled goods of the lighter sort were stored, and the butler's refrigerator below the butler's pantry, where wines and such were kept to be cooled before using. Later we even had a bouquet room, with two refrigerators where the florists stored the flowers. There was a sort of march I made along our renovated corridor and enjoyed every step of the way. One of the nicer rooms was the servants' dining room. The long table was set with crisp green runners and napkins and gay yellow plates. We had restrooms for the colored help and for the white. Then I'd turn into my own office. My new office.

It was west of the South Portico, in the corner, near the spot where the President made his talks. I could look out at the magnolias Andrew Jackson had planted, and watch everyone come and go. It had been the first office of President Adams, and now it was mine, and all my cookbooks were in it, and recipe files, and growing plants, and my collection of brass and copper shining like gold, and a nice armchair, and pictures around. It was homelike and businesslike together.

There were birds outside in the magnolias and inside too, singing away in their cages in the light of the sun or fire. Yes, I had a fireplace. There had been one, covered over, as so many White House fireplaces were, and filled with pipes for a bell communication. I argued for a fire, but the experts said it couldn't be done. The pipes could not be changed. One afternoon when Mrs. Roosevelt was down from Hyde Park to see progress, and in my room, she happened to say:

"Oh, I see you have a fireplace!"

"No, I haven't," I said, speaking clearly so the experts outside would hear. "They say it can't be done."

"Nonsense," she said briskly; "tell them to do it."

They heard, and did without my telling.

I also won a radio in a somewhat nefarious manner. I wanted one in my office, and Captain Ker didn't think I should have one. So much else was being indulged in, he said, we had to cut down somewhere.

For the first time I went over his head and asked Mrs. Roosevelt.

"Of course," she said enthusiastically; "put radios in every room."

Captain Ker was a wonderful man, and I never went over his head again after getting my radio. With a new election coming on I didn't intend to miss any of the President's speeches. We had the wonderful news by this time that he would run for a second term.

From my new office I could look through the window and see the Roosevelt boys racing their cars lickety-split through the gates, as if the circular drive were a track. Sometimes they got tickets for speeding. It made me feel bad for their father, being President of the United States, and having a son bring home a ticket. They were such attractive boys, and could charm the birds from the trees if they had a mind.

It didn't show much consideration for others, I thought. Especially for that broad-shouldered man who was working so hard in his White House study, trying to keep his strength and his wits about him, and do the best he could for the most people.

As it happened, the first real meal cooked in the new kitchen was Thanksgiving, and the Roosevelts weren't there but in Warm Springs, so it was just for the Boettigers and some guests. But of course it took a lot of cooking, for Thanksgiving dinner for the help downstairs was just as good as upstairs, even to the candy. There was one large formal dinner, a week or so before, in honor of Canadian Premier Mackenzie King and Ruth Bryan Owen. She was the "Great Commoner's" daughter, wholesome and interesting, and she came quite frequently. She gave Mrs. Roosevelt a lovely throw made of feathers, I think from the farthest North, Lapland or some such place.

A few days after this, November 14, the President signed the proclamation promising freedom to the Philippines.

The Gridiron Widows' Party was December 15 and this one was a nightmare. I always wanted these parties to be particularly nice, and this was marred by one of those annual kitchen blowups that make you think you're managing an asylum for the insane. One cook hit the ceiling and sent up six hundred croquettes, stone cold and hard as rocks.

The kitchen skies cleared in time for Christmas. Nearly all the work was through and bad feeling always cleared up then. Mrs. Roosevelt's enthusiasm for the season was guaranteed to wipe surliness from the most stubborn face that ever sulked at an order. A lot of game came in as gifts: a deer, two wild turkeys, six pheasants, eight wild ducks, and by this time I had the trick of keeping so much hot for so many down to a science, and used hot wagons that I borrowed for the Naval Hospital.

Major Harry Hooker and the President had arguments on

the art of carving. Major Hooker was a partner in the President's former law firm, and like a member of the family. He nearly always showed up for Christmas. He was a fresh-air fiend, and would tie the curtains in knots to get more air, and what those knots did to our historic curtains was a caution. Then his bed had to be made in a certain way and the girls never were able to learn how, so he always made his own. He usually carved one of the Christmas turkeys, and the President the other, and sometimes James had a third. The President prided himself on his carving, and the major was proud of his. Fields, the butler, sided with the President.

"The major carves in hunks," he told me confidentially.

I was looking forward eagerly to the new year. Nineteen thirty-six would be election year, and in the general hullabaloo I plotted to put over some White House plans of my own.

The new kitchen had whetted my appetite for improvements, and I saw need for renovation wherever I looked in the beautiful old house, and made up my mind to fight for it, no matter what I had to do to Maintenance, or what Maintenance might do to me.

Chapter Eleven

I nearly lost sight of my plans for doing over the White House in the months that followed. The start of 1936 brought the first of the Social Bureau's memorandum slips that would keep on coming until I saw them before my eyes like sun spots no matter where I looked. The first was for January second:

> FROM THE DESK OF MRS. HELM
> *The following artists will be here for supper:*
> *Miss Lily Pons*
> *Mr. Roman Totenberg*
> *Miss Cornelia Otis Skinner*
> *Mr. Arpad Sandor*

That is the way those inter-office communications came, and were all right until the next slip arrived, maybe a few minutes later, to annul the first and change our plans all over again because someone had changed his mind and was coming or wasn't.

Mayor and Mrs. LaGuardia were house guests at this time, and Ambassador and Mrs. Daniels, and Sir Arthur and Lady Willert. I liked LaGuardia so much. He was mayor of New York and seemed such a kind, friendly little man. La Argentina the dancer, appeared at one of the concerts, I remember, and the Weiner Sängerknaben, little boys with homesick faces and sweet voices from Vienna.

A letter I wrote to the family on January 7 will give you a rough idea:

"We have just finished the worst week of the season. That was a sockdolager. Starting off with a tea Sunday, after a concert. Then nine hundred and three for Monday's lunch and six hundred and ten for tea Wednesday with the Diplomatic Dinner on Thursday. All went off very nicely and Mr. Trumbridge gave us some compliments, much prized, too, by saying that we got away with murder, with the equipment we have. (He is the gentleman who made some of our kitchen equipment, who is visiting behind the scenes in the nature of seeing what our needs are, and how we conduct a dinner from the pantry side.)

"This week you can think of us as having only two affairs, a tea and the Congressional Reception. They sent out two thousand invitations and are expecting about fifteen hundred."

These were major problems. One of the worst of the minors was adjusting the help to the new equipment, and that kept on being a trial, and on January 26 Mingo's (the cook's) wife sliced her finger with the meat cutter, and there was more trouble in the kitchen. This same morning a cripple came to me for help. Later on Mrs. Roosevelt got her into some government office where handicapped people were in demand, and she made good and we were proud of her. Meantime we were rushing around preparing a tea for six hundred, and at eleven word came twelve hundred were coming, so that meant more ordering, and more slicing, and more food, and getting in more checkers to take care of the wraps. But, as usual, Ida rose in her power and threw in her kitchen force and the tea went off with flying colors. The entire month was stuffed with events, to say nothing of the Wally-Edward VIII affair, which occupied our minds a lot. We didn't talk about much else on the corridor for days. But I remember the Democratic Committee Men's Luncheon on the ninth because that was the start of the new campaign for the second term, at least it was so far as I was concerned. There were ninety-five men and the sort of food men like, sliced cold cuts —smoked tongue, ham, corned beef, braunschweiger and bologna, two or three different sorts of salads, pickles, rolls, ice cream, cake, and coffee. I think you could feed most men that sort of lunch every day for a year and they'd still be happy. January 28 was another Chief Justice Dinner, following a tea and a reception in the same day, and I'm giving the menu because it's another brand of man-size meal, the formal kind:

Clear Tomato Soup

Mushroom and Parsley Garnish

Curled Celery   Ripe and Stuffed Olives

Boiled Rolled Flounder
Sauce Alemande

Potato Balls and Parsley

Roast Turkey

Dressing

Jelly Celestial

Lima Beans   Howard Beets

Scalloped Sweet Potatoes with Apples

Pineapple and Cream Cheese Salad

Saltines

Macaroon Ice Cream

White Pound Cake

Coffee

156

By February I was able to write that we'd had the last of official affairs, that the lists of Lenten musicales, luncheons, dinners, and teas would run into double-headers and triple-headers, and that Mrs. Roosevelt had said so many nice things about the work I had been doing generally that I was all puffed up.

I took advantage of the occasion to tell her my hopes for fixing up the White House. She seemed to approve.

"We'll see," she said. "You'll have to talk things over with Captain Ker."

He was the maintenance officer, who was in charge of the White House and held the purse strings, and my financial superior, as it were.

"I'll talk to him," I said, as if I hadn't been talking to the poor man until he was nearly out of his mind. Men, especially men in maintenance, find it difficult to understand woman's craving for curtains and rugs.

Now behind Captain Ker, I was to learn, stood the Fine Arts Commission. The Commission and my drapery crusade are all mixed up in my mind with this year and the election, which was the first I had ever lived through, under the same roof, as it were. Getting cigar smoke out of the traditional draperies became one of the high points of 1936.

It was so exciting I nearly forgot my own campaign for new things. The campaign started in January, and from then on there were committees and consultations and arranging for trips and broadcasts and conventions. The Roosevelts had high ideals and the willingness to help, and to live up to them they had to play the game.

Somehow it seemed rather pathetic that Mr. Howe died that April, just as the excitement was starting. Louis Mc-Henry Howe had been secretary to the President, and friend and counselor all the way. The frail little figure took on an awesome dignity, lying in state in the East Room, and there were flowers and chairs and a minister, like a church. There was greatness in him. He gave all of it to help build another.

All the White House seemed churchly that day. Work went on, but voices were lowered, and the steps weren't as heavy in the corridors and rooms. Death was in the great house, and I for one didn't like it there. Within the year it would strike again, when August Gennerich died while visiting South America with the President.

This meant another coffin carried down the north steps, and I think the Roosevelts felt as badly about Gus as they did about Mr. Howe. It was Gus who had thrown himself before the President that day in Florida when Mayor Cermak was shot. There never was a bodyguard more devoted. He had been building a home on the Hudson, and Mrs. Roosevelt was so interested, and gave him some of the Val-Kil furniture as a gift.

It seemed as if something happened every time the President went away. He started on a fishing trip this year, and had to come back because the big floods started in the South. That was emergency, and the law holds that a President must be called at any hour, day or night, in any catastrophe.

But I remember Gus died on the South American trip because I had planned to get my holiday baking done while the President was away. And I recall the day he left. Dad and I saw him off.

All presidential departures seem exciting to me, but this more so because we were part of it. There was a procession of cars before the White House, and first the motorcycle cops started off, then the Secret Service men, gimlet-eyed in their cars, then more police, then the President and his family, then the Secret Service again, and we tied ourselves onto the tail and sailed along. Our little Ford had to sizzle to keep up, with the station wagon full of presidential luggage pushing us from behind. That was a chase, I tell you, with sirens screaming and people lining both sides of the highway and shouting for thirty miles, all the way to Annapolis.

Mrs. Roosevelt went out with the President on the little boat and aboard the *Houston* with him, although she was coming right back. The shore was lined with people waving, and Dad and I waved.

"Look, she sees us!" I told Dad, and she did, and nudged the President, and they both stood smiling and waving to us from the *Houston's* deck.

President Roosevelt did a lot of traveling this year. He went to Hyde Park and Florida and Philadelphia, and on the Midwestern campaign, and this South American tour. I think it was this same year he went to Maine with the three boys, and the Secret Service men came back simply wild from his teasing. He'd be on another boat, shouting over and pretending all sorts of things were happening, and they were beside themselves for fear something dangerous was really going on. He was eating well, and had the vitality and love for nonsense of a boy.

I often thought the bursting high spirits of the Roosevelts came from the food they ate. They ate simple, vitality-giving foods because they preferred that kind.

June filled the White House with people working for the convention, and an undercurrent of excitement ran through the place. As a result my diary pages are almost bare. So much happened I wasn't to talk about, much less write about, that I can't remember now who came or what it was all about. But events seemed portentous at the time.

Every room was bursting with relatives and guests, to say nothing of small fry. Finally I suggested to Mrs. Roosevelt that we put a cook and maid in the upstairs kitchen, to serve the six children, their governesses and nurses and the ladies' maids, to save wear and tear on the butlers. Mrs. Roosevelt jumped at the notion, so we put it to work.

I remember Premier Van Zeeland of Belgium coming to spend the night. There was so much going on I should have remembered, I suppose, from a history-making point of view, but I was too busy seeing there were plenty of sandwiches and coffee kept in stock at all hours, for convention talk and speech writing were going on in every nook and cranny. The President's old friend and political adviser, Judge Samuel Rosenman, was there, and the other speechmakers. The President would give them the article, then the facts were fitted in. The President had started giving his fireside speeches by this time, and I went to them from the beginning and never missed one if I could help. When he first started making them, in the Oval Room on the first floor, there was no fireplace, then one was found sealed over. Every room in the house had its fireplace, but some had been closed. So it was broken open and a real fire laid, and he'd just sit back and talk as if it were just to us, listening to him in the firelit room. I'd shut my eyes and picture the big family that was America sitting around their radios, on farms and in cities, and big rooms and small, and all listening.

He made some wonderful compaign talks this year, and I was grateful for my little office radio. Sometimes the doctor left his door open and turned his radio on loud, so everyone in the corridor could hear.

This was the way we learned President Roosevelt was renominated for the presidency at Philadelphia, June 27, 1936, and heard his wonderful promise:

"We are fighting to save a great and precious form of government."

A nice tribute was paid Mrs. Roosevelt at the convention, by a senator from West Virginia. He praised her to the skies as a First Lady, I remember, and it was good to hear.

The President came back for just two days, and was off on his Western trip.

I was thankful that the convention was over. The excitement wore me out, listening to the speeches and to the ovations given him.

Of course we were still constructing. Now it was the wiring, with more flooring torn up, and holes in the plaster, and the usual amount of plaster dust falling. That meant patches of plastering all over again, and painting. July was as hot as only a Washington July can be, which means it gets hotter every year no matter how many years you've lived there, and I was trying to keep down Dad's election enthusiasms because of his weakening heart, and keeping track of Patsy in odd moments. Patsy was a little black-and-white fox terrier we'd acquired. He managed to get lost two or three times this year and always when something vital was going on. The first time he ran away from our apartment when the janitor was washing him. I telephoned the police and the Rescue League, and next morning the White House guard came to my door and asked if this wasn't our pup. It was Patsy, gaunt and dirty and woebegone, and we never were able to figure out how he had made his way from the apartment to the White House. We had moved farther out on Connecticut Avenue, and he had walked five and a half miles through streets he had never seen, because he always rode on the floor of the car.

The next time Patsy disappeared and I sent notice to the Rescue League they found him standing guard over another dog that had been injured.

Dad and I managed a few nice drives this summer to Williamsburg and Jamestown and such places.

But my main purpose was fixing over the White House. I got so I talked to myself on the subject. I'd walk around through the rooms planning what I'd do if Maintenance would only give in.

"If I only had fifty thousand dollars," I kept saying, "just to spend on furniture, rugs, and curtains!"

Maybe I harped on the subject of new drapes for the East Room once too often. I had a tactful note from Tommy:

"Mrs. Roosevelt . . . thinks it better to wait until after election to get new draperies. The President wants red damask, but Mrs. Roosevelt thinks it only fair to wait and see whether they are the ones to occupy the house for the next four years."

After that I had an added interest in what would happen in November. I did a lot of praying, and some electioneering. It was my last, for after this election a law was passed saying no government employee could take the field in a campaign. But I had every reason for wanting Franklin Delano Roosevelt to continue in office. I couldn't imagine anyone else having the courage to meet all the trouble our country was in.

Besides, I could fix over the White House if we won.

At any rate I was having great fun with the linens. We had to have those. Curtains and rugs can be postponed, but no house can run without the proper amount of sheets and towels. As I said before, the linen shelves were depleted when we moved in, and I suffered when Mrs. Roosevelt had me show people around and they peeked into the linen closet, where the shelves were as bare as Mother Hubbard's. Their lack was something no maintenance officer could deny. I had to keep after the laundry to get things back in time for the next affair.

My feud with Maintenance had begun almost the hour we moved into the White House. "We have just so much money left," Captain Ker said to me after the budget was in; "we will have to divide it to finish this fiscal year."

Of course wiring and plumbing and such vital matters had to be attended to, but while I realize the importance of sanitation, I also like enough napkins to go around. Particularly in the White House.

So I said, "Well, we have to get table linen."

I remembered back twenty years, to the days I was keeping house in Duluth, when a Colson salesman had insisted upon bringing some nice linens over to the house and showing them, over my protests. They were beautiful, but I hadn't been able to buy them then.

Now, twenty years later, was he surprised to hear from me!

Mr. Langdon came to the White House, a man who knew linens to the last thread, and advised me with honesty. I wound up spending $2,000 for linens. Maybe a little over.

That was the start of my buying, and I'd never spent that much money in my life before. Necessary spending though it was, it seemed almost wicked.

Those big horseshoe banquet tables were our worst problem. Those were the ones Mr. Shepheard, the White House carpenter, had to trestle and put together for state occasions. No regular cloths would fit.

I wound up by ordering specially woven cloths four yards wide. Only two looms in Ireland were capable of weaving them, and it took a year to make just these two. They were in the Leinster design, because the dining room paneling is, and the White House is supposed to be modeled after the house of the Duke of Leinster in Dublin, a fact my Dublin-born helpmeet never failed to impress on White House guests.

Two sets of all cloths were ordered, made so they could be interchangeable.

Now, how to match the curves and borders to meet where the pattern continued! I consulted Captain Ker and Captain Lock. They were both army engineers, and they made the design for cutting the three-by-six cloths, so they fitted to the curves, and we sent to Richmond, Virginia, to have wedges made that the cloths could fold over. The engineers who designed the cloth to a blueprint, the carpenters who put the tables together, and practically every department in the White House had a hand in those tablecloths until they were almost an affair international. But when we finished, the tables were a triumph of science, and the White House had tablecloths, half-a-dozen six-by-threes, and two sets of seven-by-fours, and two sets of seven-and-one-half-by-three, and two sets of sevens—all in yards, of course—and they are still in use at 1600 Pennsylvania Avenue.

Once we had one hundred and ten people sit down in the State Dining Room.

I was frightened, spending so much money, and went to Mrs. Roosevelt. But she said she was pleased, and after this she never paid any attention to anything I ordered, unless it was something that required her final say-so.

"I like everything you have chosen," she said.

Of course we needed smaller linen, and I ordered luncheon cloths and cloths for the small dining room, and tea table cloths, and lace doilies galore, Italian and French. Then I got nervous and went to her again.

"Do we dare get so many?" I asked.

She checked over the doily order at a glance. She could get the contents of a full page with one look.

"Double it," was all she said.

We needed them all, with so much going on.

All these came from Colson's. Other linen people probably had things just as good, but I had remembered his fine goods, probably because I had been impressed by his nice attitude, after he had gone to the trouble of bringing his goods to my house and showing them, as if he loved doing it, and it were no trouble at all. Courtesy had paid off in twenty years.

When the linen shortage was about to start, my linen adviser, Mr. Langdon, warned me, and I stocked up just in time. Even so we ran short, and I almost had to get on my knees to get sugar sacks for dishtowels, when we couldn't get tea toweling by the bolt and have it hemmed any more.

Sheets had been short in the White House from the start. There just weren't enough to go around, and that's an awful feeling in any household. When we went in the beds were changed every day, by custom, but Mrs. Roosevelt told me twice a week was enough for those who lived continually in the house.

164

I bought percale sheets from Utica, and some of the hem-stitched linen sheets Mrs. Roosevelt liked for her bed from Colson's, although I told her I didn't think so much coolness was good for her. She liked linen for the fresh, clean chill it holds, and she slept in a crosscurrent too. In Hyde Park she was on a sleeping porch, almost like being out of doors. I don't think the newer theories call for quite so much fresh air.

All the napkins and towels had the shield of the President and that of the United States on it, done by hand. The monogram cost as much as a napkin. I hate to think what linen replacement cost, making up for the napkins some White House guests took with them when they departed, because of the monograms. They took the guest towels for the same reason, so when I replaced those, I purposely got the cheapest and left off the monograms. How did they have the nerve! But now, when Mrs. Roosevelt showed guests around, we had linen to show in the closets, and I was proud.

The presidential crest was on almost everything in the White House. It was on their personal letter paper, for instance, so the rest of us couldn't use it. Mine was plain white paper with the words printed on top: The White House.

There were paper matchbooks scattered around, white and blue, stamped: President's House. But the cutest matchbooks were the President's own. Match companies sent in all sorts of designs, but he chose a blue book with his initials, FDR, forming a ship. Those match people knew how much the President liked ships.

Even with plenty of linen, laundry continued to be a problem. There were so many people, and so much to sort, send, check back, and keep mended. Mrs. Roosevelt on trips would write back for a clean blouse and slips and things, to be sent special delivery. There were the President's things to be kept up, and then we had all the laundry problems of the house guests along with our own.

Guests were forever getting low on shirts, or going away

and leaving something that we'd have to launder and pack and send on.

Anna had a cute story about her brother John and the laundry. This was when John and his wife were going to South America and leaving the baby with us. He telephoned the White House, and his mother was out, so he talked with the President.

"Please call the didie company," he said, "and order in some diapers."

"Hasn't the baby any diapers?" the President wanted to know.

"Oh, we don't do things that way now, Dad. Order a hundred and forty."

"One hundred and forty!" President Roosevelt was horrified. "Is there anything wrong with him?"

John explained that that was the number, one hundred and forty a week, and they say his father did call, but I don't know if it's true. But he loved to tease, and I can just hear him:

"Didie wash? This is the President of the United States . . ."

Politics and elections took over the rest of the year. We were pretty certain the President was as good as in months before the election, but there is always the chance that something will go wrong. It was a nerve-racking wait, and only the President and Mrs. Roosevelt seemed calm.

All the newspapers seemed to be for Mr. Landon, but in the motion-picture houses it was the President that got the cheers, and the motion-picture houses are the people.

Mrs. Roosevelt came down with intestinal grippe in September and wouldn't go to bed until the doctor made her, and the President, who had intended to go to Hyde Park to see his mother, wouldn't go without her, although she begged him. It was his mother's birthday, too, but he waited until

166

Mrs. Roosevelt was well and could go along. It seemed a pity they didn't have more time to do things together. They were such good companions. But she had taken to going about a lot, always on matters he wanted done, and I guess they both thought there would be time enough for them to enjoy life later on.

Well, there never is enough. I could see Dad fading before my eyes. There had been so many years of sharing trials together, and now we were too busy to relax. But perhaps it was just as well. We were excited about our work and what was going on, and no matter how hard work is, when it's likable, that's the best life one can have.

Bobby came to visit us this October, while a new arrival was being expected in his house, and there is nothing like a small grandson to make you know how worth-while life can be.

Then we heard the big news that the New York Times was sponsoring the President and that Wall Street was betting on him three to one! The newspapermen who went with the President on his speaking tour said they might as well go home and take a rest because the returns were as good as counted already, judging by the manifestation the crowds gave him everywhere. It was appreciation by the nation for what he had done for the nation, not on party lines. Big money was set against him, but America was with him. In spite of printed misstatements against the New Deal that were being slipped into pay envelopes! From what I heard from all sections, he would be in.

November 4 was a landslide. Just the same the election staggered me with its overwhelming majority for the President. There was no thought of going home and to sleep. We were too excited listening to the returns. By midnight we were sure, and Mr. Early was jubilant, and wanted sandwiches for twelve in the office within fifteen minutes. There wasn't much in the house, as I'd let things run down with the wiring going on and the family away in Hyde Park. There was one choice Virginia ham and some bread sliced thick, and it seemed queer to be putting such a delicacy as the thin ham between those thick bread layers. But I tried to fix them as dainty as I could.

Then on November 8 the Roosevelts came back, and it warms me still to remember the welcome Washington gave him after his landslide election. Three hundred thousand people were out in the streets cheering, and he was leaning out of the car shaking hands all the way from the station. We were lined up outside the White House waiting, and even little Bobby shook his hand. The people outside wouldn't leave, they stood cheering and calling, and he had to go back three times to the front door and stand smiling and waving. His grin was wonderful, and she, beside him, was just glowing with happiness, and it was a joy to see them.

I was tuckered out with excitement and pride because the question of who was born leader of the nation had been decided by the people and not by the underhanded ballyhoo of the opposition.

How kind and cheerful he looked, and with so much trouble waiting all over the world! The Rome Axis had just been formed and the great water-front strike was sealing harbors on both sides of the United States. There was trouble no matter where you looked.

Thank God, I was thinking, he will be in another four years. And we will be.

Something else I recalled to Mrs. Roosevelt, the first time I got her alone. She and Maintenance had both made a promise, to be kept if the President was re-elected. I reminded her.

"Now we can get new drapes for the East Room," I said.

Chapter Twelve

"I warn you Mrs. Nesbitt," Mrs. Roosevelt said, "this second term is going to be hard work all the way. We'll start in January with four official affairs a week, until Lent. After that we'll settle down to musicales and teas."

Four *Official* a week! I'd been groaning over the customary one. In simple arithmetic, the second term was going to be four times as much work as the first, because of the fact that the administration had gathered momentum and more things were happening and more people pouring in on us.

The first month, January 1937, was almost solid inaugural, with something going on every hour of the day and into the night.

This was actually my first inauguration, as the affair four years before had been overseen by the Hoover's housekeeper, and I had been a guest in the White House and seen hordes of people eating and drinking, and marveled at the way she got it all done.

Now the inauguration guests were my fish to fry, and I did it without turning a hair. After feeding seven thousand in one afternoon in the White House garden I wasn't going to worry about a luncheon, tea, and dinner for a couple of thousand, more or less, on Inaugural Day.

By mistake the committee in charge sent President Roosevelt an invitation to his own inauguration. He was such a tease, he had the Social Bureau return a beautifully scripted reply on his own stationery:

The President
regrets that because of the
rush of official business
he is unable to accept the
courteous invitation to be present
at the ceremonies attending the
Inauguration of the President of
the United States

January twentieth
Nineteen hundred and thirty-seven

Under that he wrote in his own hand:

"I have rearranged my engagements and work, and think I may be able to go. Will know definitely January 19th. FDR."

Two weeks ahead I was working on the plans. The menus and lists were prepared and approved, and the hams and tongues boiled and hanging in Dad's game room. I counted on sweet potatoes. There is nothing like sweets for perking up a meal, and during my thirteen years in the White House I tried them out by every known recipe, with cream, nutmeg, marshmallows, oranges, apples, and every which way. Women usually prefer them to whites, and I'd serve them at any meal honoring a woman, such as the formal dinner for Madame Albert Lebrun, wife of the French President, when we had sweet potatoes with pineapple.

For the inaugural we'd have sweet potatoes boiled and put through a ricer, seasoned with sugar, salt, and nutmeg, placed in a buttered casserole, dotted with marshmallows, and baked until the marshmallows were biscuit-colored.

Mrs. Roosevelt liked them that way.

Maybe I've explained that these advance-order lists all had to be saved and filed, so I had thousands of them along with my other papers. The one for the inauguration dinner provided for sixty-three, and read like this:

> 81 fillet flounders (portions), 22 chickens, 10 cucumbers, 1 bushel beans, 24 bunches carrots, 4 cream cheese, 7 gallons butter pecan ice cream, 12 dozen cookies (bought ones), 12 celery bunches, 2 pecks sweet potatoes, 9 dozen rolls

This didn't include the meat course, jellies, soups, candy and such, which we had in, and also I had to figure on the band.

Matters like this had to be planned weeks ahead, and also I was baking every variety of cookie that will keep, only the kind hasn't been invented that will keep against children, even in the White House. The house was running over with the grandchildren come to see him take the oath so they could remember it always. Then Franklin was back from college looking pale and in need of building up after his sick spell on Christmas Eve when his mother had rushed off to be with him, and rushed back to be home for the tree next day. He was such an attractive young man. I happened into the family room and found him stretched out on the rug with Sistie and Buzzie, all three on their tummies with their heads together reading the funnies.

Lizzy, the upstairs maid, came down one morning laughing fit to burst. She told me she had just overheard the President playing house with the two little girls, Sara and Chandler.

"We'll play papa and mama," the President said. "And I'll be the milkman Sara, you can be the papa!"

Chandler was so insulted, she swung on Sara with her fist. Sara swung right back.

The President separated them.

"I guess Mama won't need the milkman this morning," he said tactfully.

And this was at a time when the longshoremen's strike was at its worst and the Secret Service had him confined to his office and the house for fear of cranks. I heard a President always gets threatening letters, and he had his share from the start, but they were picking up in a way that was making Colonel Starling and the others keep a sharper eye on him than on any other president. Things had never been so bad before.

One afternoon this January John Mays, the doorman who had been at the White House so many years, brought a young girl into my room with her nurse.

"This is Paulina Longworth," he said. "I knew her mother when she was Miss Alice Roosevelt."

The nurse introduced herself. "I'm Paulina's keeper."

She was only joking, for Paulina was a nice quiet girl. She came over quite often to play with her White House cousins.

My diary scribblings were brief and to the same point all January:

January 17—More inaugural preparations.
January 19—Inaugural dinner. Reception.
January 20—Inaugural. Luncheon. Tea.
January 24—Still more inauguration.
January 26—And still more.

And so on.

Weeks after the ceremonies we were still helping celebrate with those who were still celebrating.

That was the rainiest inauguration on record they tell me, and the Jackson magnolias ran like fountains through the speeches. But there had been the big dinner the night before, and right after the oath-taking hundreds poured into the White House for the luncheon, and after that there would be the tea, so I listened on the radio to the awe-inspiring words of the ceremony that made Franklin Delano Roosevelt President of the United States for the second time.

It had rained for the first inaugural, four years before.

We had the trestle tables set up in the East Room, and everyone had a plate luncheon, and after they finished, we had only two hours in which to get that table cleared off and the room cleaned, and the tables reclothed, reset, and the dishes washed and readied again for the tea. To say nothing of the trick of preparing two meals in the space of three hours.

It wears me out to think of it.

I learned by this experience. After this when we had two meals in a row we'd cover the tables with one clean cloth, put an oilcloth between, and cover with another cloth. After the first meal we'd remove the top soiled cover, roll up the oilcloth, and there was the clean one ready laid.

I was glad when that day was over.

Still, the inauguration hadn't been too bad. I had read about Andrew Jackson's inauguration party, when he opened the White House doors to all Washington, and the people came in shoals.

"Let them have a good time," Old Hickory had said. "It's only once in four years."

White House hospitality ran unconfined that day. Jackson's guests stood on the upholstery while drinking, smashed one of the East Room's priceless chandeliers, and walked off with every scrap of the White House silver.

We lost only the usual percentage, mostly napkins and spoons. Campaign overhead, one might say.

A lot of funny stories ran back stairs in the White House. Some went back a century and others were new. I heard that army and navy officers, up to majors, were under orders to attend the Hoover receptions, so they would be well attended. Ours were eagerly attended, maybe because the punch had a "stick" in it.

This was gossip, of course, and there was always a lot of it. Well, I listened, when I had time.

January 24, I wrote:

"I have had so many compliments and congratulations about the smoothness of the luncheon and tea. Mrs. Roosevelt was most enthusiastic about the way it went off and even said the President was going to send a letter to each of the heads of the various departments telling them so. Mr. Muir, myself, head butler, and cook. Won't we feel as though we are walking on clouds.

"Well, a large affair is no harder to manage than a small affair, sometimes much less so. For sometimes picayune affairs cause much more fuss and bother. However, I do wish to say that we have a fine organization here and everything did go off extremely smooth and quietly too. So I am happy."

My complacency was to have a rude awakening, and before long.

It was nice to get back to normal after the inauguration, such as whipping up a formal dinner for the President of Brazil with only one afternoon's notice. This was at the time I was trying to get rid of the President's mâte tea, an undertaking I was trying to keep under cover for the sake of Pan-Pacific relations.

The President had brought back several hundred pounds of this tea from South America, and while he insisted it was wholesome and invigorating, no one in the White House could be persuaded to take it up as a habit. Tea tastes are lifetime habits, I suppose, and none of us were brought up on mâte. Finally I distributed it quietly and in small amounts to the working people, the missions, and the hospitals.

February found us grinding away at the entertaining, and Miss Du Pont, Franklin's fiancée, came to visit, and was taken with appendicitis and rushed to the hospital for an emergency operation. Mrs. Du Pont was sent for, and Franklin was terribly upset, of course, and Sir and Lady Willert were house guests and in the general excitement Patsy the pup ran away again.

But I had caught my breath by this time and was hanging on like grim death to the East Room draperies. This time I was determined to have my way. It took me a year to get those drapes, but I got them.

Hitler repudiated the Versailles Treaty, the automobile and steel workers were on strike, and it seemed at times the world was coming down about our ears. But the White House had to be kept open, and kept up, because it was the center of the world. So I went ahead matching. samples and keeping an eye on the dusting, even in the face of what appeared to be the beginning of the end of the world.

This was where I ran headfirst into the National Fine Arts Commission.

You can't just fix over the White House as if it were any other American home. Many things must be considered and many authorities consulted, and tradition, of course, set the rules, enforced by the Fine Arts Commission. The Commission is in charge of the White House and very possessive about it. It has the say-so on furniture and such, which must be kept strictly in period and the colonial tradition. We all kowtowed to the Commission, even Mrs. Roosevelt. It controlled only the state floor, where you enter by the North entrance, and where the three parlors are, the Green, Blue and Red, and the East Room, and the State Dining Room.

Upstairs we were on our own, and Mrs. Roosevelt had her Val-Kil furniture there, and everything the Roosevelts liked.

But it was in the tradition-ridden downstairs that I began my drapery crusade.

It is tradition that the draperies of windows fourteen feet tall must clear the floor by an inch to look right, but Mrs.

Hoover had them cut short when they dirtied at the bottoms where the floors were wiped. She had hoisted them up a foot and the windows looked like gangling boys in short pants. The Commission wanted them lengthened. I explained that it's also a tradition that curtains once shortened can't be lengthened. Some we managed to lengthen from the top, under the valance, but others shrank more after being cleaned. Even the maintenance officer said it couldn't be done, and Maintenance could overrule even the National Fine Arts Commission.

So I started on silk hangings and curtains for the East Room, and as I said it took me a full year. Mrs. Theodore Roosevelt had changed it to gold, and we changed it back to its original red. We had the usual siege of bidding when the news got out that we were buying new curtains. I had so many swatches in red shades my eyes hurt, and I didn't know there could be so many shadings. The drapes had to be a particular shade of Italian red.

The President was interested in the curtains too. He loved tradition and history and a nice home, so he wanted to know about everything that was going on. I trotted up and down with swatches, and he and she would both hold them up and study them, but one was too pink and one too red and so on, and at last we had to have them dyed, and finally hit on the perfect shade.

Then the drapes had to be made, and hung a certain way, and after they were up the old Monroe furniture didn't match, so we sent it to the National Museum. We sent that mammoth gilt piano to the Museum, too, and later on, when the King and Queen of England came to visit, Steinway made a new one for the White House, just in time for their coming. Joseph Hofmann was the first to play on it, and rolled his eyes in ecstasy when he heard the tone.

I thought it high time the White House had some new furniture. President Monroe had moved into an empty house after the English burned the White House and it was rebuilt, and he brought his own furniture from his home and sold it afterward to the White House for $6,000.

A lot of the parquetry in the East Room floor was chipped. We had to replace the little wood blocks in French measurement, to matrice, not to scale, taking one piece out at a time and cutting the new to measure.

After we got the East Room drapes up Mrs. Roosevelt left me on my own, though the final choice was always hers and his.

"Go right ahead, Mrs. Nesbitt," she'd say. "I can trust you."

No sooner was the drapery crusade over than I found myself with a calculating eye on the rugs. The White House carpetry had known a lot of hard usage, and it showed. But Maintenance put its foot down on the rugs, and held it there for some time.

But the start of the first year of the second term had been a rousing success from my way of thinking so far. Then March began. I still can't bear to think about it, much less write it, but March 1937 turned out to be such a horror of a month that I'm going to tell about it fast, and then put it out of mind, the way I tried to then.

Chapter Thirteen

Trouble with Germany was coming on fast this March, and smaller troubles aimed at my rapidly graying head from all directions. It was one of those jinx months when the only escape is to spend it in bed and pull up the covers, only I had to keep going.

Most of my trials seemed to come from the direction of Canada, a country I've an especial fondness for, since it reminds me of Duluth.

First, Mr. Mackenzie King, the Prime Minister, came down from Canada, and everything was being dignified and stately, and dinner was in the President's study, as was done only for very private sessions, and Major, the police dog, bit the Prime Minister.

I suppose it suprised distinguished persons calling on the President of the United States to be greeted by a police dog and Scotties. Dogs came and went, Pap and Major, Fala, Franklin's dogs, Elliott's dogs—one almost upset the war effort later on—Anna's Irish setters and Mrs. Roosevelt's Scottie, Cricky, who was old and deaf, and once, when a newspaper woman bent over her with a kind word, Cricky bit her on the lip.

Major and I had been feuding for some time. I'd go upstairs to Mrs. Roosevelt's room and find her talking with Tommy or Mr. Early, or having her hair and nails done, and the children there, and she would be too busy to notice how all the time Major sat between us nipping my leg and rolling his eyes up to see how far he could go. He pinched sometimes, but he wasn't really biting, so I didn't complain.

It was simply that the big dog didn't want anyone in Mrs. Roosevelt's room, or in the White House either.

Then one day I had a man in the corridor outside her room measuring for the rug-mending, walking stooped over and estimating, and Major was stalking him with his eyes on the seat of his pants.

"Major!" I shouted.

Mrs. Roosevelt and the rug man jumped, and Major turned to me with a surprised look. He never nipped me again.

But another day he took the seat out of the pants of our old Italian gardener, who mowed the White House lawn with a gasoline mower, which Major detested for its smell and the noise it made. He was a very musical Italian, and was giving the lawn a final shearing one day before a lawn party while the army band was blaring away under the trees, and he was scowling, so Dad asked him if his mower was working all right.

"Oh, it's fine," the gardener answered, jogging away, "but Dio Mio, she doesn't keep time to the moosic!"

But to get back to the Canadian Prime Minister. Mr. King came from his room to have breakfast with the Roosevelts in the West Hall, and Major came up alongside and bit his hand. It was a painful situation, for the Prime Minister was put out and made no bones about it, and I couldn't say I blamed him for speaking to Major as he did.

We always had a lot of trouble with the White House dogs, usually about rug-spotting, but this was interference in good-neighbor policy, and Major was sent away, to Hyde Park, I think.

Then Lord Tweedsmuir came, Governor General of Canada, and the mention of his name still unnerves me.

Little did Lady Tweedsmuir know the anguish she caused when she asked for scones as casually as if they were pancakes! Scones may be in the line of march in a British or Canadian home, but not ours. Not one of the White House cooks had ever seen a scone, but they had to be made, and for breakfast. I'd made them years before. Mother Nesbitt had taught me, but I knew that hers, dear soul though she was, were not so light as they might be. Her recipe went back to days when they were baked on the scrubbed top of an iron range and were intended as a solid meal for rawboned pioneers.

This was a real emergency, and Ida co-operated with the magnificence she saved for crises between nations. I tore through my library of cookbooks and Ida tried out recipe after recipe, baking them two ways: on a griddle and in the oven. The scones were a White House triumph I am afraid her ladyship took for granted.

Apart from the scones, every Tweedsmuir menu had been worked out weeks in advance, for his lordship, like so many guests of the White House, was on a diet, and his list had been sent down ahead, back in October, the year before.

It was one of the most impressive-looking diet lists I ever added to my collection, which was probably, by this time, the largest outside of Johns Hopkins:

GOVERNMENT HOUSE, OTTAWA

DIET OF HIS EXCELLENCY THE GOVERNOR
GENERAL OF CANADA

Not to Be Taken

Soup of any kind. Fish, salmon, lobster, crab, trout. Smoked meats, pork, veal. Vegetables—turnips, sprouts, cabbage, tomatoes, parsnips, onions, old carrots, celery. Salads. Savouries. Creamy sweets, ice cream. No sauces

I ordered ice cream just the same, for the Tweedsmuir formal dinner that would be the high light of their visit, because a White House dinner isn't complete without ice cream, and I'd give his lordship some sort of fruit dish instead.

The ice cream was made up outside for big occasions in special molds. It was always the high minute of the evening when they came onto the tables, all fixed up beautifully, in pretty colors and shapes. At six o'clock, the night of the Tweedsmuir dinner, Ida mentioned casually that the ice-cream molds had not arrived.

I tried to telephone the shop that made them. It was closed for the night. I tried to reach the woman who ran it. She wasn't home. By this time I was shaking all over. In my desperation I telephoned Mr. Hubert, a caterer we had not been dealing with at all. He was just closing, and his driver was leaving for the night. He called back his driver, packed eight forms of plain ice-cream bricks—drugstore ice cream, we call it—and rushed them over. They arrived at the White House door just as we were clearing the State Dining-room table for the dessert, and I never gave a more thankful prayer in my life. We unpacked and sliced them in record time, and from the little dining room I could see Mrs. Roosevelt's look of shock, which she covered over fast, when the dessert plates came on with just slices of plain ice cream.

"What happened?" she asked next morning.

I explained, and she didn't say another word. What had happened, the storekeeper had left the molds out with orders that they were to be delivered, and they were still there the next morning, melted all over the floor.

It was a pity it had to happen to the Tweedsmuirs, of all people. They were a fine pair. I watched them in the dinner line that night, and although he only came up to her shoulder, they had the air of great distinction. Just as royalty would, they left a large sum to be distributed among the help,

181

and she sent me back a platinum pin from Canada, carrying the British crest and their coat of arms.

He died soon after this. All his dieting and abstinence hadn't helped. He was a sick man, and the threat in Europe didn't help him any. So many think that people in high places don't care and don't suffer over what goes on.

The diet lists I collected in the White House prove they do.

Along with my hundreds of recipe books I was gathering a small library of works on stomach ulcers. There were Jimmy's ulcer list, and Secretary Morgenthau's diet, and Secretary Hull's, and there had been Mr. Howe's, and later the President had special diets. Even the dogs had diets, vegetables with their meat, and Fala's had to be carefully watched because of his spotting the President's rug. Every menu I planned had to skirt around the ulcerites and their items, and they all had to have their foods puréed.

"Secretary of the Interior," they called me in joke.

Mr. Hull had to have lettuce, boiled chicken, tomato, green vegetables only, white bread, butter, milk, and, of all things, Swiss cheese! He couldn't eat cake, so on his birthday President Roosevelt ordered a cupcake, with one candle, to tease him.

Harry Hopkins wasn't supposed to eat anything, or drink either, but he did. Newspapers used to say Jimmy Roosevelt was a heavy drinker.

"Isn't that ridiculous," Mrs. Roosevelt would say calmly, "when Jimmy can't drink at all."

He had shown surprising gifts of oratory, working for his father in the campaign, and it seemed to bring his ulcers to the fore. Even after he went into the Army, Jimmy had to go back to the hospital and get straightened out.

Then there was Secretary Morgenthau, who couldn't touch beef or white bread. When we had filet mignon, on Mrs.

182

Roosevelt's birthday, I had French lamb chops served him inconspicuously so no one else at the table would notice. The butler didn't say anything, just served them. The next morning he came to my office.

"I want to thank you for remembering," he said.

Mr. and Mrs. Morgenthau were such sweet-mannered people. At least we didn't have to bother about Mrs. Morgenthau's diet. On her birthday this year I remembered her favorite soup and served it. Cream of almond.

He tried to keep his dieting unobtrusive, not like some of our ulcerites. It's like getting religion with some of them, they want to air their diets all the time. One morning I met him in the elevator when I knew he was lunching with President Roosevelt.

"The President is having cold cuts today," I said. "Would you like something else? Shrimps?"

"Don't bother about changing anything," Mr. Morgenthau said, and he ate cold chicken and ham along with the President.

I'd order Swedish flat bread for him, and the President would want some, and he'd eat what was left. When he was leaving he stuck his head into my office.

"Next Monday, when I come to luncheon," he said jokingly, "please see that I get pigs' knuckles and sauerkraut."

It seemed a pity to restrict his pleasure when he was surrounded by fine produce. They had a farm at Millbrook, and were always sending lovely gifts to the Roosevelts, apples and green beans and berries and everything else in season. Once, when I first knew Mr. Morgenthau, he sent in a crate of strawberries. It was a hot day when they came, and they had turned soft, so I made them into strawberry jam, which Mrs. Roosevelt liked best of all jams. He met me in the hall the next day and asked if I had served the berries.

"I served all I could," I told him, "but I'm proud to say we saved all the rest—we made them into jam." His face fell.

183

I never saw a man look so hurt. After all, they were his prize strawberries.

I couldn't say another word to Mr. Morgenthau, I felt so badly. I told Mrs. Roosevelt. She was nice about it.

"Try to be more diplomatic," was all she said.

Of course Harry Hopkins was our leading ulcerite. He was on a low-fat, high-protein, high-caloric, bland diet, and forty-eight items had to be watched on his list alone. The only fruit allowed him was puréed bananas. Sometimes I think history might have been different all around if it hadn't been for Mr. Hopkins and his forty-eight items.

You can't tell me food peevishness isn't catching. The President was too often surrounded by men who pushed their plates back and couldn't eat this and didn't like the looks of that, and it wouldn't agree with them anyway if they did. Then there were things going on in the world this March, even in our own United States, that I didn't know about just then, or I might have been able to take the events of the month a little more tolerantly and less personally. As it was, the blow came at the start of the month, March 3.

President Quezon of the Philippines came to lunch that day, a grave, fine-looking man who appeared to have a lot on his mind. He had, and it was Japan, but of course I couldn't know that. It was a stag luncheon and the men talked a long time and came out looking serious.

Up to now the President had taken every meal in full stride, never complained, and enjoyed every mouthful. Now, out of a clear sky, he blew up about the food. It was the start of his tension, and whenever he became tense, he would get peevish about his meals. I figured out later that trapped as he was by his lameness in a great, strong body yearning for action he had no other means of releasing his strain. He took it out on the food.

But it took me some time and a lot of heartache to figure that out.

Since everything the President said made news, there were headlines all over the United States:

"FDR DEMANDS NEW DEAL—REFUSES SPINACH—CRISIS STRIKES WHITE HOUSE."

His complaint, made half in joke and half peevishly, was amusing news for the whole world. Broiled calf's liver, he had said, and fresh green beans were appearing too often on his plate. Well, he was supposed to have them!

Pages were written about the President of the United States being served "liver and beans three days in a row," and "the same salt-fish breakfast four days hand running."

Mrs. Roosevelt was dear about it.

"You'll just have to be patient," she said. "The President is in a tizzy."

That was all right between ourselves, but I couldn't come out and tell the newspapers that the President was in a tizzy, that our new kitchen had been designed around his comfort and every menu set before him was made up in advance, worked out with Mrs. Roosevelt, and approved by him.

His explosions were mainly about the breakfasts, and those were ordered last thing every night by Mrs. Roosevelt, so none of the things charged against the kitchen could have happened. But it was on radio broadcasts and printed in ships' news that the President had refused spinach and didn't like eggs, which was one of the silliest charges of all this teapot tempest, as all the Roosevelts doted on eggs, and scrambled eggs and hot chocolate could pop out almost any time on the second floor. Mrs. Roosevelt was famous for her scrambled eggs, and their friends used to say you could maroon the Roosevelts on a desert island with a supply of eggs and they'd be well-fed and happy.

185

But the nation was aroused, and I had to read indignant diatribes against the housekeeping, and insulting letters came by every mail addressed to the White House housekeeper, and had to be answered as politely as I could. Lady Willert was a guest at the White House at the time and she gave Mrs. Roosevelt a list of English breakfast menus. I even had suggestions from far-off islands. Everybody wanted to help.

I couldn't say a word back, no matter what was charged. But I felt terrible. I was sensitive and overworked, and this was ridicule that curled up my very soul. The ridicule from the press and public could be borne, but not their thinking I had been belittled by the head of our nation, the man I admired most of all the world's leaders.

Mrs. Roosevelt said very gently: "Now you understand how we feel sometimes."

She told me she was getting $75,000 a year for her writing and giving it all to charity, and then they accused her of not paying taxes. And the President's salary was taxed, forty of his seventy-five thousand a year going to taxes, but the jeering had started that the Roosevelts were getting rich in the White House, and it kept getting worse.

After talking with her I felt I could bear up under anything. She and I always worked together on the menus. He'd tell her he didn't want this or that, and she'd ask what he did want, and he wouldn't know. She realized, as I did finally, that this was an outlet for terrific tension bound by physical inactivity, and she knew we were all doing our best. Every soul in the kitchen was devoted to him.

When he said, "The vegetables are watery," and "I'm sick of liver and beans," these were figures of speech.

But the newspapers didn't understand that. The public didn't know. The papers kept printing the legend that I ruled the President with a rod of iron, and all the time I was at my wit's end trying to get vegetables down him. The President had complained about peas, and crossed them off his menu.

I'd drive out to Bethesda Market before breakfast to select peas and asparagus. He loved the white asparagus, and if I couldn't get it fresh I'd get frozen, and the youngest spinach, to cook with butter and a little nutmeg, or maybe with a cream sauce with green onion tops chopped in.

As for the peas, I'd grown my own and knew he was missing the baby peas fresh from the vine, the thick cream and dewy berries of Hyde Park. I couldn't get these treats for him in Washington. But I'd bring back a whole bushel of peas, out of which we'd select only enough for maybe ten servings, and these we'd cook in water that didn't stop boiling. By such tricks we managed to get the President to eat his vegetables, though reluctantly.

I was trying everything. I'd pan broil oysters in butter for lunch, only to have him say he liked oysters in the shell. His meals went up in our new thermos conveyor, heated with electricity and chilled with dry ice, for foods hot and cold. I'd go through it after every meal to see what the President had cleaned up and what he had left, to try to get some inkling of his tastes. I'd pester the butlers.

"Tell me what the President seems to enjoy," I'd say, "or what he doesn't like." They did their best, and I'd find out one liking only to have his mood for it switch for the next time.

Mrs. Roosevelt was endlessly patient. I never saw her show anything less than perfect understanding. Sometimes, if the President was stubborn or opinionated about something, she'd laugh at him and get him laughing, too, but if it was something really serious, then she was serious with him, and with him in everything all the way.

"We'll let him decide," she said finally.

So I made up twenty-one menus, and the President discarded only one, so there! And asked for twenty more. I was doing my best. Keeping him content was my job, and it was little enough to do.

187

His was the whole world.

Not until later did I find out what lay behind his upsets. He had received important news of Japanese espionage. America was holding maneuvers in the Pacific and the Japs were watching. Japan and Germany were laying the ropes for war and he knew it was coming. Without public support he was trying to rehabilitate the Army and Navy. There was much trouble then about Guam, and the danger lay to the east and the west of us, but his hands were tied.

He must have felt helpless and frustrated, like a man fighting alone.

Still, I must have had some inkling, for right after the liver-and-beans tempest I wrote:

"Never in the history of the good United States was there such a man in the chair—the biggest we ever had. What courage. What insight into future needs. What diplomacy. What understanding of mass psychology, a statesman and politician too. He is at it too long each day, driving himself and others, never letting up."

Forces too vast for my understanding were turning in the White House in these years, and it was my humble part to help oil gigantic if invisible wheels.

When we did have food disappointments it was because of a tantrum on the part of one of the cooks, or delivery failures, or repetition because of the dieting.

There is something about working over a hot stove that brings out the best and worst in people. We had one assistant cook that kept the kitchen on edge for eight years, until Mrs. Roosevelt finally had her transferred. My hands were tied, because I wasn't allowed to fire anyone. We had another who used to tear up Mrs. Roosevelt's orders, in her own handwriting, and do what she wanted.

So Mrs. Roosevelt put her on probation.

Elizabeth Moore was an exception to the rule that cooks are bad-tempered. She had a wonderful disposition. Then there was Medina, a Filipino who had been in the Navy. He was sweet-tempered, and a wonderful cook.

Jackson, our boy, who waited on Dad and me at table and could take any cook's bad temper without turning a hair, was found to have cancer, went to the hospital, and died. I was running back and forth to the hospital to see him, and Dad came down with another attack. All in all, March 1937 was sheer nightmare, first to last.

Dr. McIntyre was a pillar of strength.

"Call on me if you need help," he said at the very start of the President's tizzies, and he co-operated on the menus and tried in every way to get the President's appetite back to normal.

He sent to New York for specialists and finally he brought in doctors from the Naval Hospital, and a dietitian arrived in uniform, and for a time the President ate everything he was told to eat, simply because it was "ordered by the Navy."

The President's reducing diet came from the Navy and was the simplest on record: Cut out all fried foods.

The President would eat all sorts of funny things when he was away from home. He'd eat baked beans and frankfurters and have no ill effects. Relief, I guess, from the strain of the White House.

I find an indignant note in my diary written at this time:

"The President is the only person in the White House this week who has worked seven days."

Chapter Fourteen

"Things will quiet down after Easter," Mrs. Roosevelt had said at the start of '37.

Well, by April, in the post-Lenten season alone, I was able to note in my diary that we had entertained ten thousand people.

A month later I wrote in a letter to the children:

"God knows it's quite a chore Mother has to go through! Fifteen hundred Monday, one thousand yesterday, two thousand today—and to have everything ready is quite a job."

It was a wonder to me the way Mrs. Roosevelt breezed through these affairs and left nearly every person feeling she had given them some part of her understanding that was special.

Crowds never seemed to tire her. Shaking hands, and not wearing out your fingers, is quite a trick. The President complained a couple of times of his hands hurting, but she never did. She had a knack of leaving her fingers limp and still pulling folks along, so the line went fast.

I saw her shake hands this spring with seventeen hundred and twenty-five Democratic ladies at three-thirty and with fifteen hundred more at four o'clock, and she looked just as fresh at the end as she had before.

The President went to California this April and Anna with him. I noticed an unusually heavy guard went along, and learned later threats had reached the Secret Service that the President would never come back alive. Mrs. Roosevelt went West, too, about this time, and came back with a lot of Indian handicraft, including a headband for Bobby.

Mrs. Roosevelt never left without arranging for a substitute hostess to take her place in the White House if Anna wasn't there. She would ask Mrs. Garner, or Mrs. Wallace, or Mrs. Hull. All three were nice-mannered women and carried things off well, though to my notion none had Mrs. Roosevelt's heart-warming way of making everyone feel completely at home. Mrs. Hull seemed the most gracious.

Mrs. Henry Wallace was nice, but there were so many contradictory stories about her husband I never did know what to think of him. He was Secretary of Agriculture for a long time, and they came a lot, to meals and evening affairs, and he seemed genial enough, but every time I looked at him I remembered the pigs. My conscience hurts when I waste anything, and I wondered if his did. If there was a surplus of food, why hadn't he divided it up among the hospitals and poor people?

Harold Ickes was another I could never warm to. As Secretary of the Interior he was in charge of national parks, so he was our superior in White House affairs. We saw a lot of him, but I can't like a man who pounds tables when he talks, so they say. His secretary called me about buying eggs and chickens from his farm, but I had to take them on certain days, so it didn't work out. He was a wonderful man for his job, but he set a harsh pace for himself and everyone else, and everyone can't keep up, and that makes for bad feeling.

Mrs. Roosevelt was dashing around more than ever these days, but wherever she went, a steady flow of letters and notes and telegrams came back, so she and I were in constant touch.

Almost always they started out, "Please . . ."

Even when she was in the White House, little notes would

191

come into my office at all hours, sent by Tommy, or in Mrs. Roosevelt's own odd handwriting.

"Dear Mrs. Nesbitt: There are twelve to fourteen for lunch, eight for tea and for dinner. See you at ten—ER."

"The President of Iceland will breakfast at nine in his room."

"Will you please have fried chicken, hard-boiled eggs, lettuce sandwiches, and whole tomatoes packed in Mrs. Baker's lunch kit Thursday morning. She is leaving right after breakfast."

"Also, will you tell whoever cooked the peas tonight that they were just as hard as bullets, though they were small and should have been very nice."

"Also, please have my brown leather lunch kit, including the box and bottle, in the ushers' office."

Other notes came on Mrs. Roosevelt's order blanks:

"Give a note to Mrs. Nesbitt or the Secret Service that the pralines are OK."

"Two broilers ready, for Mrs. Roosevelt to take to New York."

Among my food lists were the long grocery lists made out before all trips or picnics, including the vacations at Warm Springs, Hyde Park, and Campobello.

Messages shuttled to and fro from these places.

I'd receive telegrams on the White House pale blue telegraph paper. There is a telegraph and a telephone exchange inside the White House.

From Warm Springs: "Please send down two packages of wild rice in today's pouch."

"Please send a collection of cheeses by pouch."

These went by air mail.

Telegrams from Tommy, en route here and there:

"Will you please send Mrs. R a check for five hundred dollars."

"Wire from Mrs. R no laundry has come cannot understand reason."

"Mrs. R is going to Walter Reed Hospital on Christmas Day and will want cigarettes—about ten cartons."

Somehow the messages were thickest from Hyde Park. In one of her articles written there Mrs. Roosevelt told of being kept busy making lists of the bedrooms, menus for meals, and telling the various people what their duties were, and she wound up by saying:

"Doing things up here is never quite so simple as is doing them in the White House, because there Mrs. Nesbitt does all the detail work."

She'd really settle down to writing letters from Hyde Park, because I guess she relaxed more there than in any other place, and she'd go into leisurely discourses about the laundry problems, or things we were trying to get done, or about any guests headed our way, or her plans, and she signed her letters, "Affectionately yours, Eleanor Roosevelt."

A typical letter is dated May 10, 1937, Val-Kil Cottage, Hyde Park:

Dear Mrs. Nesbitt:

I will be back either late on Thursday or early on Friday morning.

The President gets in on Friday morning.

I am lunching out on Friday but at 4 P.M. I am receiving the wives of a textile group. Will you get definite information from Mrs. Helm if you haven't it?

In the afternoon on Friday, just in time for dinner, twelve girls and Miss Dickerman, Miss Cook, and Miss Goodwin will arrive.

The President says Mr. and Mrs. Elliott Roosevelt may come up with him. If they do, they can go into the little Blue Room.

"Three girls can go into the Pink Room, two in the big room, and one in the little room, and I think we will have to have an extra cot in that room.

Three girls can go into the boys' rooms, three girls into the Lincoln room and the little room off that.

Two girls in the Yellow Room.
"Miss Dickerman, Miss Cook, and Miss Goodwin
can go into Sistie's and Buzzie's old rooms.

This gives a fair idea of the master hand she was at shuffling
guests around.

The majority of our White House guests were lovely
people, who came and went without ostentation, and it was
a pleasure to have them there. However, we did have some
curious combinations.

Mrs. Roosevelt loved the White House and wanted everyone to see it, and I guess that explained some of the guests
that didn't seem to fit together, like asking Queen Wilhelmina along with Joe Lash of the youth movement, and
having Mr. Churchill and Miss Mayris Chaney at the same
time. She was the dancing one. Miss Chaney.

Harry Hopkins was also a house guest at the time.

I'd rack my brains wondering what those queer combinations found to talk about. Like having actors and titled
people and laborites mixed together. Different income
brackets, different stages of culture, different points of view.
Some of the combinations surprised even me.

She'd meet mediocre people, and people of no social ad-
vantages at all, and invite them. "They'll enjoy it so," she'd
say, and her face would glow with the thought of their happiness. "They'll remember it all their lives."

Some wormed in and got themselves asked to Hyde Park.
Some stayed on. And on.

Everyone who left cards at the White House was invited
to something. Almost every artist who asked to play there
was accepted. The Roosevelts' social lists became the longest
in White House history. House guests by the hundreds.
Visitors by the million.

Sometimes they wrote back carping letters, saying the windows in the East Room were broken, or there were cobwebs on the chandeliers, and there wouldn't be a web, or a pane broken.

Some of the house guests behaved as if they were in a hotel. She didn't know, or if she did, she never complained.

With Mrs. Roosevelt it was intellect that mattered. I don't believe she noticed a person's color any more than she did their dress.

Sometimes protocol stepped in. The usher has power of denial in matters of protocol even over the President's wife. She was ruled by her loyalties, her affections, and her desire to make people happy. Left to herself, I think she would have set the lowliest in the seat of honor. I have never known a woman, except Mrs. Roosevelt, whose motives were always pure kindness.

She never shifted loyalties. A friendship, or a relationship, was fixed. Her sons' marriages might end in divorce but that didn't change her attitude toward their ex-wives. Elizabeth Donner Roosevelt divorced Elliott, but she still came back to visit, bringing their child, and later the man she afterward married, Mr. Winser. Dorothy Roosevelt, who had divorced Mrs. Roosevelt's brother Hall, came to the White House at her request to give concerts. I was small town. This spirit of fair play was new to me, and I thought it wonderful.

Mrs. Roosevelt was not always responsible for the odd mixing up of the White House guests. The President also asked people to visit and later to stay on, and of course a lot of them had to be asked. He stood by his own words: "For no forgotten men, and no forgotten races." That should explain why such dissimilar people were asked to the White House. He couldn't go out to them. He asked them in. He wanted to know what they wanted and what they were thinking. As President and First Lady they were supposed to welcome everyone in the land, and it was easy for them, because they loved people.

"May 29, 1937—We have been having another horrid nightmare of a day with meals for the President. Conditions over which I had no control turned things upside down and the President has been so difficult to feed recently. Have one thing, then he wants another. Or when we plan for something he thinks he wants, we aren't able to get it, or not on time.

". . . the Press Party, however, was a huge success. Mrs. Roosevelt and her brother Hall Roosevelt with six or eight couples started it off with a Virginia reel which was very much applauded. They were all in costume. . . . The whole thing went off very well and we were serving beer, rye bread, sausage, cheese and crackets, et cetera, in the lobby during the evening and until supper was served.

"Supper consisted of cold cuts, salad, ice cream, cake, coffee, lemonade. There was dancing before and after the supper and later after 1 A.M. there were some Russian Gypsies, so called, who gave some thrilling performances of their dancing. Some very startling indeed. . . .

"I left at 2 A.M. and was up shortly before seven. Tonight I'm going to bed as soon as Dad and I have had our dinner."

"May 31, 1937—The President is cutting up an unusual tizzy-wizzy, as Mrs. R calls it. She said he just never fussed over his food and this is most unexpected. . . .

"I have shifted menus four times this morning, then the President at the last minute asked for fish cakes that were canned!

"Had planned giblets with rice for lunch today. Phoned for giblets yesterday, and when they came this morning they were too poor to use, so returned them. Got some from another place, but it was too late by this time for a 1 P.M. lunch, which message was sent up to Mrs. Roosevelt. She scolded me about this in her nice way but she was not fooling either.

"Phoned to see if the President's engagements were crowding. They were not. Then the kitchen phoned to say the berries had not come, nor the minute steaks that I ordered for the children, as the giblets would not be good for them. These I had sent my car down for earlier in the morning, and they had not been given the driver. Meanwhile, I had let him go to lunch.

"Got a car from the usher and sent it down to get the things. On the first trip down, early, I had ordered calf's liver, as we could not serve the rest of the family the giblets. Then, after that, I found we had fifteen for lunch, the number having gone up, which necessitated another trip to the market.

"Then, after all this confusion, the President asked for fish cakes. . . .

"Well, so it is in the White House when Congress does not behave.

"He is tense and under a terrific strain and it breaks out in this way so let us be glad it does. I do not like what repressions do to a person. It's a sight more normal to blow up and have it over."

It occurred to me the President was tired of mass cooking and hungry for home cooking, the way things were done in Hyde Park. I suggested to Mrs. Roosevelt that we open up the small upstairs kitchen and put Elizabeth up there to cook his breakfasts, luncheons, and dinners when he was alone.

This scheme, thank heaven, worked. He liked Elizabeth and her cooking and he liked the idea of "family" food. By June 13 I was able to jot down two thankful words:

"President satisfied."

June was a satisfactory month as a result.

The Windsors' marriage had me so excited I felt let down afterward, but we still had Franklin's wedding to look forward to, and John Roosevelt got himself engaged, and we gave a formal dinner to Premier Paul van Zeeland of Belgium on the twenty-third, and that same morning I met Lady Astor, who was stopping at the White House, in a bathing suit on her way to the pool.

Probably the nicest part of this summer was Dad's perking up and feeling much better, and we went up to Hyde Park to visit with Mrs. Roosevelt and see old neighbors there.

The East Room was painted that summer, and a lot of gilding and refurnishing and painting went on while the President was at Hyde Park, so as not to bother him, and we put new fans into the new kitchen over the stove.

The President came back on October 7 because Mrs. Hopkins died, and both the Roosevelts felt terrible. She had been ailing for some time, I heard. Mrs. Roosevelt went right over to the Hopkins house and brought back Diana, Mr. Hopkins's little girl, and we had Mrs. Roosevelt's little cousin, fifteen-year-old Elizabeth Henderson, with us too. Mrs. Roosevelt collected children. She'd leave Elizabeth in my charge when she went away, and we'd go to movies together, and I'd take her home.

I recall that day of Mrs. Hopkins's death very well, because that was the day we hung the new drapes in the East Room and we heard the Windsors were coming, but they didn't, and I was mixing the Christmas cakes and grinding bay leaves and such in my little coffee grinder, setting it to fine grind, and using a pestle for the smaller spices. Also, that was the day I went down to negotiate for the new crystalware for the banquet table. The glass dealer was having a lot of trouble getting experienced men to cut the President's crest.

I'd had a Hyde Park note from Mrs. Roosevelt about the crystal:

"The President says the samples of glasses which you sent are too expensive and that sixty dollars a dozen is the most he is willing to have spent."

I recall taking the first samples in to show the President. He was as eagle-eyed about detail as she, and pointed out that the presidential crest had been etched into the glasses in reverse.

198

The President's eagle looks to the left, and the United States eagle to the right.

"The eagle is looking over the wrong shoulder," he said right away.

The samples looked so pretty, I hated to give them up.

"Well, when you're drinking and see through them, the eagles look the right way," I argued.

But he said very emphatically they wouldn't do, so the etchings had to be done over.

November 16 I ordered the holiday pound cakes on ahead, for the Social Bureau as well as for the police force, and drove all the way to Baltimore to get glass jars for Mrs. Roosevelt's Christmas boxes. When I came back I found the President with another stomach upset, and the doctor had ordered him on a diet of boiled rice and milk, and the kitchen was disturbed again.

There were queer things adrift in the air. Even I caught them, taken up though I was with housekeeping details. This was the December I saw little Ambassador Saito in the Red Parlor given the direct snub by the Chinese-British contingent. Japan lost face in that moment in the White House, and I saw it happen.

Still, it was a joyous month and a lavish Christmas. One of the gayest affairs was the Gridiron Widows', when in the midst of the nonsense the newspaper women heralded "a forthcoming new volume by Eleanor St. Vitus My Day," which of course was a take-off on Mrs. Roosevelt's skimming about and the poetess Edna St. Vincent Millay.

Mrs. Roosevelt laughed hardest at some of the verses and to look at her you'd think she hadn't a care in the world:

Hi diddle diddle, the cat and the fiddle,
The cow jumped over the moon,
The moon laffed and laffed, and said, You're too late!
Eleanor passed here at noon.

Another went:

> Little Boy Blue, come blow your horn,
> The sheep's in the meadow, the cow's in the corn,
> But thinking of fences and speaking of sheep,
> When, if ever, does Eleanor sleep?

This was one of the nicest of the White House Christmases, and I served the usual family dinner, and the whole family enjoyed it, including the President, who seemed like himself again:

Blue Points   Saltines

Calf's Head Soup

Fairy Toast

Curled Celery   Stuffed Olives

Roast Turkey

Sausage   Chestnut Dressing

Cranberry Sauce

Beans   Sweet Potatoes and Apples

Grapefruit Salad

Plum Pudding   Hard Sauce

Ice-Cream Cake   Coffee

Right after Christmas I had a letter from a lady in Georgia:

To the Chef at the White House,

What a standardized, stereotyped, unimaginative dinner for a President of the United States—and that President—Mr. Roosevelt! That dinner was served at clubs, hotels, and restaurants all over the United States and thousands of our country people had a grand dinner. I wish I could have had Mr. Roosevelt at my table at Christmas. There he would have had something to eat. And something good.

Mrs. Jones

Maybe I didn't explain to Mrs. Jones, but I will now, that this was the Christmas dinner the Roosevelts wanted, the one that was being served all over America. They liked things done the old way—the way that had been America, and Roosevelt, for the past three hundred years.

Chapter Fifteen

We always had ants in the fall along with the official functions.

They were the little black fellows, and we warred on them the year round, but they came out strongest for the big affairs. After my office was made over, with the new cement floor, I was sure we had them licked.

One morning I came in and there they were, swarming all over my desk.

In the help's dining room the table legs were set in cans of water or kerosene, but the smart little pests would walk right up the ceiling and drop down.

The ants loved the second floor where Mrs. Roosevelt always had plates of fruit set out for the guests. She had mice up there too.

Government entomologists spent field days in the White House. We were the testing grounds for every new disinfectant and spray. During World War II we achieved the dubious distinction of being the first place to try out DDT.

One of my first days in the White House I walked into the elevator and the biggest bug I'd ever seen scuttled into a corner.

"Oh, that's just a cockroach," someone said.

I'd never seen such a monster.

Their breeding grounds were the ancient wooden cabinets in the kitchen, seasoned with the cooking odors of thirty-odd presidential terms. I tried to get one of the entomologists to figure up how many generations of cockroaches had grown up there since President Adams, but he just shook his head.

The cabinets of our scientific new kitchen were all of shining steel, and we still had cockroaches and ants.

The bottom floor had its own problems. The rats came from the outside, through the tunnels, into the White House. The gardeners stood watch, flanked by the entomologists, and the two forces fought the rats together, and still the enemy came through.

The zoological department entered our lives by way of the squirrels—the ones that lived in the trees, outside the White House. One morning I met Mrs. Roosevelt in her bathing suit trotting to the swimming pool—she was an early bird!

"Mrs. Nesbitt, I've had a letter about the squirrels," she said. "Someone wrote in complaining our squirrels look mangy!"

Well, if ever there were petted squirrels, those at the White House were. But I phoned the zoo, and they sent some men out, and they set traps and caught a couple, and gave them physical examinations worthy of heroes. They weren't mangy, of course, but the report came back, very official:

"White House:

"Stop feeding your squirrels so many peanuts."

The Treasury Department, the police, and the guards stationed about had all been stuffing the sassy little creatures with nuts.

These problems were as nothing compared to the moths.

When Andrew Jackson moved into the White House, following President Adams, he reported finding the East Room in a mess, and the furniture infested with every variety of bug, having been used for dozing by constituents waiting to see the President. One holiday season soon after someone sent him a fourteen-hundred-pound cheese four feet across, and he had it set up in the East Room and cut there at a reception. I could have told "Old Hickory" that the best-brought-up people spill at receptions and trample what they spill, and naturally the presidential cheese got trampled into the carpets and they say the smell didn't come out for months.

I've always held President Jackson's cheese responsible for attracting the grand-ancestors of many of our White House pests.

But I'll trade rats, pink elephants, and red, white, and blue turkeys with straw hats on, as the saying goes, against the persistency of one buffalo moth.

When we first moved in, Nancy Cook and her helpers. anxious to make the place habitable, went into the storerooms and hauled out a lot of old furniture, even platform rockers and old leather chairs, and had Sloane's cover them in colors that gave an appearance of unity to the upper west hall lounge.

The chairs were the storehouses of my legacy of buffalo moths. These horrors lie dormant for six or seven years, then they are on you like a herd of buffalo. They are at the bottom of the upholstery, then drop down, and devour anything in reach.

Five years after the ladies raided the storeroom, in 1938, I went on my vacation and when I came back my secretary Ruth met me.

"I have some bad news for you."

One end of the big Bokhara rug was completely gone.

We sent the rug and all the furniture to the storage company. They fumigated every thread with cyanide. Repairing and reweaving the rug cost $450.

Another long interval of years, and Princess Juliana was coming, and there was a great rushing around, for the slip covers were full of holes and the chairs were breaking down and so was our entire standard of appearances. I went to Mrs. Roosevelt.

"We have a little extra money," I said. "Can't we get some new furniture?"

"If Captain says we can!" Mrs. Roosevelt answered cheerfully.

So Sloane's sent in materials, chairs, and couches for the upper hall lounge, and Mrs. Roosevelt made the final decision on the fabrics, and in ten days' time they turned out fifteen completed pieces, couches and chairs, and had them in their places just one half hour before Juliana arrived!

The old furniture had taken such a beating by this time we burned a lot of it, but some of the old leather chairs were still serviceable and the chauffeurs took them into the garage, and three weeks later word came—buffalo moths in the garage!

Did I gasp with relief. Just five years had passed since the big fumigation, and our moths had survived the cyanide. We got that furniture out of the White House just in the nick of time. Was I happy, particularly since I'd bought a beautiful new Bokhara runner—at half price since it was an odd size! I had lots of fun bargaining with my Armenian rug dealer friend.

Apparently there is only one cure for moths. Burn everything.

We had a big cedar room in the White House, but you can't trust cedar entirely. Once, by mistake, after the President came back from a fishing trip, McDuffie hung his old fishing trousers in the cedar room, and I found them there and was scared to death. All Mrs. Roosevelt's good furs and the boys' winter suits were there. So I called in our exterminators and they sprayed every garment and corner. Then there was Emperor Selassie's big lion-skin rug in front of the fireplace in the President's study that the children called Leo. One of my jobs was seeing him put away against moths each summer.

But I'm getting ahead of my diary, because it was still January 1938 and I was in the thick of the moth crusade:

"Cardinal Mundelein is coming and where shall we put

him? He would come when the hall rug is being repaired. I phoned the rug man and he sent another. It came, fortunately, when the President had taken the Cardinal out to see the navy parade in the SS *Potomac*—fine for me. The Cardinal is on his way from the Pope for the conference for the Central European situation which looks bad for the Catholics as well as for the Jews.

"It must be terrible, told to get out of home and business with an hour's notice—penniless and homeless. Are we glad to be Americans. Poland has repudiated the Jewish citizens, poor victims. I thought of our grandchildren, what they will have to face to atone for the wickedness."

Some of the errands that were part of my duties were wild-goose chases, and I mean that literally. January always saw a lot of wild game as gifts, and this month brought a collection of wild geese and one large wild turkey. I took first choice for the President, as he was so fond of game that we saved any pheasant or quail or other bit of game left over from dinner, and he would have it for his breakfast. Secretary McIntyre was supposed to have one of the geese, but he said he couldn't use it just then, so we offered it to Dr. McIntyre, who had some blind people he liked to send things to.

Along with the wild birds we had been sent an immense domestic turkey weighing twenty-seven pounds which I planned to give to the help. There were so many birds, I sent them all over to our market, and asked them to keep them until wanted.

The wild turkey was for the President, and since he was planning to have dinner on the following Sunday with Franklin, Jr., in Charlottesville, I telephoned the market and asked them to send the wild turkey there.

On Friday I telephoned the market and asked them to send the big turkey for the White House help's Sunday dinner. They had sent it to Franklin, Jr. I telephoned Charlottesville.

"I can't get this big turkey in the oven," Mrs. Franklin, Jr.,

206

said, "besides, the President isn't coming to dinner Sunday after all."

That was the first I'd known about that. I asked her to please send back the turkey, which she did.

Then I phoned the market and asked them to send the wild goose to the blind people whose address Dr. McIntyre had given me.

Later on I phoned the market again, and asked them to send me the wild turkey and two small turkeys for the White House family dinner, as I had just learned the President and family would dine at home with guests, eighteen in all. The marketman explained that through another error the wild turkey had gone to the blind family instead of a wild goose.

"Get that turkey back," I almost howled, "and give them the goose!"

Well, the big turkey reached us in time for the help's Sunday dinner, the wild turkey came back just in time to be fixed for the President's Sunday dinner, and the blind family got the wild goose in time for theirs.

I was so exhausted I went home and fixed a kettle of knockwurst and sauerkraut to settle my mind. Something simple, after all that excitement, was a vital need.

That was not the only wild-goose chase of this January, only next time it was squabs. They were for the President's birthday luncheon on January 29 in the State Dining Room, and I think it was the first of the movie-star luncheons and the start of the great campaign against polio. I'd ordered thirty-five squabs from South Carolina, allowing a couple extra in case an extra guest or so dropped in.

Well, I should have known by this time! Hollywood stars increased by fives and tens, and you can't split a squab. Each guest had to have a whole bird on his plate, and nearly twice that many actors were on their way. I was cavorting around town in my Ford from market to market, trying to pick up squabs, a bird that becomes as extinct as the dodo when you need a certain number in a rush. I scraped the markets and raided hotels, and finally got sixty-five squabs. The Willard, Carleton, Mayflower hotels were always grand in crises. Ever after I'd get large birds that could be carved and allow for the last-minute expansion Roosevelt hospitality was certain to bring down on the housekeeper's head.

We had cream of almond soup and Southern beaten biscuit to start off the luncheon, and I was so busy fussing with the squabs and biscuits I didn't have time to notice the guests, but I do remember Mary Pickford.

A Southern girl made these Southern beaten biscuits for us in her own home, the way they're made in the South, where a beating block and wooden bat are standard kitchen equipment. She'd take one pound of flour, a fourth pound of lard, a teaspoon of salt, two of sugar, a fourth teaspoonful of soda and baking powder mixed, and a half cup each of ice water and cold milk. She'd work it all in with her hands and then pound on the block for a solid half hour, then cut the dough into rounds, prick with a fork, and bake. It's the beating that makes it light.

The biscuits are mostly done with machinery these days and I can't tell the difference, but maybe a born Southerner can.

For the President's family birthday dinner we had beef fillet and oyster cocktail and calf's head soup and mushrooms and asparagus and corn and chicory salad and chocolate ice cream and the birthday fruitcake that was his favorite, the dark kind, sticky with fruits.

Dr. McIntyre and Captain Calahan put on stunts for the President's birthday dinner, and for some reason they wanted an iron pot with smoke rising out of it, and put the problem up to me. I tried dry ice, but it didn't smoke enough, then went around to all the drugstores hunting for some powder that smoked red, blue, and green, such as we used to make up in our drugstore in Duluth. Nobody had heard of it, so finally

208

I went to the Bureau of Standards, and they fixed some with fuses attached like those torpedoes we used to have as children on the Fourth of July.

Then I went looking for an old iron pot with a bale, and try to find one of those on short notice! I was in and out of every secondhand store in Georgetown, and found plenty without handles, and when I finally found one that looked like a witches' brew pot, I dragged it back to the doctor and the captain in triumph. Captain Calahan was admiral later, and would be one of the first to be blown to bits in the Pacific when his ship ran the Japanese gamut.

They were all beginning to show the strain these days, but they could still find time for nonsense. The doctor's office was the rendezvous of the President and his aides, and we'd hear the haw-haws of laughter coming from there. General Edwin M. Watson ("Pa") the President's military aide, was wonderful for the President. He told amusing stories, and gave the light touch the President needed.

I've left a few days out of this January. There are blank pages in my diary and some newspaper clippings tucked in.

"Henry F. Nesbitt, seventy-two, custodian of the White House and one of the most popular members of its household staff, died today. . . .

". . . he had been at his desk all day. He studied at Trinity College in Dublin."

Everyone was kind. Mrs. Roosevelt went out of her way to help take him home to Hyde Park. "I'm free; I'll go with you," she said.

Of course I knew she wasn't, she was just making the time, but I was grateful. She'd seen so many through trouble that she was a tower of strength in an emergency.

St. James churchyard at Hyde Park is a lovely, quiet place set in trees, elms I think, and flowers bloom there in summer. My sister and sister-in-law are buried there, and the Nesbitt plot is not far from the one where the President's father, James Roosevelt, is buried. There was ice on the ground, and old friends and old faces, but I don't remember much. Mr. Wilson, our Hyde Park clergyman, officiated, the same who always came down to aid on March 4 when the President had his consecration service at St. John's in Washington. My friend Mrs. Anderson drove all the way up from New Rochelle in the cold, and Mrs. James, the President's mother, came.

Mrs. Roosevelt wrote about the funeral in her column afterward, of the little church and the neighbors, and how seeing all the dear old friends together must have given me warmth and support.

They all helped. But it would be a long time, after hearing something of special interest such as the news that the King and Queen were coming, before I'd stop thinking first thing: "Dad will be interested." Or turn quickly to say something, thinking him beside me. I still do that.

Mrs. James had been widowed many years, but she still remembered, and the message she sent turned out to be the most helpful of all.

"I think," the President's mother wrote, "that the interest of your work will be a great help to you."

Chapter Sixteen

To show how badly things were in Europe we started getting the crowned heads that spring. March 1938 started us out with a royal week, for we had the Sultan of Muscat, the new French Ambassador, and King Zog's three sisters from Albania.

"Make a showy tea for Their Highnesses," Mrs. Roosevelt said, which was a most unusual request for her to make.

Usually, for Orientals and South Americans, we had a lot of sticky and colorful sweets, colored *petit fours*, tiny cream puffs with varied fillings, and always candy and sweet or salted nuts. She'd never touch these things herself, though she was given so much candy, but would keep some out for the children and send the rest down to me to serve the household.

I recall our having a lavish sweet display for the three princesses, and no pork or alcoholic liquors, not even a light wine, for the Sultan's dinner. He arrived with his two aides, all in Arabian dress, including turbans, that they wore even to the table.

We had the grandson of the German Kaiser and his bride at Hyde Park, and the Crown Prince of Sweden visited with his wife and son and their entourage, and along with all this nobility we had labor troubles in the White House.

After Dad's death I took over the bookkeeping along with my other work, ordering the supplies and checking and recording the parcels. I took up needlepoint too. "Moron's delight," I called it—simple work that keeps you occupied without having to think too much.

A word rode me: Costs. I had to know what everything cost. The President had to know, because of taxes, and I had to be ready to produce any price list.

Maintenance had to know just how I was spending my share of the general budget, so I was still keeping track of the three accounts, and blessing my stars for having learned bookkeeping in my drugstore days.

There were labor troubles everywhere in the world, including the United States, and a lot of the labor upset centered in Washington, and the spotlight was on the White House. Mrs. Roosevelt said the eight-hour day had to be. It doubled our expenses, and also the help got the day and a half free every week the Government ordered to give more people work, but even this brought on a lot of bad feeling. There are always grouches in a domestic staff. In our first White House year the girls had worked all day, and the butlers, too, and not a peep out of them, but that had been in hard times. Now, with easier times, the complaining began.

I labored over schedules along with estimates, trying to get each worker satisfied as to the days he or she wanted to work. The butlers were taking the brunt of things. They had to serve the breakfasts with lunch pressing them, waiting upstairs and down, carrying trays, serving teas all over the house, getting tables ready, serving dinners, and after dinner snacks, and trays of drinks. . . . This routine had to be divided up so there was fair play for all, and it all had to work out into minutes as well as dollars and cents. I tell you I was stumped for a while.

Mrs. James came down to visit during these troubles, but she didn't say much.

She and her daughter-in-law had more in common than the Republicans seemed to think, only they looked at things from different age angles. The main trait they shared was their wish to be kind.

Eleanor Roosevelt believed in being practical and Mrs. James believed in doing good, and I think that was the difference. Mrs. James came from a social group that believed in low salaries and perquisites, or, in other words, making up in gifts for what was lacking in the salary envelope. That was the old way.

Mrs. Roosevelt, on the other hand, wouldn't stand for "tote," or carrying food home, because she said that was like giving the servants handouts. "I believe in giving good wages, not perquisites," she said. This was while labor was struggling for a living wage.

A great deal of Mrs. Roosevelt's desire to help people was native in her, I think, and some may have been cultivated by the mother-in-law who practically reared her and was almost like her mother. I don't know what a letter from Mrs. James to Mrs. Roosevelt is doing in my files, but evidently Mrs. Roosevelt turned it over to me with a request for help. It reveals the way they both tried to do for others, each in her own way.

Mrs. James had sent a notice of a new hospital, and wrote:

"I hope that you will read it, and despite the many other demands made upon you at this moment, will feel the pleasure of helping those in misery to find a place to go where doors are never closed. . . ."

On November 18 the commercial treaty was signed, at 4 A.M. in the East Room, between Canada, Great Britain, and the United States. It was an impressive spectacle with Ambassador Sir Ronald Lindsay, Prime Minister of Canada Mackenzie King, Secretary of State Hull, and the President in the seat of honor at the old Jackson cabinet table.

Right after this the President wanted a stag dinner, which

usually calls for roast beef, but I was not sure of putting it on the menu, as he had been refusing beef in any form for several months. "It's too hot," had been his reason, back in summer, but now it was winter and he was still anti-beef.

I phoned Mrs. Roosevelt. She was in the President's office, and I could hear the questions she asked and his answers, and his were all "No!"

"Would you like roast beef for the dinner?" she asked, and I heard him most emphatically say "No!"

"Would you like steak?"

"No."

"Fillets?"

"No."

By this time she was laughing, and seemed amused by it, but it didn't sound funny to me, all those "no's," over the phone. She went right on, good-natured as ever.

"Pork?"

"No."

"Veal?"

"No."

She spoke back to me, "Well, he doesn't seem to want anything, so get a young turkey." So the men had turkey, and the next morning she brought up the subject.

"The President seems to be off his food again," she said.

"Well, he has me worried," I admitted. "He has been refusing beef for two months, and won't eat pork or veal, so lamb, fish, fowl, or a steak are all the changes I have to work on."

The President didn't seem to consider a steak as beef for some reason.

"He has his Dutch up," Dr. McIntyre used to say when the President got into such moods. Both she and he had the Dutch stubborn streak, that on her part showed in her sticking more strongly to anyone under attack. The more that was said against Mayris Chaney and her dancing, for example, the more Mrs. Roosevelt stood by her.

Miss Chaney was occupying the small Lincoln Room this December, and the Canadian Prime Minister was with us, and Mr. and Mrs. Jimmy Roosevelt were in the Rose Suite, and Mr. Johnny in the Yellow Room, having been turned out of the little Blue Room, where he usually slept, by guests. More guests came, and Mrs. Roosevelt gave up her own bed, and slept on the couch in her room, and caught the flu, and that was the day we had Lady Lindsay and the Anthony Edens for tea, and the cabinet dinner for ninety, and three hundred in later to the concert, and still later the supper for the artists. Also this December Miss Eleanor Roosevelt, one of the cousins, made her debut in the East Room, with a few hundred invited for supper and dancing, and we had the big diplomatic reception, and affairs for the Egyptian Minister and Madame Hassen, and the Irish Minister and Mrs. Brennan, not to mention the usual phantasmagoria of getting ready for Christmas.

For Miss Roosevelt's debut alone I ordered one hundred and sixty pounds of link sausages, seventy-five chickens for the salad, six cases of eggs, dozens of different kinds of cakes and cookies, to say nothing of gallons of ice cream, coffee cream, celery, olives and such, and brandy, champagne, and white grapejuice for the punch.

And in between I was stirring up the plum puddings and fruitcakes.

It wasn't often Mrs. Roosevelt was really put out, and showed it. I never saw her angry, though I saw her when I knew she was, and she'd get emphatic then, and put her foot down. She was so long-suffering I often thought she forgave too much.

Only once did I see her indignant under attack. I was up

215

in her room one morning after a congressman had charged she used her position as first lady to sell the Val-Kil furniture.

"You know that isn't true, and you must retract it," she told him firmly. "I will give you until just ten o'clock, because I'm meeting the press then, and if you don't, I'm going to tell them the whole story." He promised to come up to meet the press and retract before them, but he didn't come, so she told them the truth.

Usually, she laughed things off, and no matter how indignant the rest of us became over some printed lie, she'd never let it show.

But she came down firm-handed on the young couple that crashed the White House in January 1939.

It was the start of one of the strangest years in history, and the atmosphere in the White House was tensing to the snapping point. Italy had turned Fascist, Spain had "capitulated to Franco," and the Third Reich was solid Hitler under his hooked cross. Europe was ignoring President Roosevelt's cabled appeals to "preserve the peace." There were meetings and conferences going on, and a feeling of dread over everyone, and I noticed Colonel Starling's men kept a sharper eye than ever on those who came through the White House doors. So in the thick of onrushing disaster this young couple made a bet they could crash the White House.

They won by an odd coincidence. Mr. Morgenthau had told the doorman a couple of his young relatives were expected, so when this young couple appeared at the door and said, "We're expected," the doorman thought of course they were the couple, and let them in.

They didn't even wait for the elevator. They just sailed on up the stairs and in on the Roosevelts in their living quarters.

They shook hands with the President, and were making themselves at home, when Mrs. Roosevelt came out of her room. She knew right away they were strangers, not invited.

For once she was upset and showed it.

"You would both have been shot on sight with no questions asked if the Secret Service men had seen you," she told them. "They are here to guard the President and see strangers do not get in. You have done a dangerous thing, as well as a rude one."

After that the Secret Service pulled their ropes tight around the White House. They forbade any visitors on the top floor. The ushers and detectives were more careful than ever about getting the names of everyone who entered the White House doors, and one could feel the sense of precaution and tightening up in the air. I, for one, was glad of it.

The clubs, groups, organizations were starting in on us full swarm, and I was appalled by all the wholesale entertaining this year was to bring.

I didn't have to read the papers or listen to the radio—though I did both—to realize how dangerous things were in Europe. I could tell by the President's appetite. He was difficult as the year started, and I knew things would be worse. A gift came in of five buffalo tongues, which were lifesavers, as any food oddity whetted his interest, and Ambassador Kennedy sent a barrel of stone crabs for the President, and Mrs. Roosevelt sent me some for myself, with the message, "Meet them and eat them," which I thought odd, coming from her.

Hendrik Van Loon, the writer, came in January, and I always looked forward to seeing him because he usually sent back wonderful Dutch cheeses to the President, and, besides, I admired his personality.

Also we had Franklin, Jr.'s baby and his nurse staying with us, as their house in Charlottesville had burned down. He was an adorable youngster, and Mrs. Roosevelt and I played with him every morning she was home, and then she'd take him in to the President.

By the start of February everyone from the President down was worn out by the social season. The ushers were so weary they were almost hysterical, and I was ready to drop in my tracks, and we had three more big affairs to go. After that, the President and Mrs. Roosevelt planned going away for a rest, she to Mrs. Boettiger's in Seattle—Anna was having another baby—and he to Southern waters for some fishing. Three of the kitchen help were down with the flu, and Elizabeth Henderson, and Miss LeHand, and, finally, the President. I heard Mrs. Roosevelt phoning Dr. McIntyre, and she said the President's temperature was over one hundred, and he was perspiring in a way that was very queer.

The President was not taking his illness well, because he had a luncheon coming up for Oswaldo Aranha, the Minister of Foreign Affairs from Brazil, and after that he wanted to go fishing. There were only fourteen invited, and the President said, "I will be at the lunch!" and Dr. McIntyre, just as stubbornly, said, "No!" and Mrs. Roosevelt was tactful and didn't say anything.

All this kept me sitting on the fence with meals and plans. Meals were being canceled and reordered continually, and it was like juggling, because it takes a certain amount of game to feed a certain number and I had to keep particular game until the numbers were right, and I was hoarding those buffalo tongues and four wild duck.

The doctor won, and the Brazilian luncheon was postponed, but I was glad the fishing trip wasn't, because the President so dearly loved being on the water.

From then on most of my thoughts in '39 were on royalty. Mrs. Roosevelt told me for certain in February that the King and Queen of England were going to visit the United States, and would stay at least two days in the White House.

It was the first time in history a ruling head of England had visited the United States, and Lloyds of London had taken bets against their making the trip. But on February 25 I wrote in my diary:

"The English King and Queen are really coming!"

As usual, I took advantage of the event by starting a rug-buying campaign. This time everyone backed me up, because the White House was badly in need of new floor coverings. At least six million people had tramped through the President's house since we came in, back in '33, and no matter how much care rugs get, they will wear thin.

We had been so tight on money at first that I hadn't dared ask.

Mrs. Roosevelt had a two-tone blue carpet in her room and when we moved in the edges were so worn it kept breaking apart. Mr. Marvin McIntyre got a new rug in his office, and I wanted her to have one, but she insisted the old one would do. So I spent thirty-six dollars to have it resewed, and she had used it up till now, and having so many dogs around hadn't helped it any.

But now, with Their Britannic Majesties coming, we had to spruce up, so Sloane's were sent for in the usual rush. We never did things in a leisurely way, as in other houses—but Mrs. Roosevelt had a new rug in her favorite blue.

The rug in the President's bedroom was also badly worn and spotted, but we found a nice rug on the *Mayflower*, the President's new yacht, and used it.

The rugs in the little red dining room and the Red Parlor were coarse Turkish red and blue affairs, and in the little dining room the butlers walking around had worn grooves in the nap of the rug so that when the table was extended it wobbled, so we banished it to the upper room and replaced them all with broadloom. Then the big controversy was on whether we should save the big rug fresh for the King and Queen, or put it down for the Press Party.

We decided to wait, press affairs always being so messy, since they are popular and so many come. And a good thing we did, because after this one we swept up a full bushel of cigarette butts.

The President was showing a lively interest in all the new things, and wanted to be in on it all. He had the final say on glasses, dishes, rugs, and anything like that, and on the whole he was shrewd and had a good sense of values.

Mrs. Roosevelt told me that when Val-Kil cottage was started at Hyde Park, he looked at the plans and estimates she and her group had had drawn up.

"You're paying too much," he said. "I'll bet I can get it put up at a fourth less."

The ladies just hooted at him, and told him to go ahead, and he did!

Once, after a trip to Warm Springs, he came in to me.

"I have a good story for you, Mrs. Nesbitt," he said. "Down at the Springs a salesman came to see me, gave me a good sales talk, and showed me a rug. Persian antique, he said, and I fell for it. Well, later I found it was American-made."

I was indignant.

"Did you box his ears?" I asked.

The President chuckled.

"No, I bought the rug."

He seemed to think it was a good joke on him. He didn't often get sold.

We had the Red Room done over with fresh dark red damask on the walls, chairs, and settee. It was the informal reception room.

The Blue Room, which is oval like the President's study, was hung in blue silk which was splitting, and I had it copied by Cheney. The walls and curtains had borders hand embroidered in the Greek key on them, and there were starred valances with gold eagles. Here all the presidential receptions were held, the army, navy, judiciary, diplomatic, congressional, royal, and here he received the credentials from his office, and I'd peeked in to see Haile Selassie's emissary give him that lion rug that lay before a fireplace copied from Fountaine-bleu.

There was a lot of history to consider, along with matching silks and two-tone rugs.

The ugliest rug was the taupe one in the diplomatic reception room, and we sent that out and had it dyed a deep rose to match the rose curtains, and it made a dramatic and dignified room.

Sloane's were putting new rose all-over carpets in the Rose Rooms, which would be the Queen's, and the Joels, my interior decorator friends, came and helped put the suite into solid colors, pink and cream, with just one little pink-and-cream carved chair.

I was wildly matching up glasses, too, and counting them, and found we had only eighty-one champagnes.

"We'll be short for Their Majesties," I told Fields. "Well, if necessary I'll buy some in the five-and-ten."

But I ordered more with the President's crest instead, and began filling out the dishes. Mrs. Woodrow Wilson started the Lenox set when she was First Lady, but conditions had changed since then, and we needed more, and besides, there is a lot of breakage no matter how careful people are. The Roosevelt china had a cobalt-blue border with a feather design in gold inside the blue, taken from the Roosevelt crest, and in the center of the plates the President's crest, with the eagle looking to the left.

Mrs. Wilson, being in the jewelry business, had also started the White House silver service for twenty in the Minuet pattern, but that wasn't enough for us. Before her day the White House silver had been made up of conglomerate designs, and wasn't as nice as the silver in the Blair House, which is a sort of annex to the White House. The Blair House was a historic mansion occupied by members of that family, and filled with rare and beautiful antiques, even Paul Revere silver. Early in the war the State Department took it over, and when foreigners came and brought their families and retinues they were cared for in the Blair House and the State Department paid their official expenses, I think.

I spent most of March wrestling with rugs.

Now the news of the royal visit was out, people began pestering me, asking how I was preparing for British royalty.

"Same as for other guests," I'd say, "cleaning, dusting, putting up fresh curtains, replacing the worn out, getting the chance at new things—only everything on a larger scale."

I was fingerprinted and photographed for a gate pass, to use when Their Majesties came, which interested me greatly, as I had always wanted to be fingerprinted.

One morning I was out under the trees when I noticed a camera grinding away in my direction. I ran inside, and the cameraman followed and kept on grinding. It turned out they were from the British Secret Service, taking pictures of the White House, its grounds and inhabitants, to be shown to Their Majesties ahead of the American visit.

We were anxious to please their tastes in every way, and Washington drinking water is chlorinated and does not make good tea, so we asked London to send over samples of the drinking water, and our American water was "torn down" and then built up by American chemists "to a queen's taste." Upon the doctor's orders we also sent along the drinking water for President Roosevelt's trips, whether in this country or abroad.

There were a thousand threads of detail to tie together, here and overseas, and I made out the longest shopping lists ever. "Towels for bathrooms . . . shower curtains and johnny covers for the King and Queen. . . ."

Months ahead I began getting advice from perfect strangers as to how I was to conduct White House plans, and warning me of the wonderful service the King and Queen were accustomed to.

I'd give everyone a smile and the same answer: "Oh, we'll muddle through somehow, as the British say."

Mrs. Roosevelt was flitting about faster than ever these days, and I blessed her for her ability to make quick decisions. She'd back me up in all that was planned.

I was being snowed under with advice and menus and suggestions. A famous chef sent me stern advice. I showed it to Mrs. Roosevelt and she patted my arm.

"Don't let them worry you, Mrs. Nesbitt. We have our plans made, and we'll stick to them."

In almost the same words she had told me of plans she and the President made, when we came to the White House six years before.

Well, the British Government wasn't leaving much to chance in preparing for the visit. I was swamped with official orders months in advance of the King and Queen:

CONFIDENTIAL

General Remarks Concerning the Sovereigns
and Their Suites

In all rooms: No bolsters—two pillows. Notepaper—penholders, inkstands, writing pads, etc.

Ladies-in-waiting: Hot-water bottle (belonging to them) in each bed. Two or three glasses and spoons.

Countess Spencer: Thermos bottle of 1/2 liter to be filled every night with hot milk.

Marshal: Big desk table, and second table for papers. In all bathrooms: Glasses, soap.

Numerous vases to be prepared for the flowers offered to the Queen at the receptions.

Special linen room for the Queen, enabling her second maid to press gowns and linen without the attendance of any outsider.

In that room there should be a large supply of white tissue paper and string of various sizes, to be used when repacking.

In the Queen's wardrobes, hangers should not be placed too high, since Her Majesty seldom wears dresses with trains and her dresses should be easily reached.

Light muslin cloths should be provided with which hanging clothes should be covered.

A second linen room for the King's valet and the suite.

All servants' rooms: Glasses, soap, wastebaskets, notepaper.

There should be, in the room of the King's valet, a large solid table for cleaning shoes.

Newspapers: For Their Majesties: *The Times, Daily Telegraph, Le Figaro, Daily Sketch.*

Never should be produced: Daily Mirror, Sunday Pictorial, News of the World, Daily Express, Daily Mail (read, however, by part of the suite and the servants).

Breakfast and Refreshments

HIS MAJESTY

8:00 A.M.   Plain tea

9:15 A.M.   Complete breakfast with tea, toast, fruit, bacon, and eggs.

HER MAJESTY

8:00 A.M.   Plain tea

9:15 A.M.   Complete breakfast with tea, toast, and fruit.

Service is always made separately, on trays, the latter prepared by private servants of Their Majesties.

Whenever Their Majesties come home, tea should always be kept ready for them. Moreover, when they come back at midnight, ham sandwiches should be prepared.

The King generally brings his own liquor and spirits. His footman will need a tray with sets of glasses, pump and crushed ice, decanters of lemon and orange juice, and everything necessary for the preparation of cocktails and various drinks.

In all rooms a tray with mineral water in ice, and glasses, should be constantly renewed.

Fruit is not kept in apartments, but is often asked for during the day.

Suggestions for the Furnishing of Her Majesty's Room

Large Bed

No bolster—two pillows.

Bed cushion supplied by Her Majesty's maid.

Light, but warm, blankets with silk cover.

No eiderdown coverlet—a soft silk cover folded in four on the foot of the bed, with one corner turned up.

Bedside table with lamp.

Bathroom

A large dressing table, or table for the bottles.

Four glasses, one of which is graduated.

Bathrobe type of bath towel.

Quantities of hand towels.

Basket for putting linen after use.

Bath thermometer.

Several spoons, large and small.

225

Dressing room or Boudoir

Dressing table perfectly lighted day and night, with armchair of corresponding height.

Near the dressing table a small table with drawers for hairdressing and toilet articles. This table should be easily removable.

Very comfortable settee with soft wool blanket.

One or two ash trays and matches for the King. The Queen does not smoke.

On the desk: Inkstand with blue ink; thin penholder with "J" pen (or similar make) of medium size, red pencil; blue pencil; ordinary black pencils with very sharp points; ordinary and typewriter erasers.

Suggestions for the Furnishing of His Majesty's Room

Large bed "de Milieu" (in center of panel) with the head against the wall. (Never with the side against the wall.)

No bolster—two pillows.

Special bolster supplied by His Majesty's valet.

Warm, but light, blankets with silk cover.

Very soft eiderdown quilt, which can be accordion-pleated at the foot of the bed.

On each side of the bed a bedside table with lamp.

In the bathroom or bedroom (according to possibility) and preferably in window recess on account of light, a dressing table with triple mirror, high enough to enable contemplating oneself when standing.

Very comfortable settee.

226

Ash trays, matches, cigar, and cigarettes for guests, His Majesty having his own cigarettes.

Great number of hangers; some of them with wide back slightly curved; others with a double bar for trousers; no special clip hangers for trousers.

On desk an inkstand with two inkwells; one full of blue-black the other of red ink.

No toweled bathrobe. His Majesty prefers large bath towels. (I bought sheet-size.)

To be ready to supply, if requested, gamet-red and white carnations for boutonnieres.

Chapter Seventeen

The royal visit takes up most of my diary's pages for '39.

There were so many problems, and so much cleaning and refurbishing, and so many social events, before and after the English King and Queen.

"One thing we'll get out of all this royalty," I told Mrs. Roosevelt, "at least the house is clean!"

We had the Crown Prince and Princess of Denmark about this time, and the Norwegian Prince and Princess, and a little later Prince Consort Felix of Luxemburg, his son the Crown Prince Jean and nephew Prince Felix of Baden, and sandwiched in between would be affairs for the Minister of Finland and the Prime Minister of Ireland, Mr. Eamon De Valera, and on May 7 Ruth and I ran out of doors to see and hear General Somoza, the President of Nicaragua, come up Pennsylvania Avenue, to a twenty-one-gun salute, with seventy-five hundred soldiers, sailors, and marines as escort, a cavalry formation, swarms of motorcycle police, sixteen army tanks, an echelon of our wonderful new American bombers followed by forty-two pursuit planes.

It was a thunderous spectacle.

One of the Secret Service men shouted to us to stand back, since no one was allowed to stand on the lawn while the South American president came into the White House, and there was an ominous note to the affair that made one realize

Europe and its gathering troubles were not as far from the Americas as some people liked to think.

The reception, I wrote in my diary, "was a magnificent dress rehearsal for Their Britannic Majesties!"

Well, George and Elizabeth had their problems, and Mrs. Nesbitt had hers. Where were we to feed the royal valet, the royal maid, the royal equerry? How was I to settle the argument between the water company that had kindly made up twenty gallons of pure drinking water for the royal tea, only to have a rival water company pop up with the announcement that they had been supplying the royal party with its water in Canada and why not in the United States? Then I had to quiet down the clamors of the wine companies, who were down on us like locusts, begging for the honor of supplying this wine or that, foreign or domestic, red, white, or tawny.

We were deluged with gifts of wine by dealers who didn't stop to ask, and although I was forbidden at the time to say which wines were finally used, there is no harm now in telling the wine was sent in by Mr. Bullitt, who was then Ambassador to France, and was his gift to the White House for the occasion.

The French Embassy also sent four cases of Pommery champagne, tawny port, Tokay, and Hungarian white wines.

The advance preparations were made more confused by our phones ringing constantly and folks wanting to know about everything we were doing, which added on to all we were trying to do.

The staff was briefed like a small army. We received orders from the ushers as to the duties of our floor men and women. The women were to stay behind the screens in the North Hall second floor until the royal entourage were in their rooms, then they were to contact the maids of Her Royal Majesty, and her ladies' maids' maids, and find out what they could do for them. The head floor man, Caesar, would be downstairs with the floor men to disentangle the royal luggage and get it into the respective rooms, then contact the royal valets and wait on them.

Maggie, the upstairs head maid who had been my right hand from the start, having worked in the White House thirty years, had been retired in May, but I was keeping her on, on a per-diem basis, during the royal visit. She knew the ropes and we all loved her, and I figured this would be an exciting finish to her long years of service.

Of course my desk was running over with warning notes on protocol, but, thank heaven, it was not my headache. Edith Helm, in collaboration with the State Department and the British authorities, figured out who sat where, and while it all sounded solemn, protocol was still comic opera to me. It was figured out to a hair's breadth, and Anglo-American relations balanced between.

There was one vital decision to be made between two large chairs and two small for the royal dinner, or four large ones for the royal pair and the Roosevelts. The subject occupied a lot of thought all around. The King and the President would have the large chairs, Mr. Crim, the head usher, told me, the Queen and Mrs. Roosevelt smaller chairs. The President and Mrs. Roosevelt would sit opposite each other at table. The President and the King would be served at the same second and the Queen and Mrs. Roosevelt would be served together directly after.

Then Mr. Crim told me the two large chairs were still a question in his mind, and he was having four large ones ready, just in case.

That was the way matters stood for a time, and we all prayed they'd stay there, for the State Department had a habit of making last-minute changes that threw our Social Department into a tailspin by changing places at a formally arranged table governed by protocol.

I wrote: "Hope this won't happen. We are having only

eighty-four. This is a relief, for we can give smoother service when there are less than ninety."

Protocol kept pouring in orders right up to June and the visitation.

Here are some samples, though not of this affair, to show how such orders ran:

"Protocol:

"To the right of the President, Mrs. Henry Morgenthau, Jr., Professor Einstein, Mrs. Henry Morgenthau, Sr., the Secretary of the Treasury, Mrs. Roosevelt, Mr. Justice Cardozo, Mrs. Schneider, Bishop Atwood, Mrs. Henry G. Leach, Mr. Henry Morgenthau, Sr., Mrs. Einstein . . ."

One of the first I received, way back in '34, went like this:

"Protocol:

"President, Representative Greenway, General MacArthur, Lady Lindsay on President's left, Mrs. Roosevelt across table with the Ambassador of Great Britain on her right . . ."

And these had been for fairly ordinary affairs, so imagine the stress on protocol with the heads of a great nation come to pledge the peace!

Mr. Bullitt helped a lot by sending the instructions that had been made out in France during the royal visit of the year before.

As we neared on June the orders flew.

Memo to Mrs. Roosevelt from Mrs. Helm later changed:

"I understand that the President will keep the gentlemen in the dining room after dinner, also that you will leave the table after dinner, and go around, and get the Queen, and go with her and the ladies to the Green Room."

I'd have to see there were coffee and cigarettes in there for the ladies. Mrs. Roosevelt smoked sometimes to be companionable, but she did it so badly the Gridiron widows once did a take-off of her smoking.

Memo to Mrs. Nesbitt from E.R.:

"I will want four butlers and Mrs. McDuffie and Mac at Hyde Park over the visit of the King and Queen.

"Mrs. McDuffie can take care of the top floor and do any maiding which Miss LeHand will require.

"Send Williams, George, Mingo, Jack."

I was glad they were all going up to Hyde Park afterward, so I'd get a chance at straightening out after the royal visit.

Her responsibilities were so great, I sometimes wondered why the extra anxieties and burdens were forever being heaped upon her. The private heartaches she never let show. Just as she was leaving for Hyde Park to make the final arrangements for the King and Queen, word came that John and his wife had lost their first baby, and I knew how she longed to be with them, to give the consolation and encouragement only her strong soul could give. But she had to go to Hyde Park instead. Amid all the glamor and show I wrote of Mrs. Roosevelt: "Her cup is full."

I was buying and refurbishing up until the last day. There were some old lamps I'd found in a storeroom and had regilded and fitted with white silk shades that turned out beautifully for the Queen's room. Everything had to be just so. We couldn't let the British think we were an inch behind them in any way.

We had to ask some guests to move out of the White House, to make room. The royal dinner was planned to the last breadstick a month ahead of time. We had been offered some especially prepared terrapin for the occasion, and I asked the President if I could serve it.

"I'll try anything once," he said merrily.

He was feeling fine just then, and not fussing about the food. I could see he was looking forward to meeting the King and Queen, and I knew how he felt, because I was going to meet them too. I was to be in on the diplomatic reception.

"What on earth will I say to Their Majesties?" I asked Mrs. Roosevelt.

"Oh, just say, I'm pleased to meet you, and mumble something," Mrs. Roosevelt answered.

She took protocol the easy way. I could mumble all right.

There was a lot of last-minute fussing about the bathrooms for the artists. The Roosevelts were having mixed entertainment after the royal dinner, as being representative of America. I had my orders to see that the singers were distributed through the two floors, and that all had the proper accommodations. Lawrence Tibbett got the President's bedroom and bath, Marian Anderson had Mrs. Roosevelt's bedroom, Kate Smith had her sitting room, and downstairs on my floor the library was equipped with sanitary arrangements, and so was my office. There were a great many artists to be accommodated, Lomax the guitar player, and the North Carolina Negro singers, and these all had to be sorted out and distributed around, with separate bathrooms for the separate groups. We had our instructions.

"Protocol in the johnny," I explained to Ruth.

On June 9 I was up with the White House birds to see everything was in readiness for the British King and Queen. If I do say so, the lovely old house shone like a brand-new stove!

Just before they were due I had a telegram from my younger.

"Good luck, old gal. Signed, Buck."

I scolded him afterward. The idea, sending a message like that over the White House wires!

Chapter Eighteen

They turned out to be just like any other young couple, more quiet-mannered perhaps, and with more on their minds. I was surprised to find King George and Queen Elizabeth so very young, and almost shocked to find them so human.

One associates kings and queens with fairy-tale descriptions of golden thrones, ermine trains, and golden crowns on heads held high.

None of this for England's royal pair. They came into the Diplomatic Reception Room with Mrs. Roosevelt and took their places on either side the President's chair, the Queen on his left side, the King on the right. She was such a little person, pleasant and nice-looking, in her soft light gray dress scalloped at the hem, with a white hat off her smiling face, and white gloves. The young King looked tanned and pleasant in a much-decorated uniform, with white gloves, too, that he pulled off for the handshaking.

Miss LeHand, Tommy, Mrs. Helm, Miss Connochie and I were taking it all in. Mrs. Roosevelt had asked us to meet the royal pair, and Miss Connochie, the children's governess, was especially interested because she was Scottish-born, like the Queen.

I was still out of breath from the slip covers. I'd waited until the twenty-one guns began saluting at the station before putting them on the chairs, because I wanted them daisy-fresh. Well, try pulling a slip over a long cushion when you're in a rush! It was beastly hot, too, over ninety degrees, and the soldiers picketed on the lawn had stacked their guns and laid down under the trees, and just got them up in time to present arms as the first car tore up the circular drive.

I'd heard over the radio that people had been standing in the streets since dawn, and hundreds fainted in the heat.

The King and the Queen were smiling as if they didn't notice how hot it was, but you knew they wouldn't let it show if they did.

Their escorts and attendants came in, Mackenzie King in full uniform, Lord and Lady Lindsay, the King's equerry and private secretary, Mr. Lascelles, cousin to the Earl of Harcourt who married the King's sister, and Mr. Canning, the Superintendent of Scotland Yard, and his men. They were combining forces with our Colonel Starling's staff to see no harm came to the royal guests.

Then the three Roosevelt sons came in with their wives, and Mrs. Roosevelt was buzzing in and out bringing folks in to be presented, because that was the President's job, and he couldn't. Afterward she took us up, Mrs. Helm, Miss Connochie, and Tommy and me.

I mumbled something, as Mrs. Roosevelt had told me, but you couldn't worry about protocol with such a pleasant-speaking pair. They were just plain nice, and I found myself thinking I might have traveled long and far along more ambitious lines before meeting on such intimate terms the rulers of a great country, and I only wished, as I so often did, for Dad to have been here for this.

The Queen stood chatting, easily and simply, of this and that, but her eyes were on the younger Roosevelts on the other side of the room, and one could see that she was missing her own little girls on the other side of the Atlantic. Suddenly she excused herself, crossed the floor, and began talking to them in the sweetest way.

Then the President lined them all up and took them into

235

the East Room, where our diplomatic corps was waiting, and I raced off to see about luncheon, which was comparatively simple; minted melon balls, broiled sweetbreads, asparagus, saratoga chips, and strawberry shortcake, and to cast a weather eye out toward the dinner, which was the high spot of the royal visit.

So far, all was running to schedule, only I'd had to shift the strawberry dessert to pineapple, since the British Embassy was giving a lawn party that afternoon, and counted on strawberries, in English tradition.

Well, of course, late in the afternoon I learned the corn sticks that were to go with the terrapin had not arrived.

I didn't dare leave them to chance. I ordered my car and started out. The streets were jam-packed with people hoping to get a glimpse of the royal pair en route to the Embassy, but the heat had gone down a little, and it was only a little under ninety. I had along an old split shower cap of the Queen's, that had been given me by one of the Queen's maids with the request that I get two more like it, because it seemed the Queen wanted to take a shower at 7 P.M. and I also had some of the Queen's laundry that I was to take to Nancy, our laundress, with orders to have it ready by next day.

Well, of course all the stores were closed, and the store people out on roofs and in trees to see the royal couple go by, and my driver climbed the fire escape to the roof of Magruder's store and got a clerk to come down and give me the corn sticks.

By this time it was five-fifteen, and just as the clerk and I came out of the store, a blaze of motorcycles tore by and there was the Queen, smiling away under her parasol and looking so dainty and cool. The crowds were enchanted. They broke through the police, and were out into the middle of the street as close to her car as they could get, and I felt pretty good, because under my arm were the corn sticks. But still the rubber caps she'd need, less than two hours away, were still unfound. There was nothing to do but navigate the mobs back to Garfinckel's.

Well, I got the caps exactly like hers, and very nice, but they were oiled silk, and not rubber. I handed them to the doorman, asked him to give them to Her Highness's maid, and dashed to my office. A hundred-and-one items had come up, and there were sandwiches to make for the Social Bureau, and the fifty-nine concert artists were all to be served refreshments in their respective rooms, and I had to get into my formal dress for the dinner, and just as I was sailing into action in came the Queen's second maid, to say the caps would not do.

I dashed up to the maid's room and explained to the Queen's head maid that it was too late to get others, and I was very sorry.

She went into a fit of hysteria worthy of grand opera. Then she flew into a temper.

"Then get the first cap back," she ordered.

I stared at her. I must say I was surprised.

"In the first place, it had a tear in it," I said, as reasonably as I could. "Secondly, in my rush to get back, I left it in my shopping bag."

"Then send for it," she snapped.

"That will take too long."

She flounced around like a spoiled child.

Then Marie and Ivy, the upstairs maids, had a grievance to air.

The Queen's maid had made them warm over her lunch three times. She was a tartar, they said, and they didn't want to attend her.

Mr. Crim came in with a story about the same maid, but he was amused.

He said he had been upstairs leaving a message for Lady Katharine Seymour, the Queen's lady in waiting, and the maid was sitting in a chair before the Queen's door.

"I've a message for Lady Seymour," he explained, but she cut him short.

"I want you to understand that I am not Lady Seymour's maid. I am the Queen's."

"Oh, a big shot!" said our Crimmy innocently, and the maid gave him a murderous glare and flounced out of her chair and away.

Well, I had the big dinner to see to and our own to get out of the way before the other ended, so the ushers and Secret Service men could be on hand when the guests came out of the State Dining Room. For these two days I'd have nine to meals in my office, as the ushers, the Secret Service men, and Mr. Canning of Scotland Yard would have their meals with Ruth and me. Mr. Canning was quiet and ruddy-featured, and had little to say.

He told me in confidence, "We caught that fellow who had been threatening the King—up in Canada."

Since I hadn't known about any threats, all this was news to me, and I didn't ask any questions. I had problems of my own. I didn't have time to eat anything, and wouldn't until nine that night.

By seven-thirty I was at my post in the little red dining room, where I could watch the serving going on in the big State Dining Room, ready to pounce on any errors if Fields had to leave the scene for a minute. The table looked beautiful, with the gold Monroe plate and the new crested glasses and new Lenox and Wedgewood pieces, and the flowers were exquisite, small white orchids, lilies of the valley, and maidenhair fern. They'd been selected especially for Queen Elizabeth.

Then—dinner was held up.

Mr. Crim had to keep Their Majesties and the President and Mrs. Roosevelt waiting from ten to fifteen minutes and I was praising the Lord we were having domestic fowl that wouldn't spoil. Franklin, Jr., and his wife and the King's aide were late. Finally Mrs. Roosevelt said they would go down to dinner anyway, and just as they were getting into the elevator the aide arrived and got in line. But Franklin came tearing in with his wife so late that they had to wait in the ushers' office until the line of eighty guests had passed into the State Dining Room before they could join it. Fortunately Jimmy and Franklin had the exchange for dinner partners, so they made a rapid switch as Jimmy dashed by.

The rest of us were chewing our nails on the side lines.

It was wonderful the things that could happen and Mrs. Roosevelt never turn a hair.

The Queen, coming into the dining room, looked like the queen in the fairy stories, in a sheer white dress spangled over with silver sequins, diamonds at her wrists and throat, and a delicate diamond tiara glittering on her soft dark hair. But Mrs. Roosevelt, across the table, looked every inch a queen, too, and with fewer jewels. She didn't have many gems, one lovely big square diamond that was her engagement ring, I think, and a diamond necklace, and she'd had some beautiful pearls, but she gave these away, a strand each to her daughters-in-law. As for the President, sitting at the head of the horse-shoe table, well, he was America's Commander in Chief, and looked it.

The Queen not only looked like a fairy-tale queen, she ate like one, and just picked at her plate. We had heard she had dieted six months before coming over, and she was very slender, and ate very sparingly now. She refused the clams and soup, just tasted the terrapin and capon, had a few beets, and drank her coffee.

But the King seemed to be enjoying everything, and so, thank heavens, did the President. The King ate his clam cocktail, calf's head soup, terrapin with the corn-bread sticks, sliced tomatoes, peas and beets, the boned capon with force-

239

meat and cranberry jelly, sweet-potato cones, the frozen cheese and cress salad, maple and almond ice cream, and coffee. It was a marvel to see one so slim enjoy so much.

A vile thunderstorm started during dinner, and the guests could hardly hear one another speak, but it did cool the air.

But it was still hot. Ninety-five degrees.

I was seeing the salad course on when Mr. Crim came in and handed me a slip of paper. I was terrified—something dreadful must have gone wrong. But when I opened it, it was the King's order for his breakfast.

The Queen's was to be a light one, just fruit and plain tea, but the King wanted a full meal and was leading off with ham and eggs, fruit, cream, bread, butter, tea, and glucose.

"What on earth is glucose?" I asked Mr. Crim. "Syrup?"

He didn't know, so I tore out of the little dining room and downstairs and found one of the Scotland Yard men.

"What is glucose?" I panted.

"It's a sort of powder," he explained, "for sweetening tea."

"Oh, you mean dextros!" I exclaimed. "We give it to the babies. Now where can I get that this time of night?"

"Don't worry about it," he said; "your Mr. Fields has it already."

I started to totter back to the dining room on my high heels that I wore only for state affairs, and were already beginning to hurt my feet. All that worry, and in the midst of dinner! But a new tow-row had started in the halls. The maids were dashing around carrying heavy blankets that had been put away for the summer and smelled of moth balls.

"What are you doing with those?" I wanted to know.

Our maids explained that the British maids had ordered them.

"They want all the hot-water bottles filled too," they said.

And we were gasping for breath!

I went down the hall to Lady Seymour's room, and found a maid sitting outside the door.

240

"You don't mean to say you want heavy blankets!" I said. "And the hot-water bottles?"

She was extremely haughty.

"My lady likes to sleep warm," she said, "and I would like some milk heated for her, too, when she comes up."

Hot milk—and we in the midst of dinner! And with all else going on, butlers scurrying all over the house with trays of the extra meals.

I went to my office and let my maids struggle with the problem. All that bedding had to be changed, and we had bought a dozen summer-weight blankets especially for them as ours were rather shabby and the winter ones smelling of moth balls. But the English nobility slept under them, with hot-water bottles, hot milk, and the thermometer bubbling close to a hundred when I reached home, dog-tired, at two that morning.

The heat was less next day. Down to eighty-eight. I was at the White House by seven-thirty with a royal day ahead, winding up with a tea in the garden, but at the British Embassy, praise glory! Everything went off easily, as planned for, months ahead.

The final dinner was at the British Embassy too.

That night I saw the King and Queen for the last time. Just as I came out of my office they were leaving the elevator, on their way to the Embassy dinner. She was wearing a pink net evening dress similar to the white, spangled with pink sequins, and I realized she must have been wearing hoops to make the fluffy skirts stand out so. She wore her diamond tiara and no wrap. The King was in advance, and she followed him around the corner and I tell you she was going fast. King George was loping on ahead like any other husband whose wife is late, and she was so little, she had to gallop.

From the British Embassy they would board the special train for New York, she still in that exquisite evening gown.

The secretary of the King and Queen, before leaving, had

sent down a large sum of money to the ushers, to divide among the help. The ushers were each given gold cuff links. I was given a beautiful little satin box containing a platinum and gold pin with their crest and the British crown.

During their visit they had not made a single demand. Royal guests take things as they are. It is their retinue that do the fussing and put on airs. The arrogance of some British servants could only be compared to that of some of our American guests who came to the White House, and stayed on, and made life a horror for the help.

But the English King and Queen had left an impression of simplicity and goodness, and when I think of her it is a pleasant-faced little woman I remember flitting across the hallway, prettily dressed, and into the room of the King.

The King and Queen didn't have the same room. He had the Blue suite and she the Rose across the hall, and she ran to and fro. I'd heard theirs was a love match. During their two days in the White House it was easy to see this was true.

When General Anastasio Somoza, President of Nicaragua, visited the White House this year, he complained to friends because he had not been put in the same room with his wife. He did not like that, he said. But it is White House tradition that the highly placed and wedded have separate suites, and England's King and Queen had theirs.

They were kind, good people, and my heart ached for them a few months later, when the blitzing of England began.

As souvenirs of this visit, the last fragment of pleasure that was theirs before England's travail began, I treasure their platinum pin. With it I keep a note from President Roosevelt:

"I want to express my appreciation for your fine service during the recent visit of Their Majesties, the King and Queen of England. It was a satisfaction to me to note the

242

efficient manner in which these additional arrangements were executed."

Mrs. Roosevelt wrote, too, a letter from Hyde Park, after the British guests were gone:

"I want to congratulate you on how well everything went during the royal visit. Let us hope we will have no more excitement this summer."

The President's summer fishing trip was interrupted. On August 24 he came back from Nova Scotia twenty-four hours ahead of schedule because of the gathering horror in Europe. He had written Hitler before, and Hitler had not answered, and now he wrote him that the cause of world peace was the cause of humanity.

It was a letter written to a madman.

September 4, 1939, I wrote in my diary:

"Again in my lifetime a great war is in progress, with subs from Germany over in our waters. The shock was so terrific to me that I cannot grasp it yet. It means so much more to me this time as my sons are men and will be drawn in, with all our wishes to stay out. The President's speech of last night was practically thrown back at us by the actions of Hitler. . . .

"Here the President is at it night and day. He stayed up all of Thursday night and called Mrs. Roosevelt at Hyde Park to tell her that Germany and Poland had started fighting at 5 P.M.

"Was told that it takes a sub two weeks to cross the Atlantic, consequently they must have started long before the fighting began between them on the Polish-German frontier. Dastardly work, and why with us, when we are neutral and so far across the ocean? Cannot get their plan or idea.

"Cabinet is called and no doubt the calling of Congress is only a matter of days. . . ."

Well, I went ahead with my work, baked one hundred

cakes ahead for Christmas, saved all the cantaloupe rinds and made pickles, and in between times balanced the White House books. That reminds me, two checks of Mrs. Roosevelt's are still out! The payees kept them for the signatures. Together they amount to only four dollars and eleven cents, but I couldn't balance the White House books for months because of them, and finally had to write them off.

The *Graf Spee* was interned. The tension grew.

People continued to write in asking for White House souvenirs. I accommodated those within reason.

But one man wrote asking for a wishbone "the President has eaten on."

Another: "Please send me a mousetrap from the White House."

The night before war started in Europe, Harry Hopkins moved into the White House. He was a sick man, who had not been able to keep on with his job as Secretary of Commerce because of his stomach ailment, and he was unable to take a desk job, the President said. But now he would be working at all hours, and dashing over to Europe and around the United States, to see how the war was going over there, and later how the war efforts looked over here. He reported all he saw back to the President, and Mrs. Roosevelt was shuttling back and forth, bringing back to her husband all she heard and saw.

Mr. Hopkins's diet list was already in my files, along with all the others, and I was going to learn all forty-eight of his forbidden food items by heart until I could recite them backward and forward, even in my sleep.

Chapter Nineteen

We were drawing near the end of the second term, and every move in the White House after 1940 started spelled exodus. Mrs. Roosevelt didn't accumulate things any more, but sent them to Hyde Park or gave them away. We were clearing out the storerooms, packing and shipping to Hyde Park; in fact, the Roosevelts were closing up.

We even shipped home the children's toys, including the sleds, and when Anna's children came to visit and a nice snow fell, I had to rush downtown and pick up sleds, and when I got back they had taken out the big aluminum kitchen trays and were sliding on them under the White House trees.

"We'd rather have the trays," Buzzy said, and they went on sliding.

Talk of his wanting a fourth term is silly. He didn't even want the third. I could see how they were looking forward to freedom. It was in all their plans and all they said. President Roosevelt intended to write history, and he was assembling his historical papers and sending them to Hyde Park.

No doubt of it, he counted on retirement. So did she.

She told me once, "I've never seen the lilacs bloom that I planted at Val-Kil cottage." She sounded wistful.

Often I'd speak to her and she'd smile and I'd know she hadn't heard a word. Smaller personal matters were forgotten in the White House these days, with every ear turned to the radios, and Europe, and the war. Mrs. Roosevelt was going so many places, and trying to do so much winding up of affairs, that sometimes she'd just be in the White House overnight, or maybe for an hour, between trips.

She'd make a beeline for the President's study the minute she came in, and they'd talk together, and then she'd be out and away. Usually she'd make time to drop into my office, to check and see how everything was going.

I wrote January 14, 1940:

"They are packing these last weeks so full I cannot see how it is possible to have the time so closely filled and do it all. Not my part, but Mrs. R's. Each day we are getting from three to five notes filled with new engagements. The President and Mrs. R are lending their help and prestige to project after project. They want them thoroughly understood and established before they leave the White House, so far as they can, and their part is concerned. God bless them and their long, hard work with success."

I go on to write how Franklin's two dogs, a great Dane and an Irish setter, had made a mess of my old office, where the aides now kept their wraps, and lounged, and had sandwiches and coffee, while off duty, at state dinners.

It was partly my fault, I admit, for not having turned the couch to the wall and placed the chairs so the dogs couldn't use them for beds. "Even the carpet will have to be cleaned," I wrote. "They are nice dogs and I like them, but I do wish there was a place here where one could feel they were happy and comfortable, especially for them."

The prospect of freedom seemed to have the President cheered up. His outburst of good spirits started on January first, when he was chuckling all through dinner like a small boy who had won a game. It seems he had placed the war in the enemies' camp; namely, Congress, by placing with them the responsibility of raising the taxes for additional naval defenses, and this during an election year!

He was feeling pretty happy about it.

A few days later the President set a barber pole wound with red and white before the doctor's door on our corridor, with a big sign on it:

MCINTYRE, FOX AND MAYS

BARBER, CHIROPODIST, AND MANICURIST

Dr. McIntyre was not amused. Usually he had a lusty sense of humor, and they had some high old times in his office, but this time there was no reaction. That night the President spoke in the East Room on "The Children in the Democracy," and I went in to hear the broadcast, as I always did when I had time. The President came rolling past the doctor's office just as one of the stenographers came out.

"Which did you get, Roberta?" the President asked, all innocence. "A manicure or a foot treatment?"

I wrote that night: "A good thing he can play!"

Dr. McIntyre, General Watson, and Mr. Early were in my office over cups of coffee that January 25 when my phone rang, and the operator said, "Helsinki is calling General Watson."

It seemed awesome to me, remembering how I'd used my first wall phone in Duluth as a woman grown, that Finland should be speaking right there at my desk from thousands of miles away. But "Pa" Watson took it calmly, and talked away as if they were right next door, and later he said Helsinki had called him, or the President, every day for the past week. The men went on drinking coffee and talking over my head about Hoover and the Finns. It made me feel inside world affairs.

Little Johnny Boettiger stayed on with us that January, the only child in the White House for the time. The White House was no place for a single child, the grownups were always busy, and only when they came in groups did the little ones have fun, Diana Hopkins was with us a lot; in fact, she lived in the White House three or four years after her mother's death, and I'd catch her chasing the guards with lipstick, trying to paint mustaches on their faces. They were young fellows, and just as bored as the child.

Mr. Hopkins behaved like one, when he was sick, and he was sick a lot of the time. He'd ring his bell, and have Caesar, the head of the second floor, come into his room to give him his medicine when it was right there by his hand.

February brought a deluge of rain and the Youth Congress. Cots were lined up in every available room, and we were going at top speed, trying to keep up, and shorthanded, because so many of the help were sick. Five thousand of the youths stood in the rain in the south grounds on the tenth, listening to the President, who was also standing in the rain without his hat or topcoat, to be one with them. But the boys were dressed for weather, and he wasn't, and I was sure he'd catch his death.

The Youth Congress, standing in the rain, was nicely and firmly spanked by the President. At least they received some guidance and a better understanding of their position and conditions that they had not taken the trouble to learn before coming to Washington. The President put himself on record with them and with the people of the United States who were listening to his broadcast, as disapproving of any organization that went off half-cocked without bothering to gather its facts. Unfriendly newspapers would garble whatever he said, but the people could listen to his words and form their own opinions.

The moneyed interests, who owned the papers, were afraid he would run again. By this time, no matter what the sacrifice, I hoped he would! The youth movement proved to me that our country was in need of a strong and understanding hand.

This was the day I learned even radio can show prejudice. I was standing under the porch with the operators, and when the President closed his talk, and the boys applauded, I noticed one operator close his key so the applause did not carry over the wire.

I asked him about it and he said he had cut it off, then he

started, took a quick look at me, and said quickly, "Oh no, you're mistaken. I turned the other key."

I wasn't mistaken. Neither was he.

With the youth movement running all over the rooms, I wrote:

"Gosh, I hope Roosevelt, for the sake of the United States people, will go in and get the third term. It terrifies me to see what narrow-minded, ignorant, and untrained minds would do in this job of being President. During these days of world turmoil it takes a wise and careful mind to make and weigh moves before putting them into effect. I hate to think what the heritage of our children may be should a wrong man fill the chair.

"We are teetering on a social upheaval again, and a complete change of policy will certainly bring chaos about us and also disaster. The monied classes will fight to the death again to get the reins. Then, with this social unrest interwoven with communistic tendencies, God help the middle class who are the backbone of the country. Our President understands all this, and how wisely he is handling them with his understanding of the right psychology. . . .

"Here we feel we are sitting on something that may explode any minute. This communistic element weaving into the social side, about which we can do little except teach them to open their minds to what it really means. . . . There seems to be several organizations that are communistic within the larger Youth Congress. Being a democracy we cannot muzzle them, and shouldn't, for it is better to have them out in the open than growing under cover."

This last explains why they were in the White House.

They were young. President Roosevelt wanted to know all kinds, all ages, all points of view. He tried to learn the thought impulses of all people in all lands. He questioned, read, asked people of all classes, creeds, and races, and studied their histories and backgrounds. That was why, I felt more and more strongly, he was the only man who could steer us past dangers both within and overseas.

Hitler's subs, prowling off our Jersey coast, were no more dangerous than some of the thoughts of our young people.

After the outdoors talk the President called a closed session of the Youth Congress in the dining room, where he and Mr. Hopkins would meet the leaders in an informal way and answer questions. It was a hush-hush proceeding.

It was a drizzling February night, and more of our help were sick, and the youth movement didn't bother to wipe its feet. Crim and the other ushers had foolishly set up the room for smoking, and we had the new specially woven carpet, and several hundred boys, and I think they all smoked. Some didn't bother to use the ash trays, just threw the cigarettes on the floor and stamped them out with their heels.

I was watching with Mr. Crim, and wished I hadn't done away with the brass cuspidors I'd banished from the White House when we first came in, along with the feather dusters.

One youth leader was asking questions of the President and not taking the trouble to hide his obvious sense of superiority. It was easy to see he and his followers didn't think much of the President, or the United States, and certainly not of the White House carpet. But the President was listening just as gravely, and answering with patience and courtesy, knowing all the time it would be meat for the anti-Roosevelt grinders.

The youth movement served to bring Mr. Joseph P. Lash to our attention, and after this we had him often as a White House guest, in fact, for weeks at a time. But I will say he was easy to care for. Ask him what he wanted to eat, and he'd give one answer.

"Steak!"

Of course, after rationing started, I prayed for him to order anything else, but he never did.

That spring social season was a horror, with double and triple headers, big garden parties for thousands in the afternoon, maybe, followed by a formal dinner. We'd get the garden cleared up just as the first cars arrived. We had several variants on the usual procedure, once the ice didn't arrive for the clam cocktails, and during one party a woman guest was brought into my office drunk, having had a few too many before she arrived. She came out all right after black coffee. The Veterans' Party was larger than ever this year, and Mrs. Roosevelt and the President received under the magnolia trees, and afterward, as he was climbing into the car, the President's coat slipped up, and she reached over and yanked it down, still talking. A little group of us standing around were amused. It was such a wifely gesture.

But if it were something he needed to do alone, like holding himself upright, she wouldn't make a move toward him. It wasn't lack of sympathy, because no more sympathetic woman ever lived, but her way of sparing him, to let him recover, hold himself up, and carry on his way. Mrs. Roosevelt wanted every person to have his pride. She awarded it to the most humble around her, and most of all to him. All that racing around was for him. Later, it was for people in general.

Party rushed after party, and order followed order. Notices came to change the orders. Five changes, for one order alone! One canceling a tea for 1,200 on May 3 was changed to 4,200 with refreshments—whee!

Conventions, two in a day, nearly five thousand to tea . . .

When on April 18, 1,175 people were hand-shaken through the line and ate seventy-seven pounds of cookies and drank their punch, all within thirty minutes, Mrs. Roosevelt and I agreed it was the fastest on record.

Raspberry purée, fudge squares, honey drops, I dreamed about them. Roast turkey, baked ham, sweet potatoes. Congressmen are the heartiest eaters. I was sick of food. So was the President. He was getting peevish again. He had foreign troubles and troubles with Congress, plus a cold, and no wonder he was unreasonable.

In April he complained that food didn't taste like anything. He scratched more things off the menu in two weeks than he had in the past two years.

At first I'd just note the President was off his food, and feel responsible. Now I learned to look for the disturbing factor behind his upset, and could usually find it.

The menu scratches were thickest in June, when news came of the bombardment of Paris.

That was the trouble with living inside the White House. One knew when to be afraid. My sons and their children were living on the border of Washington. Their lives were well started. They were happy. Then I learned Buck had applied to join the naval reserve. I sat in my office, June 10, after hearing that, with a black curtain over my mind. I couldn't believe this was happening to us. Not over here. France, even England, was on the other side of the world.

Dr. McIntyre came in.

"Mussolini has come into the war," he said. "He's joined with those sadists."

I couldn't say anything. I started up some coffee. But the doctor walked up and down as if he couldn't stand still.

"Those maniacs!" he said. "Those sadists! England will fall into their hands!"

I began making plans for moving the children into the Catskills in case trouble came. We had English cousins—maybe their children could come over. England was holding, England would hold. But how long?

Someone else on the official staff dropped into my office about this time.

"If we're not drawn into a war of defense," this person said, "we may have a revolution here, with all the reds and Nazis we have."

Our corridor was a wonderful place for rumors.

Captain Ker dropped in on June 29 and told me, very

quietly, that President Roosevelt would have to run for the third time.

"Willkie hasn't a chance," he said. "Willkie is a utilities man, and the farmers hate the utilities."

For my part, I couldn't imagine any other American capable of the job ahead. The President had smuggled in a few days of rest at Warm Springs and Hyde Park, and on his boat. He felt fine. Germany, for some ominous reason, was lulling her attack on England. There was a feeling of new hope in the air now we were certain he could run for a third term.

The President seemed cheerful, now he'd made up his mind, but by September, all conversations led to war.

Women were attending the house and senate sessions in silent protest against conscription. They wore long mourning veils, and weeks went by, and they were still sitting there.

Colonel Starling moved into my old office. He needed it, with all the extra work piling up on him. The President signed the Selective Service Act this month, and was going to travel about a lot from now on, looking over army posts and the plants working on defense. The police took to wearing their pistols outside, with belts of cartridges, which they had not worn before.

Things were happening fast this September. Germany, Italy, and Japan signed their pact, we started getting bids for decorating the Blue Diplomatic Parlor, and Crown Princess Martha came for a visit.

I was accustomed to the simple manners of royalty by this time, but Princess Martha was the most informal. Her country, Norway, had fallen to Hitler, and Prince Olaf, her husband, was in England, but she was making the best of things over here. The Roosevelts were very fond of her. She came with her suite, a countess, a baron, the two little princesses, and little Prince Harold and his nurse. She had the Rose

Suite, and Harry Hopkins had the Blue, and Judge Rosemann and his wife were someplace else, the Yellow I think, or maybe Joe Lash had it at this time. Judge Rosemann was back because of the new campaign, and he always helped the President with speeches. He was modest, unobtrusive, and quiet, of small stature but with a beautifully shaped head. He came for weeks on end but didn't live in the White House, and he never made any trouble.

As for Princess Martha, she and her whole entourage made less trouble than one or two house guests I could mention. When she arrived on the second floor Mr. Crim asked her to sign the guest book.

"Do you object to my using my own pen?" she asked, and got up and went into the bedroom to get it. Her lady and gentlemen in waiting were in the room, but they did not offer to rise or get the pen.

We were continually surprised by their democratic, friendly ways, and the way the children went in and out, like normal, healthy children, not at all like little princesses in exile. Only, they were not gay, like our American children. None of these exiled people were gay.

Princess Martha didn't eat beef or lamb, and was almost a vegetarian. I'd give her chicken, the white meat, when others had meat. I prefer dark meat, myself, and to my way of thinking the white meat is just for salads and clubhouse sandwiches.

Martha was concerned when the President toyed with his meals, and even though she was a vegetarian, she brought in a Norwegian recipe for pigs' feet in sour sauce.

"It will tempt his appetite," she said, and, to my surprise, it did, and became one of my favorite recipes, both in the White House and in my own home.

This is for four:

Pick out four nice clean white pigs' feet and simmer in salted water until nearly done. Add one half cup white vinegar, two large bay leaves, one medium onion cut in quarters, eight peppercorns, six cloves, and cook till tender—about two hours in all.

I usually let the pot stand overnight and take off the hardened grease.

Then bring it to a boil, thicken the gravy with arrowroot, add perhaps a dash more vinegar and some sugar, and serve it with mashed potatoes.

Princess Martha's Pigs' Feet has a place of honor in my files.

I had to get started with the chandelier washing and cake baking, and by November the house was swarming, with ten or twelve each night working all night long in the Cabinet Room on the campaign and speeches. Mr. Hopkins and Judge Rosenman and Mr. Robert Sherwood—he wrote plays—were among those working at the speeches, which for some reason always have to be done at night.

I'd fix sandwiches and thermos bottles of coffee for the midnight snack.

"We don't want any more dead sandwiches," Mr. Sherwood told me once, meaning the cold ones, so after that I had a doorman stay up to make hot sandwiches.

One morning about nine-thirty I met Harry Hopkins and he looked as if he'd been through a wringer.

"I don't know if I'm asleep or awake," he said. "I didn't go to bed until five-thirty."

"You should be in bed right now," I told him.

Mr. Hopkins almost set fire to the White House. Caesar found a lighted cigarette in his bed once, with the windows open and a wind blowing. When things got tense he'd walk by in the corridor without seeing me. Whether he let things prey on his mind more, because he was sick, or whether worry brought on his spells, I never could make out. But the President seemed to depend on him more and more.

There were a lot of campaign buttons out with mean sayings. "We Don't Want Eleanor Either," and "Put a Size Fourteen in the White House." But President Roosevelt won for the third time, and when he and she came back from Hyde Park Washington was out three hundred thousand strong to cheer them, and we were all lined up outside the White House, and little Bobby shook his hand again.

There was a sad note, even in the congratulations, because the first draft numbers had been drawn from the fish bowl, and sixteen million of our young men would be called. That was the answer America gave to the President's campaign plea to make our country "an arsenal of democracy." I went around these days with a steady prayer on my lip, not for our country only, but for the young of all lands.

The President got another engraved invitation to his own inaugural, and sent it back to "Pa" Watson with a note scribbled on:

"Pa—Tell them I will go if I can arrange it—FDR."

To my surprise I also received a lot of congratulations about my staying on four more years, which warmed me up considerably.

He was feeling fine these days. They invited another exile, Crown Princess Juliana, of the Netherlands, and we were planning a large state dinner in her honor on December 18. I was pleased because it gave me the chance of getting some new furniture and a Bokhara rug for the West Hall, which made it into a beautiful lounge. This was the place the family liked best, and where he read the *Christmas Carol* each Christmas.

There were fourteen or fifteen pieces of new furniture, and Sloane's got the last piece in place just thirty minutes before Juliana came!

On the morning before Christmas 1940 Mrs. Roosevelt called me up to her room. She was just back from New York and the last-minute buying. We had a lot to discuss, including the red Santa stocking filled with little gifts and yummies we were sending to Nancybell, who had been our linen maid and was in the hospital fighting t.b. The colored help had already chipped in and sent her a small radio so she could listen to the Christmas carols.

The President came in just then, anxious to see Mrs. Roosevelt, and glad to see her back. Fala, his little Scottie, was prancing around.

"Fala is on a real diet," the President told me. "He's had the hookworm."

"Isn't that unusual for a dog?" I asked.

"Yes. But he had it."

The President was in a happy mood. He was just bursting with news.

"Eleanor," he said—as a rule he called her "ma"—"the Crown Prince is coming for a Christmas surprise for Martha, and she doesn't know it!"

Those two just beamed at each other.

"How is he coming?" Mrs. Roosevelt wanted to know.

"By clipper," the President said. He was as pleased as punch. He added gaily, "I arranged it."

It was a big secret for only a few hours, then the papers splurged it—a crown prince in exile being flown over from war-torn England to spend Christmas with his family. Princess Martha had taken a house down Rockville way. They were sober, gentle people, with little lightheartedness about them, and I was glad that for a few days at least they were together.

It was like the President to think of that, with all else he had on his mind.

Chapter Twenty

There were more guests than ever for the third inauguration, but we kept inside the budget and just spread it around.

By this time I had inaugurals down to a split-second schedule, and January 20, 1941, was mapped out to the last sandwich weeks ahead.

One hundred and fifty extras came in to help, drawn from my special list—butlers, cooks, assistant cooks, maids, waiters, busboys, dishwashers, and checkers.

We served twelve hundred guests a buffet luncheon, from soup to dessert, inside an hour, and got them all outside in time to see the inaugural parade, which was more impressive than ever this year, as war preparation was written all over it, and they tell me those soldiers and redcoated bands were a sight. I didn't have time for parades, though I did listen in on the radio.

Lunch was a hearty cold-weather meal—tomato soup, a plate of salad, beef, ham, and tongue, cake, coffee, and ice cream. Everything prepared in the White House, which saved money.

The guests ate standing around in the East Room and State Dining Room, and after they went outside we had just two and a half hours to get the rooms cleared, the red carnations straightened up, the linen changed, and all those dishes washed and reset in time for the big inaugural tea at five.

Everything went off fine. Three electric dishwashing machines in the mezzanine pantry and kitchen and help's dining room made short work of all those dishes, and it seemed like no time before all the guests were back, multiplied. Four thousand people spread over the East Room and State Dining Room, and ate cake and sandwiches by the wagonload, and drank one hundred and thirty gallons of tea and sixty gallons of coffee.

We made the tea ourselves, but the coffee came from a caterer's and arrived hot in thermos jugs.

I had to borrow two hundred extra cups to go 'round.

The usual "family celebration dinner" that came right after was a letdown, with only a dozen extra house guests.

By the end of January all the inaugural guests were gone, and we were still up to our necks in the usual lather of entertaining, including a big coming-out party for Miss Morgenthau and social affairs for the Grand Duchess of Luxembourg and her husband, Prince Felix. She was a tall, distinguished woman with six children, and I recall her coming down to dinner in pale blue, wearing a single strand of diamonds, but they were large ones. Then Lord and Lady Halifax came from England, and went to the British Embassy, where he was taking Lord Lothian's place as Ambassador. The subs were thick in the Atlantic, so the route they took was hush-hush, and all of a sudden one morning the President drove down to Annapolis to meet him.

A whole lot going on now was not to be talked about, and I tried not to guess too much.

There was a sense of waiting about everything. We kept open and kept on, but always with that sense of expecting anything to happen at any minute.

It was after the excitement of the third inaugural, as I was slipping out of my high heels one night, that it occurred to me I was nearer seventy than sixty. When we came into the White House I'd still been in my fifties. I was getting on, and so were the Roosevelts.

259

I'd been too busy to pay much attention. Not that I minded moving on in years. It's a comfortable feeling, and I'd been noticing more people who came to the White House told me how much I reminded them of their mother.

Just the same, realizing you're edging on to seventy comes as a surprise to any woman.

I was having a lot of fun spending our $50,000 expenditure fund, which was allotted us at the start of every new term, and had to be spent, or obligated for, by the end of our fiscal year, in June. Congress had made the stipulation that we had to spend it right away, instead of when things were needed, over the full four years. I thought this poor housekeeping on their part, but did my best, and laid in a lot of linens, in case the war in Europe lasted longer than we feared and we couldn't get any more from Ireland.

Four years of constant wear make any house shabby. There were new drapes, new carpets, new dishes, and so on needed, to replace the worn out.

"Spending Brewster's Millions," I called it.

Captain Ker had a lot of fun kidding me about it.

Then, in March, he left us. Summoned to Fort Belvoir. A lot of our help were also leaving. Some were called to duty, and some were drafted, and a few enlisted. By spring we were shorthanded, not only with our regular staff, but in per diems. My list that had been so long shrunk by the hour, and in getting new names I had to put them through the mill of the Secret Service, and medical, and so on, to say nothing about their being able to do the work. And Buck was in uniform, taking his shots for Puerto Rico. We still kept hoping against hope America wouldn't get in.

I did a lot of free speaking in my diary this March.
March 3:
"The Senate is acting up and the President has a head cold

and is staying in his room, and everything is wrong with the food.

"Mr. Van Loon back. I've a soft spot in my heart for him.

"Mr. Alexander Woolcott here. In the play *The Man Who Came to Dinner*. He certainly is. Came to stay a week and has stayed two. . . .

"March 9—At last the Lend-Lease Bill passed the Senate members. . . . Anyway the President can get busy now and push on the reins after he signs the bill. From the papers he has been lining up the program for weeks. Good thing he has the foresight and can make up time while the others are fiddling away. I'll wager he will be considered the greatest President in our history.

"March 14—Fala a problem. Poor little chap in President's bedroom at night, does not get down early enough to prevent accidents . . . they cannot always be cleaned up before the secretaries come up. I suggested feeding him much later.

"March 22—This house is seething, and was seething before the President left for his southern cruise. Gosh, Harry Hopkins had a group in his room for dinner, the President another in his study, and downstairs Mrs. R had eighty for dinner in the State Dining Room, with a speakers' table and small round tables each accommodating six, and all at the same time. The butlers had some sprinting to do. All connected with work for defense and conditions arising from defense activities. . . .

"I am still buying rugs, replacing those that are shabby and worn out."

We had a flurry of excitement this month when Mr. Crim came in to tell me the couch in the President's office looked as though someone had shot it full of holes with a shotgun. "Buffalo moths again!" I said, and we galloped over to the office and my heart was in my shoes. We'd just had that couch done over, but it was as he said, and I called the interior decorator, to start getting out the President's furniture and go through the cyanide treatment all over again.

The decorator came and looked at the couch and then at us.

"That velvet," he said coldly, "is woven that way, to look antique, and it cost nearly twenty dollars a yard."

Mr. Crim and I felt very foolish.

Again in my diary:

"Mrs. R back for breakfast, out for dinner, here for supper.

"In the house she always goes at a dogtrot, so fast she bends forward. Somebody said she can give you enough work in five minutes to keep you busy two weeks. But she drives herself hardest of all."

She made appointments by the minute, and kept them.

I could tell how Congress was going by the President's appetite. But it was growing plainer by the minute that a lot of his upsets came from the peevishness of some of his house guests. I wrote in my diary:

"The President in his generous hospitality tries to please his guests and makes a fuss about the food in order to satisfy them. We really have many of these experiences from guests. One would be surprised. I think the friendship of the President inflates their ego to the bursting point and it comes out in this way.

"I do wish Mrs. R would come back and could stay until we straighten out things, for she can do it so beautifully. The President is our first concern and it is him we want to please. If the others do not like what we serve it is just too bad. This happens more often when the President is worried, all but sick with worry, then his appetite fails. It is easily understood.

"The hitch comes when his guests refuse what has been sent up, even if it is their diet, and order something else, through the butlers, from the kitchen. This crew changes every eight hours, and the ones on duty do not always know what food has preceded that day, so they do their best to substitute something else they think will please. . . .

"I have seen an order sent down for hamburger in place of

something else they had enjoyed a few days before. Well, Mr. Hopkins is a sick man, too, and should be very careful about his diet. Has repeatedly ordered popcorn; in fact, so often that I reported it to the doctor. Very irrational in his eating.

"Dr. McIntyre, I think, brought in Dr. Cushing, who made out the menus for the Pres. for Saturday and Sunday. A very frugal fare, small portions, etc., without dessert. Mr. H sits in on these meals and eats with gusto and even sends down for more when small portions were the doctor's order. It puts one in a quandary to say the least."

Dr. McIntyre was understanding and sympathetic, and went on working miracles in the diet changes. Mrs. Roosevelt kept on being comforting.

"It's his tizzy-wizzies," she'd say. "You mustn't mind."

But she'd be off again, because he wanted her to. Her wonderful talent for organization was being pushed to the limit by all this defense preparation. They made fun of her traveling about so much, but she did it for him, to find out or do things for him. And she always had things running smoothly before she left. It wasn't her fault if some of the house guests acted up.

And the affairs went on. Oh, the affairs. As a young woman, after large parties, I'd come home and weep. I always hated swarms. But we had to keep going.

It was nice when we could dovetail proceedings, and fit things together. Like the big Press Dance this May 21. I had thirty-five items on that order list, including twenty-five hams, twenty tongues, ten pounds each of cold cuts, and twenty-four pounds of potato chips. Well, the Veterans' Garden Party was the next afternoon, and a lot of the leftover pound-cake and angel-food cakes stayed fresh and sweet in the big iceboxes, and we had those, as well as over one hundred more cakes, and a hundred gallons of ice cream, and a lot of other food, sandwiches and such.

We were more careful than ever before about the White

House food. Threatening letters were thickening, and I had quite a lot of crank mail myself, and turned it over to the Secret Service. We kept milk and everything else in locked boxes, and all the people we traded with had been investigated, still there was the danger of tampering during deliveries. Colonel Starling came to me and asked what could be done, and I was ready with an answer because I'd been wanting a delivery truck of our own for years.

"Just the thing!" he said, so we bought a truck, and one Secret Service man stayed in it while a second went inside the store to watch every sliver of food being cut, weighed, and packed.

Now, if I telephoned for extra groceries, I'd be careful who I spoke to, and never once mention the White House.

I'd be stopped at the little house at the gate, and have to show my identification card to a man I'd known perfectly well for ten years! But I was glad things were tightened up.

One Secret Service man at the gate was trained to detect cranks. A salesman I had known for years started talking funny in my office one day. He demanded to see Mrs. Roosevelt. She was in, but I said she wasn't, and called the gate after he left and reported him. He turned out to be a mental case who had been in an institution, and was dangerous, and put away.

Another time the man who sold us our gift-cake cartons came in looking uneasy and told me about a queer conversation he'd overheard in a restaurant the night before. Some men were talking in whispers, and he only heard mention of "the elevator on the corridor," and "we'll get him there."

Being in and out of the White House a lot, he'd seen the elevator, of course, and he hadn't liked the sound of those men. He told me, and I told Colonel Starling, because by this time I knew almost anything could be more serious than it sounded, and it didn't pay to take rumor too lightly. Colonel Starling told me a few days later that it had been no idle guesswork, they had caught the men. Another time some men with drawn revolvers appeared outside the White House, demanding to see the President.

He needed every ounce of protection we could give him. Now, when he spoke on the radio, he referred to that man in Germany as "Hitler," not bothering with the Herr, and he told him off in frank terms.

A lot of people right here in America didn't like that.

Every single soul associated with White House deliveries and procedure was investigated, all over again, by the Secret Service.

These were tense times.

I felt personally grieved when word came that the Duke of Kent, King George's youngest brother, had died in an air crash. The year before we'd vacationed in Canada. We were jogging along the road near Victoria when a car behind began honking us to clear the way. We were American visitors, and up to the speed limit, so we stayed put. But the honks grew fiercer, so finally we pulled over, and we could tell it was a Very Important Personage in the car by the glares we got from those around him, and we figured out it was the Duke of Kent, a guest of Canada at the time. So I got back home and there he was, a guest of the White House. When Mrs. Roosevelt went to England she visited his widow and took two dozen oranges for their baby.

June 11 we planned tea for eight, which changed to one hundred since there would be a broadcast, which grew to three hundred and forty, then six hundred, and at two-thirty they told me eight hundred and four were coming! We had only forty-five pounds of cake on hand, and no chance of getting more, so I prowled the kitchen and unearthed a can of cookies and some fruitcakes left over from Christmas.

"These sessions will certainly bring on heart failure sometime," I wrote in my diary. "They are hard to survive."

While Ruth was racing around enlarging the equipment,

dishes, et cetera, I was nursemaiding Diana Hopkins, who wanted to take a little friend into the pool. I told the guards to come running if they heard me scream, because I was no swimmer and in no condition to do rescue work.

On top of this word came that Mr. Hopkins was raising whoozy about his laundry. His shirts hadn't come back on time.

Caesar, the floor man, who was well educated, very formal, was very unhappy about it.

"But, Mrs. Nesbitt, Mr. Hopkins only has three shirts," he said with a pained air.

I told Mrs. Roosevelt, and she laughed. "Tell Caesar to get him more."

Caesar was commissioned to go down and buy six shirts for Mr. Hopkins. "And next week," I said, "get him six more."

Mr. Hopkins had been in the hospital and was now back, though against the doctor's orders, ordering popcorn again, and when I said we didn't have it, saying we'd have to send out for it. He was forbidden cantaloupe, so he ordered that too.

To add to the confusion, I found some feather dusters still extant, after I'd burned them all, I thought, eight years ago. The boys were using two on our new Venetian blinds.

As I say, I tried not to see too much or know too much. I thought the President was on a fishing trip this August, until I read in the papers he'd met Winston Churchill on the Atlantic Ocean, off the coast of Newfoundland, and signed the Atlantic Charter.

After he came back he and Mr. Hopkins were both pickier than ever about their meals. I often thought if they'd eat apart it would be better for both, but they had so much to talk over. I'd scour the town to find some tidbit to tempt the President. Mr. Cammerer of the Park Service gave me quail, a pheasant, some buffalo tongues, and elk meat from the game preserves. I'd go to the brook hatchery and beg for brook trout. And I sent all the way to Duluth for the whitefish he loved.

He was working too hard. His worries were too great. Nothing tasted right.

Mr. Hopkins was on his strict diet, and not supposed to eat what was sent to the President, but he was always there and interested, and he'd prefer the President's tray to his own. As a result they'd both get upset.

I was glad when Anna or the boys could get home on visits. They kept things livened up, with their friends running in and out, and the President took on a healthier attitude, and ate more and laughed more. The White House was lots more cheerful when they were there.

Sometimes we had Mr. Hopkins's two sons too.

Hall Roosevelt, her brother, died that September. The last of her close blood kin. She had been with him in the hospital all night long, for a week, till one wondered how she could bear up under the strain. Fortunately the East Room was freshly cleaned for the fall season, and he lay in state there, with all the flowers. We had to stretch carpet across the room because of the newly waxed floors.

We went tiptoe, as always when there was sorrow in the house, and I was going quietly past the President's office when the door opened and two visitors came out—the Duke and Duchess of Windsor. They looked very sad to me, their faces like masks of tragedy, and no wonder, with the England they'd left staggering under the blitz till we almost gave up any hope she could hold.

The President's mother died that same month at Hyde Park.

Sara Delano Roosevelt hated confusion and ugliness. She left this world just in time.

November was the lull before the storm.

Mrs. Roosevelt called me upstairs one morning to talk over the day's appointments. When I reached her room the

President was there having breakfast with her, a treat for them both, as their times never coincided any more, they were both so busy.

Mr. Hopkins was back in the hospital again, but he kept in touch with us. He was supposed to be submitting to the orders of the navy doctors, but he phoned up and said he wanted a game dinner sent over.

"And with it I want some oysters on the half shell, celery, avocado, two grapefruit with French dressing, sweet pickles, raspberry and currant jellies, and I'll let you know later what else I want," he said.

I wonder what those navy doctors thought.

Later on he phoned the pantry he wanted some small pork sausages and some salted codfish before 8 A.M. next morning.

December 7, 1941, fell on a Sunday. I was in the White House every Sunday the Roosevelts were, and I had on my list for the day: "One P.M. small lunch, about thirty-four, in State Dining Room."

I phoned Harry Hopkins that morning to learn the plans of the day. He sounded disturbed, but that was nothing new with him.

"I am eating in the study with the President," he said.

I couldn't make that out, since they had the luncheon arranged, so I phoned Mrs. Roosevelt. She was calm and sweet, and didn't know anything about the change of plans.

"I'll see the President right away," she promised.

I waited, and she came back on the phone. Her voice wasn't as steady as before.

"The President has received important dispatches and will not be at the table, but will have his luncheon in the study with Mr. Hopkins," she said, then she hung up quickly, which wasn't like her.

Buck was back from Puerto Rico, and in Communications, the naval end of G2, stationed in Washington. He and his family were quartered with me for the time being, the housing shortage being worse in Washington than ever before. I was outside, just leaving for the White House, when he came running out.

"Did you hear it?" he shouted.

That's how I learned what the dispatches were, that Japan had bombed Hawaii, Guam, and the Philippines.

Buck dashed down to his office and stayed there, sleeping on a cot and sending out for drugstore sandwiches and coffee, and we didn't see him again for a week. By that time Germany and Italy had come in against us, and the United States was at war with the Nazi world, and Mr. Churchill was on his way over to the White House, and so was Mr. Litvinov of Russia, and representatives of China, Belgium, Canada, Australia, goodness knows how many more.

I was at the hairdresser's on December 20, having my hair done, when Ruth, my secretary, phoned to say Prime Minister Churchill was arriving by plane, and the President had missed his lion-skin rug that Haile Selassie had given him and I had stored at Garfinckel's. He wanted that rug on the floor, to show Mr. Churchill when he came, and he wanted it there right away.

Everyone was rushing around preparing for the arrival, so I had to go. The store was closed when I got there, and I had to get someone to unlock the store and open the storeroom and unpack that confounded rug. I came back around the White House by way of the South Drive, and the State Department and White House were all blocked off, and guards set, because of Mr. Churchill's arrival. Worse luck, I had forgotten my pass, and the military guard wouldn't let my car through the gate.

"But I'm on an errand for the President," I argued. "I have to get this rug in ahead of the Prime Minister."

He wouldn't listen.

I jumped out of the car and ran on foot to the door to the police guard, and told them to get the usher.

269

Of course I was reported. Mrs. Roosevelt spoke to me next morning.

"You came close to being shot," she said reproachfully. "After this, always keep your pass with you."

I promised. I felt pretty good. Leo the lion, smelling of mothproofing, was back in place on the President's floor, and we could get on with history.

Goodness knows I'm not making light of things. There was sorrow and grieving worldwide, and in my own small circle it was Major Garven Nesbitt and Commander Trevanion Nesbitt, and the years ahead were to hold endless heartaches and anxious prayer. Dear lads and great men would die, due to war. But it's a woman's job to keep the home fires burning, and there was a fireplace for every room in the White House and four in the East Room alone.

Chapter Twenty-one

The items in my White House diary shortened after Pearl Harbor.

Too much was going on. Too fast. Too important to write about. "Hush-hush," "Confidential," "V.I.P." are written across lots of pages. "Mr. B in Rose." "So and so's Secret Mission." No explanation. Just a list, a menu for an important dinner, or foodstuffs to go overseas.

Looking them over, I remember Mr. Churchill being one of the V.I.P's (very important personages), and "Mr. B." was Molotov, who came from Russia soon after Pearl Harbor, and stayed in the Rose Suite under the name of Mr. Brown.

I never did catch a glimpse of Mr. Molotov, because we were shooed into our offices when he came through the corridor, and I didn't see Lord Beaverbrook either, though he was in and out a lot. I wasn't supposed to peek, and besides, I was too busy. Mr. Churchill was not one to hide his light under a bushel, and we always knew when he was a guest in the White House.

Right after Pearl Harbor Mrs. Roosevelt took a plane to the West coast to get her part of the defense organized there, and we canceled all affairs, so the White House was virtually blacked out and closed. This gave me a chance to finish the Christmas baking in peace, and I made *Lebkuchen*, *Springerle*, and the last of the fruitcakes. It would be a queer Christmas, with raid shelters being dug in the White House

271

lawn, to spirit the President off in in case of attack, and the Treasury Department had ordered our blackout curtains, and when I could get only one roll of black sateen, they went to the trouble of commandeering more, so I finally got every window in the White House either painted black or covered with black sateen. We all carried little dimmed-out flashlights, and getting around nights in Washington became a problem.

All around the White House streets were blocked off and bristled with soldiers, police, and Secret Service men.

The talk was ugly. "Strange planes off Florida. Subs off New Jersey. Santa Barbara shelled by Jap submarine."

The big house at 1600 Pennsylvania Avenue had become the war headquarters of the United Nations.

But with all affairs canceled, and even our annual egg-rolling considered too dangerous, we were doing a hectic amount of entertaining behind those blacked-out windows. Everyone who came now had something to do with the war.

I saw to it we saved all the fats, waste paper, and tin cans, and wound up a first-aid course, and went back to knitting, and was surprised to find my fingers had grown rusty. For the first time I wanted the clock turned back. I wanted to be younger and take a more valiant part in things. As it was, I was working harder than ever before.

The war was doing a lot toward bringing older men to the front—Hull, Knox, Borah, and older women too. It seemed a pity that it took world tragedy to make people realize their possibilities. I'd get scared of everything sometimes, but my metaphysical training helped, and what had helped me most through the bad time after Dad had died was my going to and fro between the White House and home with the car pool. My boys, and a half-dozen others, shared Buck's car, and they'd take me along on their way to their offices, and it would be wolf calls and whistles all the way to the White House door.

Not dignified, but it took your mind off things.

And the war brought so many young folks into Washington, and my spare couch was hardly ever empty, with beds so hard to find. Young folks, with their problems and triumphs, keep us knowing it's all worth while!

To get back to Mr. Churchill. The ushers were on duty twenty-four hours a day while he was there, and I never knew how many for meals. He and the President were always together, and they'd have in the Army and Navy and State Department heads, and other high officials, and there was organizing and plotting and planning going on all over the place. Once there was a big conference on in the Cabinet Room, and Mrs. Roosevelt asked them all to stay for lunch, and there they were all sixty-eight, on very short notice. In your own home you can open up a package of spaghetti and make out, but not in the White House. I was trying to buy close and not get extras in, but that wasn't easy, with the English around.

Even Mr. Churchill looked poor-colored and hungry, though he was heavy-set and, one could tell, had enjoyed good living. But they had pared to the bone over there, holding Hitler at bay, so I tried to feed them up while we had the chance. Every time the Churchill group came, it seemed we couldn't fill them up for days. Once we cooked for guests who didn't come, and offered it to some of the Englishmen who had just risen from the table, and they sat right down and ate the whole meal through, straight over again.

I was surprised, when I first saw Mr. Churchill, to find him smaller than I'd expected. The camera was misleading in his case, as in so many others. Mrs. Roosevelt, for one. I'd almost cry over the way some pictures made her look. They couldn't show her queenliness and kindliness, and the deep, warm human friendliness. How could they call her homely! She was beautiful.

Mrs. Roosevelt said one had to be philosophical about pictures.

I'd watched the experts setting up colored maps all around the new map room, with the door locked, and an armed guard before the door. This was our first map room, put up overnight in the Monroe room for Churchill's first visit, and later, when war was declared, a regular map room was fixed on the lower floor, next to the doctor's office. After seeing things set up I never saw the maps again, just rapped on the door when I wanted anyone, or had to take a boy in to clean.

"Send us a dumb one," they'd say, and I'd pick out one I knew wouldn't be interested in military plans, and when the boy and I would go in, the maps would be covered over. Just the same, that room had to be immaculate.

When the waste paper was carried out, officers up to majors would march out with the waste to the incinerator, and watch until every scrap of paper was burned.

This was where I met Mr. Churchill, looking all preoccupied, because he was planning a speech. I'd seen him only in photographs before and he looked enormous, like a mound, so I was surprised to see that in reality he looked almost slender and dapper in his dinner clothes, not over one hundred and sixty pounds, I'd say.

He went around in zipper suits, and the house boys we sent down with him on a two weeks' visit he made to Florida reported that he went swimming in the nude, and the Secret Service boys were upset.

This first visit Mr. Churchill's secretary phoned me.

"Could you get any soap for the Prime Minister?"

"What kind would you like?" I asked.

"Oh, any kind. Just soap."

He sounded as if he couldn't believe I could.

It seemed pathetic that while we could still get English

soaps, they couldn't. His valet came down and picked out over fifty dollars' worth and paid me, and I guess the Prime Minister wanted them as gifts, because he never asked again. But no sooner were they back in England than back came his photograph, with a nice message and a message for me, signed, Winston Churchill. I was so pleased that he would be that thoughtful in such terrible times.

It was a relief to know they'd reached home safely. Submarines had been lying in wait in the Atlantic for his departure, but he fooled them again, and went by air.

Mrs. Churchill, too, when she came over, was just as friendly. She sprained her ankle, and had asked me to come up to see her and had me perch on the bed so we could talk. She was interested in the way the White House was run, and how we managed rationing, and all sorts of things. She had true beauty, with a lovely English skin and large, expressive eyes, young as a girl mentally, and as animated when she talked.

She gave me her photograph, too, signed.

Once, after she left, she sent me a note from 10 Downing Street, Whitehall, London, saying she was returning some books she had been reading in the White House and packed in her luggage by mistake.

I got quite a few notes like that, with spoons and napkins, usually, that had been taken by mistake, but usually they were anonymous, or just signed "a guest." I was always glad to get them back, especially the napkins.

One woman sent me an old pillow. Her beloved husband had died on it, she wrote, and he had admired the President so, she knew Mr. Roosevelt would want it.

We started running short on linen, though I'd stocked up ahead soon after the war started. The men sat so long at table, and were so interested, that a rash of cigarette burns broke out in our tablecloths. They couldn't be replaced, and had to be rewoven, and I was desperate.

I asked Mrs. Roosevelt, "Do you think the President can keep an eye on the tablecloths?"

"Of course not!" she said, pretty sharply for her, and I realized it had been a preposterous suggestion.

So I asked Fields to watch, and he came down grinning.

"The President burnt a hole himself," he said, "and when he saw it, he looked around guilty-like, and put his salt cellar over it quick."

That story that went the rounds about Mr. Churchill and the orange-blossom cocktail, well, I let that go in one ear and out the other. I don't believe it. If he offered the Prime Minister gin and orange juice, he did it as a joke, and he wasn't playing in a light vein in those days. Also, he was too good a host. He drank scotch when he drank, and kept it in a panel in his study, and the Prime Minister was also a scotch drinker. They liked the same foods: grilled kidneys, and roast beef, and game. The President was particular about the menus these days, anxious to please our guests and Allies. We were all doing our best to make the Churchill group feel happy and at home.

I remember his ordering creamed chicken for "Mr. Brown." Maybe Mr. Molotov wanted to taste it, as an American dish.

Somebody in Greenland sent the President the hindquarter of a musk ox frozen solid. It was dark and looked dreadful, and the Secret Service tested it, but the President liked it.

He knew how he wanted everything. With all the stress of World War II coming down on him, he'd write me little notes:

"FDR to Mrs. N—Feathered game should never be plucked until just before it is eaten. Taking off the feathers dries up the meat."

March 17, 1942, was Mr. and Mrs. Roosevelt's thirty-seventh wedding anniversary. I'd planned an extra nice dinner, with turkey and all the things they liked, and sprang it on her as a surprise that morning. She seemed so pleased.

"I'm especially happy," she said, "because I've asked the Norwegian Crown Prince and Princess to dine with us."

So for once I was a jump ahead of Mrs. Roosevelt.

She had a little pot of shamrock on her table. Mr. Reeves, even with the greenhouses closing, had not forgotten. It gave me a queer turn, remembering Dad and the way life had turned over for me, and how the world itself was turning upside down. Then I went back into my office, and there was a little pot of shamrock. Mr. Reeves had not forgotten how Dad had started the shamrock tradition, and even sent off for seeds to Ireland.

It was just as if Dad had left it there.

We were certainly breaking out in a rash of company.

This summer we had Lord Beaverbrook and President of the Philippines Quezon—his land was in the hands of the Japanese—and the Minister of New Zealand, Mr. Nash, and President Prado of Peru. He was the one who ordered the funny breakfast, including cauliflower. Nearly all the South American Presidents came. And we had the Duchess of Luxemburg again, and the King of Greece, with full honors, and King Peter of Yugoslavia, and Queen Wilhelmina, and Alexander Woolcott and Joseph Lash.

I find in my diary quite often for this year: "Send car to meet Mr. Woolcott."

Mr. Woolcott talked on the radio.

He wanted service, though he did it with humor, and I must say having Mr. Woolcott and coffee rationing arrive at the same time were a strain. He was irascible and impatient, and the floor boys were afraid of his sharp tongue, then he'd say something funny to make them laugh, so they couldn't resent him.

Mr. Churchill was also outspoken in asking for what he wanted, but he was never unpleasant about it.

277

People used to wonder how Joseph P. Lash came to be an honored guest in the White House. We'd gotten him along with the youth movement, which wasn't allowed to meet in the White House any more but had to go to one of the auditoriums. Mr. Lash was one of the leaders. Well, the answer to him was, I think, Mrs. Roosevelt's belief in freedom of speech. He tried to get a commission, and couldn't, and had to enlist as a private.

There were a lot of questions asked about Mr. Lash visiting so often in the White House.

I thought I knew why Mrs. Roosevelt wanted to shelter so many. To give them a chance. She knew at second-hand how tough the world could be. And when others criticized certain people practically living in the White House that Dutch streak in Mrs. Roosevelt would widen and she'd hold on to her friendships, and you wouldn't have her any other way.

Queen Wilhelmina had breakfast on the White House porch during her stay and was honored by the Army and Navy bands playing in the rain. I'd expected a homely woman, but she was lovely. I gasped the first time I saw her coming in to dinner, all in black lace and pearls, with her gray hair beautifully done, and her walk so graceful. I wonder how royalty learns to walk so well. She and Mrs. Roosevelt took the worst pictures of any I know.

She was simple in her ways and absolutely without ostentation, but I was told she was the richest woman in the world, one of the shrewdest of businesswomen, and the best informed. The way she carried herself, with such dignity, and the calm, quiet air she had, sitting at dinner on the President's right, you'd never know she was one of the world's most powerful rulers, now in exile, having been driven out of Holland before Hitler's bombs.

She stayed only a short time, but her daughter Juliana came often. She was plainer than her mother, and very friendly,

278

and both the Roosevelts liked her. We worked up quite a romantic feeling about Juliana, because her marriage to Prince Bertrand was a love match, and we heard she was over here saving the dynasty, so we were all happy when a third child was born in exile, in Canada, on Holland soil. They fixed it somehow so that it could be done.

Maybe I leaned too heavily on sweetbreads during the Queen's visit, because after she left I had a little note:

August 8, 1942—Memo for Mrs. Nesbitt:

"I do not want any more sweetbreads until October first —FDR."

King Peter of Yugoslavia came in this month, July, and was officially greeted under the magnolias, and I rushed outside to see if everything was all right, and to get a good place to watch from, and I collided with the President sailing around some bushes in his chair. I almost pitched over him.

"Well, that was a near spill!" he said, with that great big wonderful grin, as if he hadn't a thing on his mind. He had his entourage around him, and he was always cheerful when they were with him. But sometimes I'd come into a room where he was alone, when the jovial air had dropped off and he looked tense and tired. Withdrawn is the only word I know to describe him. Only then could you see what he was going through.

Once, in New York, I stayed over at the Roosevelt home and she put me for the night in the President's room, since he wasn't there. I couldn't sleep, looking up at all the paraphernalia over and around his bed, pulleys and weights and stretching devices that had helped that mighty will of his to make him walk again. Once he told someone the biggest moment of his life had been when he found he could wiggle his toes.

Only a man as brave as that, who could smile like that, was capable of carrying the world burdens that were on him now.

When I saw King Peter I was glad we were having a hearty meal for him, with chocolate and raspberry ice cream, coconut balls, and candy for dessert. He was only nineteen, just a slip of a boy, but no look of boyhood to him. He tried to be pleasant and smile, but he looked hunted. With or without a crown, youth was being pushed around in this new world. I pity all people wearing crowns, particularly if they're young. Underprivileged, you might call them.

We had another social event this July. Mrs. Roosevelt ordered a wedding cake for Mr. Hopkins, and twenty-four little boxes with the bride and groom's initials on to give to the guests.

"I think it should be fruitcake," she wrote. "The lady's name is Louise Macy."

His southeast suite had to be done over. He was so busy with his job and the war that he didn't notice anything about his room, and the canopy of the bed fell down once, and he hadn't said a word about it.

His irregular fare still had me in a tizzy, but he'd been skimming around a lot, among other places to England and Russia. He'd taken along some Virginia hams, one hundred razor blades, twelve dozen cartons of cigarettes, toothpaste and shaving cream, and had seemed surprised when I'd made him produce his empty toothpaste tubes before he could get full ones.

On July 30 Mr. Hopkins and I met in the hall, and he was on his way to be married in the study, and looked real nice.

He was always friendly when he felt well.

"Come along and see me married," he said, but I didn't, thinking it was Mrs. Roosevelt's place to ask me, if anyone did.

All this summer the lower hall was torn up for the new water and sewer pipes, and we teetered along on planks, expecting to break our necks. We were going on ten years in the White House, and still remodeling. Each time the

President and some V.I.P. went through the hall, the poor fellows toiling away in the heat would have to lay down a temporary floor and go out, and come back and tear it up again after the President was by.

A lot of my war troubles started in November with the coffee rationing. Mayor La Guardia in New York said we should "save the grounds and boil them again," and the President made some facetious remark, and I opened my mouth and put my foot in it. "I'd rather have one good cup of coffee and go without the next," was all I said, but the papers played it up and people took it seriously, and pretty soon I was swamped with letters, praising or scolding. It didn't seem of vital importance to me, considering all else going on.

I met Mr. Hopkins in the hall again this November and he just stared right through me without speaking. Not one hint of recognition. Trays came back just barely mussed up. There were more burns on the tablecloths than ever. I didn't know what was brewing, but the war heads were thick in the White House, all in conference, and they'd come out of the map room stary-eyed with concentration.

Captain McCrea, who was always passing quips, didn't even speak.

As usual, I didn't want to know. I just prayed. November 7, 1942, I learned along with the outside world what the tension meant.

That day our troops invaded Africa.

I felt better when the President announced this Thanksgiving was "just another Thursday" and we were to "work as usual." It made Thanksgiving easier to bear with our boys away fighting. I worked on the fruitcakes, not so many for the White House this year as for the boxes for boys overseas. Mrs. Roosevelt was sending thirty-three, with a fruitcake in every box, to say nothing of other things. But I made up my mind that the White House would have its plum pudding as usual, and I worked on that.

Mrs. Roosevelt went over the Christmas menu and crossed off some items. We were getting ready for rationing.

The Potomac flooded, we conserved heat and had to wear sweaters inside the White House. Prime Minister H. E. Wladislaw Sikorski came from Poland, Mr. Woolcott and coffee rationing descended on us together, and all of a sudden 1942 was over.

It had been the swiftest and strangest of all our White House years. It had left us names to weep for—Corregidor, Lidice, Dunkirk. I still couldn't take it in. It seemed hard to believe American boys—boys we knew—were fighting alongside British troops on the sands of Africa.

Chapter Twenty-two

The President came back from Casablanca in time to meet Madame Chiang Kai-chek, who visited us in February '43 and again in April.

February 17 Mrs. Roosevelt gave me a ticket to hear Madame Chiang talk in the Senate, and I went to hear her, and must say I was impressed. Her plea was for China, and she swept us all off our feet speaking of freedom and democracy, and using some words I'd never heard before. She stayed ten days, but I never saw her close. She wasn't democratic like the Queen and Mrs. Churchill.

All the while she talked before the houses I'd been thinking of the sheets. She wasn't well, and spent a lot of time in bed, and every time she got out, even for a short time, both sheets, the two pillow slips, and the blanket spread, silk with lace insertings and lace edges, had to be changed fresh. Even the sheets were soft, and she'd brought them with her. The fresh spread had to be sewn back on, so no touch of blanket could harm Madame Chiang, as it seemed she was allergic to wool. I couldn't help wondering how she had managed, as a girl in that Wesleyan Methodist school in the South, or while she was campaigning with the general in China.

I forgot how much it cost to clean the sheets and spreads, but it was very fussy and expensive, her getting in and out.

Mrs. Roosevelt knew about it, but of course she wouldn't

mention it, any more than I would. We'd been raised in the same faith about guests—when they are in the house, they dominate. All guests are honored guests. That was the rule in my home, and she had been reared by it too. So we never mentioned things.

The President would argue with a guest, but in such a cute way, both sides would be laughing. All the Roosevelts argued among themselves. It was part of their high spirits—they each had an opinion and wanted to voice it.

Those silk spreads were on all the White House beds except the President's. He used seersucker, because he liked his books and papers with his breakfast, and the children climbed up, and Fala.

Two nurses sat on duty in the room next to Madame Chiang's, night and day, and I set Maggie to wait on the nurses. We did all we could to make her stay comfortable, and I think it was, for Madame Chiang seemed to enjoy her meals, all light foods.

While she was with us this February I started wrestling with rationing along with every other housekeeper in the land.

The Office of Price Administration would allot us rationed foods, two months at a time, on the basis of the number of meals served. I went back through the whole period of 1942, broke it down into months, then into meals, and compiled the quantities of the different kinds of food now rationed, sugar, coffee, meat, canned goods, and so on. Then I had to translate the ounce weight of the canned and packed goods into pounds.

The catch was, the ration board picked out our past three months to judge from, which happened to be "family months" and the lightest in White House entertaining. But they rated us by these, and when the outburst of spring entertaining started, we began running close to the grain.

I had counted on just the Roosevelts and Hopkinses, then

284

in one month I had to stretch our points to feed four Presidents, one Prime Minister and his war-starved entourage, and a return engagement of Madame Chiang Kai-chek.

We had to send back some wonderful thick steaks and beef roasts that Amon Carter sent up to the President because we did not have enough stamps to pay for them. Ration stamps. This was keen anguish to me. They were such luscious-looking steaks they made my mouth water. Cruel, I'd say.

But the Board wasn't interested. They wrote us down as an institution, which classed the White House in with vessels and tugboats.

Also, because we had a sugar surplus of three hundred pounds, though it was no more than our share, I was able to check back some sugar coupons, which made me proud at the time, but later, when I wanted lemonade sugar for our veterans, I came to rue this nobility.

Of course we cut down the big-scale entertaining to about half, and served only three courses to a formal dinner, soup usually, the entree, and dessert. But the steady flow kept on to lunch and afternoon teas.

I thought smaller meals a fine idea, sending people away from the table satisfied but not stuffed, and I don't think we'll ever go back to those teeming dinner tables of our mother's day. Those days, a woman felt ashamed if she couldn't put her guests down to three or four kinds of meat, fish, and fowl, and half-a-dozen desserts.

The Roosevelts, even the children, were brought up on simple meals and preferred fruit desserts to the richer, which I still hold to be the secret of the bounding Roosevelt vitality. He and she both preferred cheese and crackers and fruits to dessert. So now desserts were for guests. They loved chicken and fish and eggs, so rationing for the Roosevelts would have been no problem at all.

But some of our house guests objected, and the help complained most when we had to cut down on meat.

It was a puzzle to make the cooks understand there was a war on. They just had to have more chocolate, more sugar, more butter, they said, or they couldn't cook.

Well, they learned. We had meatless days, as I thought that was the best way to stretch. Butter for breakfast only. Dry rolls in the White House for dinner and lunch. No more whipped cream on the clam bouillon. Food sautéed in bacon fat instead of butter. One cup of coffee a day, except for foreign visitors, with a pitcher of hot milk alongside, so the drinker could "stretch" his own. Mr. and Mrs. Roosevelt, fortunately, liked their café-au-lait, but I still say I'd rather have one demi tasse than a gallon of whitish coffee. We couldn't get corned beef for a time. Nor ham. Not even the ham hocks we liked for flavoring pea soup.

For the first time I learned the value of stew. It takes art and a knowledge of herbs to make a good stew. The Europeans have it all over us in that respect. They had to learn the trick of superior dishes, with their inferior meats.

Some of our sweet-saving salads were Bar Le Duc—cottage or cream cheese on lettuce, with currant conserve, and a French dressing flavored with tarragon or mint.

Another was apricot salad, of sliced canned cots on lettuce covered with walnuts chopped fine and French dressing.

For these sweet salads we made the dressing of cider vinegar with the juice of peaches or apricots.

Apricots with broiled chicken breast is a nice luncheon dish, especially for ladies.

Dishes like these took the place of dessert.

We did all right at first, and I decided rationing wasn't too bad. Then I met my Waterloo in Mr. Churchill and the roast beef of Old England. That was in the spring, a couple of months after rationing started. We had the usual rash of heads of nations, including the Presidents of Bolivia, Czechoslovakia, and Liberia, which last was very interesting, a colored man from a colored country. All were received with full honors and given filling official meals.

Anthony Eden arrived in March, and was no trouble at all, taking things as he found them. He was one person who looked handsomer in pictures than in real life, though he was a handsome man naturally. He was Foreign Minister in the British Cabinet, so as a friendly gesture I thought up a foreign-sounding meal, and we had Russian borsch for the soup, roast beef and Yorkshire pudding for England, Harvard beets in honor of the President's college, and spinach for America.

Senator Connolly of Texas was at the dinner, and I heard he asked Eden:

"Wouldn't this be a good repast for England?"

Eden answered ruefully, "It would."

He was leaving at noon, March 30, and at eleven twenty-five the President sent down word he wanted to send along a parting gift with Mr. Eden—grapefruit, lemons, limes, and bananas. A truck raced downtown to bring back fruit packed on the double.

May brought Mr. Churchill back, and others coming and going, all planning the winning of the war. Once I looked out on the lawn and saw at one time the President and Prime Minister Churchill, Field Marshal Sir John Dill, Lieutenant General Sir Hastings L. Ismay, and goodness knows how many more. It was a garden party, and I counted twelve noblemen who were war leaders, among them Lord Halifax.

All these admirals, lords, commanders, generals, chiefs of staffs, and deputy chiefs were, to me, so many hungry mouths to feed.

Because one member of Churchill's party happened to mention that in England each person was allotted one egg a month, I ordered plenty of eggs for our English guests and all the orange juice they could drink.

These were unrationed, but also, I knew their love for roast beef, which was practically non-existant in England, so I splurged. Our allowance of beef was in the deep freeze, but I hauled it out, and we prepared to treat our British allies.

Well, the usual happened. At the last minute extra guests! I had to scurry around for more beef, and for the next three or four months the entire White House household had to skimp along on twenty-one points a day.

I wouldn't go whining to the ration board for extra stamps and get us all in the papers.

Mrs. Roosevelt got home one morning in time for breakfast after a defense trip, and I told her all about it.

"It's chicken for company from now on," I warned her.

"Then chicken it is," she said cheerfully. "Chicken and fish."

Some of the house guests complained, of course, but they were complaining anyway. In thirteen years in the White House I learned one odd fact. Big people do not complain.

Now I had two sets of affairs to balance, the White House money and the ration books. Since we were an institution, I drew on my ration account at the bank. Both accounts had to balance.

Also, if anyone in the White House left the White House, the President, or Mrs. Roosevelt, or any member of the family, and was away for more than seven meals, they had to take their ration books with them. I just came across his among my papers. Issued to Franklin Delano Roosevelt, and so few of the stamps are gone. I'll turn it over to the Library of Congress, with other papers. I kept all the ration books in my office, and counted noses, and did my best.

Ruth had married, and I had a new assistant, my neighbor Mary E. Sharpe, whose husband was overseas. Later she took over as housekeeper for the Trumans after I retired.

Housekeepers came to the fore along with the war effort and a lot of people were interviewing me. Newspapers and magazines wrote I was noted for my thrift and way with left-overs. But some anti-Roosevelt papers claimed the White House was getting food illegally.

Let me say now we adhered strictly to every law laid down.

We had to serve wines with all this royalty coming over, which was only done in the family on festive days. This cut into our budget so heavily that the State Department paid for it. Dad had fixed the wine cellar, with the racks across, where we kept the wines, and the President and General Watson and Harry Hopkins kept their private stock there too. The President kept his key upstairs, and only he and his guard had access to it, and the head butler and I had the other keys.

Now, during the war, the wine started disappearing, then our whiskies and fine brandies, even champagne.

Our staff was all out of the White House nights, so they weren't guilty.

I reported to the Secret Service. I was feuding with them just then over the damask couches. They got tired and bored nights, no doubt, with nothing to do, and they'd lie on the couches upstairs, leaving oily stains, until I sent them pillows. Padlocks were put on the wines, and they still vanished.

Not only liquor, but food. The butter shortage was on, and our butter and fine cheese just melted. Dad's storeroom, where he had kept the olives and canned delicacies, was constantly raided.

The Navy Department fixed straps over the iceboxes. Those boxes were padlocked and strapped in ways that would baffle Houdini. It didn't help.

It got so bad I was bewildered. I told Mr. Crim, "Here are the keys to the wine cellar. I want nothing to do with it." One day he brought in Charles Frederick, the President's new bodyguard. He seemed a nice, refined person.

"You can take over my storeroom," I told him.

I kept cooking liquors, brandy, rum, sherry, port, wines, et cetera, in my storeroom, and they were vanishing too. So I gave Mr. Frederick the keys.

After that I'd come in mornings and hear of things vanishing in the night, and I didn't care. It was out of my hands. Shortly after he took over the situation, things stopped.

In November I went shopping for seventeen yards of green felt to cover the forty-eight-foot table in the East Room where the Treaty of All Nations was signed on the ninth. That was the United Nations Relief and Rehabilitation Administration, and an impressive ceremony. The President looked magnificent sitting at the table signing with the flags of the Allied Nations behind him, and the green felt showed up wonderfully well.

Christmas this year was planned for Hyde Park. It was their first since coming to the White House, and perhaps their happiest, because they liked things best at home, with their big family around them. Their hearts were on the Hudson, and they were packing and shipping things back, because another administration was ending, and they were both tired. He wanted to write history, and he wanted to write the peace. He thought he could adjust the peace where Wilson had failed.

So we went ahead with plans for Christmas. Mrs. Roosevelt wanted a tricycle for little Haven Roosevelt, John's son, and they weren't to be had in wartime. I found a secondhand one for $16.75, and had the White House mechanical department fix it, and the paint department paint it, and we sent it West, good as new, to the President's grandson.

On December 4 the Hopkinses said they were moving out of the White House. She wanted her own home, she said.

The President's appetite had been getting poorer, and he

had gone on a diet that simplified our rationing plans as far as he was concerned at least. He cut out the chocolate desserts he loved, and got so he was almost eating salt-free. The doctor said his dieting was unnecessary, but he was on a reducing streak and wouldn't stop. It was a relief all around when Anna came back and took over. She was wonderful with him, acting as his secretary and right hand, and she could get him to eat when no one else could. She could make him laugh too.

I was certainly glad to see her back. Mrs. Roosevelt was traveling more than ever, and she had to leave me in charge, knowing I'd do my best. But I could relax and know all was well with Anna there.

Sometimes Mrs. Roosevelt would tell me when the President left on trips, and where he was going, and sometimes she didn't. The Stars and Stripes is supposed to fly over the White House only when the President is in residence, but they kept it flying there all through the war. If I did know he was away, I never wrote it down. These were dangerous days, with saboteurs caught landing off our coasts who had been reared in American schools, and the more shame to them.

I tended to my knitting and tried not to know too much.

As a result I was just as surprised as our own American soldiers in Africa were when they looked up just before Christmas to see President Roosevelt driving by in a jeep.

This was in December, and he was returning from Teheran. He and Mr. Churchill and Mr. Stalin met there and agreed to work together "in war and the peace to follow."

They would have, too, if he'd lived.

They said the boys in Africa were dumfounded. "My God, the President!"

But he was home in time for Christmas, and they spent it in Hyde Park, as they'd been longing to these three successive terms.

He wanted to go back. To the sloping hills, the peace of the valley, the Hudson. We all wanted to. Once, before his mother died, I told her how much I longed for Hyde Park.

And she said to me then, in the queerest way: "But you'll never go back."

I wondered later if Sara Roosevelt hadn't been thinking of him as well as of all of us. Once we get out in the center of things, few go back to the quiet and content, until we're carried there by old neighbors.

There was the fishing tackle he kept in his bedroom. He talked of shipping it home, but he didn't get around to it. Meantime it had to be dusted, and while that oil painting of Dolly Madison is considered a White House treasure, I tell you it received no more reverent care than the President's rods and tackle.

The car he could drive himself was at Hyde Park, and it was another reason he had for loving the place. He could drive about and feel free.

There was no freedom in Washington. He was getting seven thousand letters a day. People waited to meet him. Two hundred were waiting the day he flew in from Teheran.

People swarmed in on him, and he loved them, but sometimes he had a look about him, like the loneliest man in the world.

The pictures of his four sons in uniforms were on his desk, along with the little knickknacks he treasured that had to be dusted every morning before breakfast. I think he missed James's arm most. The boys didn't agree with him maybe, but they argued and wrestled, got teased—they had been his companions.

The ugly talk grew worse than ever in '44. The opposition was afraid he'd run again. All sorts of queer stories went the rounds in word and in print.

There was the story that Fala had been left behind on an island in the Aleutians, and that the President had sent a destroyer back to get him, at terrific cost to the nation, of course. The President made a cute talk about it.

"Fala's Scotch soul was furious," he said; "he has not been the same dog since."

But he couldn't always laugh. Not when one of his sons said bitterly, "They won't be satisfied until one of us is killed."

We had no privacy. Not one of us escaped.

Big money didn't want him to stay on. But the people came to the closed White House, and stared from across the patroled street, and you could read the faith on their faces. They were the ones with blue stars in their windows, and gold stars, and Red Cross signs. They were keeping their ration books, saving scrap and fats, and writing letters to their sons overseas. These were the people he was trying to help, and it was for them he ran again, this year, for the fourth time.

Sundays, if I didn't have to go to the White House, I'd stay home and cook. It was my indulgence.

I'd make all the things I liked that couldn't be served in the White House. Old-fashioned, homely dishes that have been part of our family way of living for hundreds of years. Hasenpfeffer, pigs' knuckles, sauerkraut, Sauerbraten, potato cakes, stuffed veal. Now I'm retired, I still like to cook. The grandchildren run in and out, five of them now, the darlings, and there are pretty nearly always cookies tucked away in a jar, with caraway or anise in them, the way my mother fixed them long ago.

Sauerbraten is one of my favorites.

For it I take four pounds of chuck or shoulder pot roast, one large onion cut in quarters, six whole cloves, eight peppercorns, two small bay leaves, and a heaping teaspoon of salt. I place the meat in a deep vessel with spices and vinegar and water to cover, and let it stand two days.

It won't hurt it to stand a week.

Then I drain the meat, heat a dutch oven greased with suet, and brown the meat well all over. It has to cook dry before the browning begins.

Then I add a little of the spiced liquor at a time, cooking it at low till tender. Remove the meat, add a half cup of cream, sour or sweet, and bring up the seasoning to taste.

This is nice with wide noodles, dumplings, or mashed potato, and Hasenpfeffer is made the same way, only with rabbit. Venison can be fixed like this too.

Sauerkraut is a healthy dish, rightly cooked, and is nice boiled with pigs' knuckles or a ham hock. I try to get the kind they make in a barrel around Baltimore. I put the meat right in with the kraut, with water to cover, and caraway seeds, and cook for two hours.

Spetzle are nice served with these. I used one egg, one cup milk, a half teaspoon of salt, beat well, and add enough flour to make a rather thick paste. Have a deep, wide kettle of boiling salted water on the stove, and hold the bowl over it, running the dough into the water and cutting it into thin strips from the edge of the bowl. Cook a few minutes, drain into colander, and keep hot over the hot water while you fry some fine dry bread crumbs in butter until brown. Place the spetzle on a hot platter and scatter the crumbs over.

Cooking such dishes for my family and friends, and making some needlepoint covers for the Monroe room footstools in my spare hours, helped take my mind off the war for a little while at least.

It still takes my mind off anything I want to forget.

Cooking, my mainstay of a lifetime, remains my means of relaxation and medium of social exchange. When I like people, I fix them an apple pie, and when I take a sugary, crusty pie from the oven and set it to cool, I feel the way an artist must when he's finished a picture.

It seems to me when girls, and boys, too, don't learn something about cookery, they rob themselves of a lifetime of pleasure, and it never hurts anyone to learn how to make the best out of little. For young folks trying to save I know of no shorter cut to independence than through the kitchen.

While I miss having a big family, and detest eating alone, still I try to make each meal a separate experiment and adventure, even if it isn't the convivial celebration the simplest family meal can be if it's planned and prepared with affection.

Love has a lot to do with it. Loving people, or liking them, makes one want to tend them well.

Young mothers and wives can find home-making a never-lifting burden unless they learn to think of it as their creative chance to build bones and brains and human life. Stirring in a little love helps lighten the work.

Another thing. I warned my sons when they married, "Don't ever tell your wives how your mother used to do anything!"

The girls worked things out for themselves, and are both wonderful cooks. When the time came that they asked me for recipes, I knew I'd passed the acid test. The ghosts of too many mothers-in-law have darkened the sun in many homes.

I'm getting through this book just in time to start the Christmas baking. Nothing much, compared to what the White House Christmases used to be, but I'll enjoy it down to sugaring the last cookie. Christmas isn't Christmas to me without *Springerle, Lebkuchen*—the little dark cakes made with honey—and stollen, a raised cake with citron, raisins, nuts, and orange and lemon peel. Through the lean years and good, the smell of these cakes baking has lifted the hearts of me and mine.

Chapter Twenty-three

June 6, 1944, I spent the night with my son Buck in his home. Buck was in Communications. At twelve-thirty-seven he was called to the phone. Message censorship. The Allies had crossed the English Channel and invasion had begun.

We made coffee and drank it and waited.

They called again at three-forty-five. General Eisenhower had sanctioned the news broadcast. This time Buck dressed and dashed to his office. I sat on, drinking coffee without tasting it, thinking.

D-Day. This was what we had been waiting for these tense years. I tried to picture it. Then I tried not to. Many of our young friends were fighting this morning, maybe dying. One intimate friend I knew was in the landing. I kept thinking of him.

Probably for our own protection, human imaginings go just so far. This same month a million Chinese died of famine. But we couldn't see those skeleton bodies, not even with the pictures before us. We don't know until it is ours that is malnourished, or in danger. Fear has to strike home with most of us before we know.

That was the strange thing about the Roosevelts. They knew! They knew how frightened people could get, and the way courage can be sapped. I think that was why they listened to so many strange, misplaced characters, brought them in, cared for them, kept them on. I think they would have liked to bring everyone living into the White House and take care of them. Rambunctious youth and dignified old age were listened to there, and with the same respect.

That is the word for them. Respect. They had it for everyone everywhere. You couldn't name a land they didn't know about, or a kind of people they didn't know. It's been said he enjoyed knowing royalty. He certainly did. He also enjoyed knowing and conversing with the White House gardener, Duffy, and a lot of others.

In spite of all that was going on on land, sea, and air, my diary makes no mention of such things, but concentrates on menus and social events, mostly small teas. This was one of the fast years. So much was happening. There were the usual White House upsets, tea and lemonade orders for the spring events, and never enough sugar, and having the Entomology Department in to check up on our cockroaches and ants, and a heavy rain flooding the East Room floor just as we were preparing dinner for Lord Beaverbrook, so eight men were swabbing away at the last minute with brushes and sponges.

I have one item: "Lord and Lady Halifax—shower caps," but I don't recall what that was about.

General de Gaulle arrived and had to be served broiled chicken since we were all but stampless, but we made up for it by giving him a smoked ham and two smoked tongues to take back to France.

The parade of war and official dignitaries kept on. Among other affairs was a stag dinner in honor of the President of Iceland.

Maybe it was he who sent the ptarmigans. The Secret Service men passed them, and when I went into the kitchen to see about fixing them, I was amazed, they were so cute. They weren't like birds at all in their little feather panties and feathered boots, like snowshoes, and all white. They came from Greenland.

The President was getting some curious food gifts this year.

After his Teheran trip teal ducks came from the King of Egypt. Princess Martha brought in a large jar of crayfish, to be used as a course. While he was running for the fourth time Mr. Jesse Jones sent in six pheasants, and he had one for dinner the night he came back from his election.

We kept books on gifts like these, to be sure he got them all.

That time a cold pheasant was eaten by the help, and he asked for it, he was cross because he considered pheasant the greatest of delicacies, not to be wolfed down like a leftover chicken. He could carve a pheasant so one would do for eight. Sometimes I'd worry if we had enough, but Mrs. Roosevelt was always calm.

"Don't worry, the President will manage," she'd say, and he always did.

Three pounds of smelts came in this summer, and the President insisted he wanted some made into fish cakes. This might seem a waste of good smelt to some, but the President loved fish cakes.

We still had an occasional explosion about the food. During the invasion of Normandy, and in other tense times, he'd get into his moods again of not knowing what he wanted. He still had the aversion to beef.

Once he almost shouted: "Damn it, I don't want beef."

"Then what do you want?" Mrs. Roosevelt asked, just as gently.

He calmed down right away.

"I want a steak!"

I was with Mrs. Roosevelt, and that "damn" sounded awfully loud over the phone. That was the only time I ever heard the President swear.

Only when his nerves were drawn to fine wires did things like this happen. I'd see him in the study, against the great map of the world, and think of the power he had, and the

298

struggle to use it well. His was the greatest responsibility of any man alive.

He looked thin and worn, but his mind was acute—too fast-working for the rest of us, I'd think sometimes. It seemed as if a lot of his worries came from having thought too far ahead, and he was worn out waiting for the rest of us to catch up.

His meals were all he had to vent his irritation and worry on, and he did it only when worries were too great. Mary, the Irish girl we had inherited from his mother, was the President's cook, and he liked her cooking. Mary was awed neither by ration points nor Presidents, and did things her own way.

It made me cross, in October, seeing the President leave for New York, to drive all over those drizzly streets with Mayor La Guardia in the campaign.

"It's cruel, his driving around like that," I said to Mrs. Roosevelt. "Why do you let him?"

"He loves it," she said.

She meant he loved people, and he truly did. He wouldn't disappoint the New Yorkers waiting in the rain.

They were at Hyde Park on election night, and there was a torchlight parade. We'd been pretty certain all along he would be elected President of the United States for the fourth time. No one else had the world situation grasped so completely.

He was back on the tenth, greeted by three hundred and thirty thousand Washingtonians, with seven bands, in the pouring rain. We gave him a rousing reception in the Diplomatic Reception Room. Everyone in the White House was there to receive him and congratulate him.

He had a big, excited grin and a warm handshake for everyone. He seemed joyous.

November 19, 1944, I wrote:

"I am at present making plans for the FOURTH inauguration, the first in history.

"The President is going to make the inauguration very simple, as will be the collation. No parade. This will· do away with all the building of grandstands and save lumber, time, and expense. For this I am profoundly grateful, for this means that I do not have to feed sixteen hundred people after the President is sworn in and before the start of the parade. . . . We cannot have sandwiches, since there is no butter in any such quantities, or filling either."

I was wrong again. Two thousand were asked.

The pinch of rationing made itself felt worse that December.

Even chicken, our standby, was scarce by this time. I put over what I thought was a masterly deal, buying three dozen chickens from a farmer. But it didn't work out after all, because the chickens weren't frozen properly and weren't much good.

My December diary is mostly food worries, and though the Battle of the Bulge was on, and I spent every spare minute by the radio, there is still no mention of world events. I never wrote anything down, no matter if the news had been released. The safety of the man who was America's only fourth-term President was the major concern of all who were close to him. Everyone who had access to my office had been investigated. Still, one never knew.

Safest to stick to menus and dinner lists. I had a self-made ruling. If it's vital, don't write it.

December 10, 1944, my diary:

"We are going top speed and no fooling. Christmas boxes to pack. The shipping clerk has been busy with Mrs. R's boxes getting them sent off for some weeks. . . .

"Mrs. R has been entertaining the veterans and still is, each Sunday and two days a week. They have movies and then some beer and pretzels, potato chips, or something of that sort, and punch with cookies. On the afternoons they go to football games they are served hot coffee, cake, and cookies.

"This has been continuous since early in November."

Fruitcakes were out this year. Materials were too hard to get, of too poor quality, and too high when you found them.

I had been making them for the Roosevelts every Christmas for eighteen years.

But I made my mind up there would be a plum pudding on the Christmas table! That was the supreme moment of the Roosevelt year, when the pudding came in on its silver tray, set in holly, with the blue flame of the brandy lighting up the circle of old and young faces. No matter what President Roosevelt's worries were, he looked his happiest then.

So I made the plum pudding.

This is the old English way, the one my mother-in-law taught me, and the Roosevelts liked it best.

One and a half pounds each of grated bread crumbs (use bread a day or two old), seeded raisins, currants, brown and white sugar (half and half). One pound kidney suet chopped fine. One half pound each mixed orange and lemon peel and cut walnuts. One teaspoon each nutmeg, mace, cinnamon, one fourth teaspoon cloves, and twelve eggs.

I beat my sugar and eggs to a cream, mix in the suet and bread crumbs, then blend in everything; moisten with sherry, grapejuice, or brandy, and steam in molds for three hours.

The Christmas pudding looked fine that year, and I'm still glad I made that particular one.

Just before the fourth inauguration the President came downstairs. He wanted me to go into the vault back of Dad's office and find his family Bible. This was an heirloom, printed in Dutch, that had come from Holland with his family, and he always used it in taking his oath of office.

He waited, and I searched, and it wasn't there.

He sat waiting in his chair, withdrawn and so quiet, I found myself holding my breath, not to intrude. Usually I found him overpowering, not in manner, because he made everyone around him feel of equal importance, but I felt I had nothing to offer by way of talk, as my ideas were so insignificant compared to all he was going through. Besides, my contact was seldom with him. I belonged on the distaff side of the White House, so to speak.

Now I looked at him, the massive head, the fine, proud features graying. He looked drawn, not as bad as the newspaper pictures made him, but tired to the point of an inhuman loneliness.

Sitting there, with his head sunk down and thoughtful, the whole world seemed pulling him down. He hadn't wanted the third term. He didn't want this fourth. But he was the only man who could carry things through as planned and hoped for. The only one who knew all sides, and could hold them firm.

I could hardly speak.

"I'm sorry," I said. "But the Bible isn't here."

He looked up, slow and surprised, thinking I was upset about the Book.

"Don't worry about it," he said kindly; "it must be some other place."

He was drawing near the end. We all felt it. We prayed for its coming, thinking it would be the war's end, not his.

Chapter Twenty-four

President Roosevelt wanted chicken à la king for his inaugural luncheon, but I had to say, "No, we can't keep that dish hot for two thousand guests."

So Mrs. Roosevelt said, "We'll pare to the bone," and we compromised with the President, and planned for chicken salad, rolls without butter—I hoped the salad would be rich enough to make them forget the butter—unfrosted cake, and coffee.

That called for ninety gallons of coffee, two hundred chickens, one hundred and seventy dozen rolls, one hundred and sixty-five cakes, and one hundred gallons of coffee. Three buffet tables, one in the East Room, one in the State Dining Room, another downstairs on the lower floor, and one hundred extra waiters for those who couldn't reach the tables.

Two thousand for lunch was really too many, but I didn't say anything.

This was one inaugural I was determined not to miss. I had everything seen to in advance, and went outside under the South Portico, and saw it all.

The other inaugurals had been spectacles. This was quiet. Family prayers inside the house, and outside the oath-taking, and the band playing "Hail to the Chief" for the fourth time, followed by prayer. Mary Sharpe and I stood under the magnolia trees while the President took the oath.

No parades this year, no military crushes, no crowds to jam

traffic, no balls. The gray pressure of war cut these away. Just a semi-private back-porch talk of about twenty minutes, and this January 20, 1944, closed down on the first fourth-term inauguration in America's history.

I thought back over the others. To the first, when frightened millions had heard him launch his war against fear. To 1937, when the streets were jammed in the rain, and 1941, when Pennsylvania Avenue shook to the tanks and guns and marching lines, and planes droned savagely over the city, and we knew America was wakening.

This, the quietest, was the most impressive of all.

Suddenly I realized a mild-looking little man was taking the oath of office, and it was Mr. Harry S. Truman, who had been elected Vice-President. I didn't take much notice of him because I had to skip back into the house, since the ceremony was ending and two thousand would be stampeding inside for lunch.

The toughest stretch, as usual, was the interlude between two and four that afternoon, when we cleaned up in preparation of the tea at four-thirty. Eighteen hundred new guests came in then to find the tables spruced up and set over, with tea, cookies, and cake. Two hundred dozen cookies, very small ones, and one hundred unfrosted marble cakes did for the tea and reception for the electors and Democratic party leaders, and that night for the family inaugural dinner I splurged all my ration points on a rib roast—their first in months.

Like everyone else that wasn't buying black market, we were doing the best we could.

January 22 a·note came downstairs from Eleanor Roosevelt:

"I want to send you this little personal note to thank you and all who worked with you—particularly Fields and all the men in the pantry—how grateful I am to you for handling so efficiently the very large crowd which we had on Inauguration Day. Everything went off smoothly, and I know it meant

304

a great deal of work for everyone. Please thank them all for me."

On that same day I find a list in my diary:

Twenty-four dozen eggs.

Caviar.

Oranges.

Two cases of scotch.

One case gin.

Old Grand Dad.

Bottled waters.

I didn't write that these were for the President, and he was taking them with him to Yalta.

Several weeks later, in a place at Yalta, Stalin, Churchill, and Mr. Roosevelt made their plans for the final blasting of Germany.

I saw pictures of them together that made me furious. Since Casablanca, when he'd been taken with Giraud, De Gaulle, and Churchill, the photographs of him were calculated to make him look worn-out and old. He didn't look that poorly. A deliberate plan, it seemed to me, was behind this attempt at making him look so worn.

The photographers of certain papers had always done awful things to the President, and to her, but this year the pictures were worse than ever.

She was looking harassed these days, and people tired her who never had before. There was a limit even for Mrs. Roosevelt. Once we had been relaxed and chatty at the morning conferences, and she was still unfailingly sweet and thoughtful, but I felt I was taking time, and tried to clip our talks. Her minutes were scheduled, she had conferences even at breakfast, and when I read her day's appointment list it would be ten minutes upstairs, ten down, and fifteen minutes at some function or other.

Once she could spare me only three minutes, and wrote of it in "My Day."

Still the notes, memos, letters poured in. She was always in touch with me and with the running of the White House. My desk was piled daily with lists of groceries to be sent here and there, servants to be sent places, the juggling of meals, guests, visits, affairs of all kinds. She kept her eye on all things, like the great housekeeper she was, but when she was gone weeks at a stretch we'd have to carry on.

Someone wrote her a sizzling letter this January:

"Why don't you stay home and keep house like other women?"

His work was her job. When she went places, like over to the war-infested Pacific, when she rubbed noses with that Maori woman, she did it for some purpose that belonged to the President of the United States. The world was her house. She had to keep an eye on its affairs as well as on her own.

We were retaking the Philippines this January. General MacArthur and his troops were rolling toward Manila. Mr. Churchill in London was demanding the unconditional surrender of Germany. Our fourth inauguration had been carried out while a red-hot crusade was going on against the high-priority plane ride given Blaze, Elliott's bull mastiff.

We had trouble with our White House dogs up to the end. The suite the Hopkinses had lived in for so long was just being restored to use again, with the rugs cleaned and mended where Susie, their dog, had done her teething on the corners.

March 13, 1945, I wrote:

"Have twice as much work these days as in the days of yore. So much red tape. The points at times drives one nuts. I have turned this all over to Mary Sharpe."

March 27:

"At the House here we have been entertaining royalty." First Princess Juliana, then the Earl of Athlone who, as Governor General of Canada, received full honors as head of that country. Princess Alice was with him. They had out the bands of honor from the Army, Navy, and Marines, with the Marine

Band playing the national anthems of both countries, first Canada, then ours, all standing meantime at salute out on the South Lawn. The President and Mrs. R. met them at the station."

Every year I think on the fourth of March, the President had a private rededication communion service of his own, in St. John's across the way. I dropped in, as I often did, not knowing this was going on, and was surprised to find the President and his cabinet there. St. John's is Episcopalian, and the Roosevelts were, and our family, too, and I'd seen my sons as choirboys on Christmas Eve and wondered, can those angels be mine!

Once inside I stayed for the service, and marveled at the look of humbleness on the face of a great man asking for guidance.

There is just one item in my diary for April 12, 1945:

"Rep. and Mrs. James W. Trimble of Arkansas will come to lunch."

After that, empty pages.

My diary says the President had gone to Hyde Park with Mrs. Roosevelt on March 24 to spend the week end. The President came back from Hyde Park on March 29 to stay a few hours in the White House, then leave that night for Warm Springs. We had terrapin, one of his favorite dishes, and a man came in from one of the hotels and cooked it, in cream and in the shell, just as he liked it. I was pleased that we had terrapin, and that it turned out just right.

Everything was turning out all right. Everything was turning our way. One thousand planes, in one day, had bombed Berlin. Our planes had bombed Tokyo. Our flag flew again on Mount Surabachi and Corregidor, and the pictures of its raising were enough to make any American cry like a child. Every day showed victory on every side of the world.

307

Nothing but good news—so much, you couldn't take it in.

The President looked weary but happy, and of course he was always eager to get to Warm Springs.

He chatted with the polio patients at the Foundation, played with them in the pool, and taught them the exercises that had made him able to walk again. That cottage they called the Little White House was the place he loved next to Hyde Park. I was never there, but I know that going there, to him, was going home.

April 12 I wrote:

"The President has been away for over three weeks and I do hope he has had a fine rest. He always needs that.

"They tell me, 'they' being Dr. McIntyre, that the President is feeling fine and looks well. I am so happy, for he did look weary when he left.

"We are all weary."

Mrs. Roosevelt looked tired out, but she carried on in the White House, entertaining more veterans than ever, including some servicemen who had been war prisoners.

April 12 I got home from the White House and tuned in to catch the last of the evening's broadcast. My hand was still on the dial when I heard the tag end of the words . . . "The President died."

"The president of some railroad," I thought to myself, then I said it out loud. But I must have known, because I stood by the radio as if I was frozen there. I just stood still and couldn't take it in. Not even when another voice came on: "Franklin Delano Roosevelt, President of the United States, died this afternoon at Warm Springs . . . in his fourth term . . . age sixty-three . . . cerebral hemorrhage . . ."

I stood by the radio a long time. Not listening. Not even thinking. I was still standing there when Garven telephoned from the Pentagon Building to confirm the news and ask if I was all right.

Then I called the ushers at the White House and talked over what had to be done.

When I went down the next morning the flag was at half mast. Mrs. Roosevelt had left for Warm Springs. It was a house of death, but there was no pandemonium, all went smooth as clockwork.

A houseful of people were coming, so I made preparations. Food and meals must go on. Even death could not close those tall white doors.

I had to get things started.

But I felt paralyzed. This was worse than Dad's dying, because Dad had been just ours. This was world death, and the loss of a valiant fighter for that world.

I planned meals, but my mind felt fuzzed, and I couldn't think.

All traffic would be stopped when the cortege came, so I ordered deliveries made, in advance, and filled up the shelves with supplies.

His train came into Washington by night, I think, under guard. The cortege seemed to take forever, moving up Pennsylvania Avenue. So many relatives, and the sons in uniform, and Anna, completely overcome. They all had so much poise, but they were silenced by grief. Mrs. Roosevelt looked tall and slender among them, but under the black veil her face was stricken. Even then she was troubled by the grieving of others. The help were in tears, they were truly mourning, and now the House itself was so paralyzed, I didn't see how I was ever to get it in motion again.

Through the silence and grieving inside came the babble of a woman from New York, who had once sold Mrs. Roosevelt some dresses, and talked her way into the White House. She was as excited over the cortege's arrival as if it were a show. "Oh, isn't it wonderful!" she kept saying. "Isn't it exciting!" She made me think of a bluebottle fly, buzzing away.

From the North Hall window I looked down on the flag-covered coffin, on its caisson, coming so slowly through the North West Gate. All Washington seemed out in the streets, weeping to the sound of the half-dozen bands playing the slow, heartrending music, and there were entire companies of servicemen, Marines, Army, and Navy.

They carried the coffin up the steps and into the White House, and it was like the end of the world—the world he'd hoped for.

Mrs. Roosevelt went right to her room.

Even then she had a million things to remember. She had so much on her mind. She sent for me, and when I went in she was calm and efficient with all plans made. We didn't say much. I do recall my telling her having so much to do would help, just as the President's mother had told me it would, and how it had worked for me.

I don't think anyone saw her cry. But I knew she did. Her words to Mrs. Truman, whose husband was our new President, that she felt sorrier for the people of the United States than for themselves, were prophetic of things to come.

After leaving Mrs. Roosevelt I went in to the East Room and made my way between the flowers. The air was heavy-scented with the funeral pieces, they were stacked to the doors, and that room is eighty feet long. He lay where the dead always lie in state, opposite the corridor door. The casket was shut, and a flag was spread over it, and a soldier stood on guard by his side.

I heard later that in the rich night clubs in New York they lifted champagne glasses that night because he was dead.

Vinegar against the wounds, long ago, of another who looked too deeply into the hearts of the poor and the frightened. Their tears never count for much with those who can toast the death of a great and good man in champagne.

For a time the man lying in the East Room had given back courage and kept it alive. Now the world outside was weeping, and fear spreading again.

I could hear the sound of it, outside on Pennsylvania Avenue, even with the windows of the East Room closed and the
air inside drugged with his flowers.

That was Saturday. Services were at four in the East Room.
Interment would be Sunday, at Hyde Park. Mrs. Roosevelt
sent down word she would like me to go.

It was a sad, slow trip to the station, through all those
weeping faces, and in the Annapolis group that marched on
guard beside his body I saw Bill Lagen, my young nephew,
stiff as a ramrod in his uniform, and his face white with grief.

We boarded the long train and went straight to our sleep-
ers. It was a train of sorrow. When we got off at Hyde Park
it was morning, and when I saw the familiar station and faces
I couldn't help but remember the other times he'd come
home, with the cars and station wagons lined up waiting, and
the familiar welcoming faces.

The day was cold and windy, and I stood watching a freight
car filled with flowers being unloaded. The rose petals kept
blowing off in the wind, which for some reason seemed too
pitiful to bear.

It was all so familiar. The little church again, and the rector,
Rev. Anthony, waiting, and the services at Hyde Park, and
the funeral.

I'm not going to write about it. I don't want to think about
it any more.

Monday morning I got down to the White House early
and went right up to her room for instructions, as if nothing
had happened. We had come down from Hyde Park on the
same train the night before, but I hadn't seen her. She had
all her clothes out of the wardrobes and over chairs, and was
sorting them.

"I'll be out by Friday," she said.

I was thinking she'd never make it, with all there was to do, but at the same time I knew she would. We worked like beavers. There was thirteen years of accumulation to sort out. She wanted to give mementoes of him to so many people, and we had to dig all these things out, and sort them, and send them. She wanted everyone who had known him to have some little thing to remember him by.

She gave me some handkerchiefs, the beautifully embroidered ones with his initials she had made for him.

Everyone in the White House was remembered, and we were sent copies of the wonderful letters of condolence that poured in from all over the world.

I got busy identifying the furniture. Their own furniture had to be sorted out and crated, his bed and hers, and many of the tables were Val-Kil. There were things in the store-room that belonged to the White House, among things that she had paid for, and these had to be identified and packed. We had one stenographer listing, and Mr. Shepherd checking the packing. Books were kept on everything, inventory made, and lists of the contents of all boxes, as storerooms and gift rooms were sorted out.

The worth-while gifts were packed for Hyde Park, and those that were plain junk disposed of.

If anyone had any possible use for anything, Mrs. Roosevelt wanted them to have it. She liked to see things used.

A lot of things went to the colored help, for nearly all had their poor to give to.

Six army trucks had brought the Roosevelt furniture from Hyde Park, including my own bits of furniture, when we came to the White House in 1933. Now thirteen trucks left for Hyde Park, and nothing of mine among them, and so much had been shipped before, in the third term.

She had purchased so many children's things. I think I felt worse when the high chair I had bought was carried out. The

White House had looked bare when we moved in. Now it was not quite so bare, but it seemed empty.

I guess her worst time came when she said good-by to the staff. That was on her last afternoon, April 20, 1945. She said good-by in the East Room to the office staff at three-thirty and to the house staff at four-thirty.

Anna was with her, and Mrs. Helm and Tommy and I, and we were all in tears.

Not one, white or dark, but had some special kindness to remember.

I stayed on until the Trumans got settled. Things seemed quieter and more sedate in the White House. Three people can't fill up a big place like that, and they were a quiet family anyway, and not much given to company.

The first Christmas after his death, 1945, Mrs. Roosevelt sent out cards with pictures of their family group with him in the center, smiling the way we remembered.

The harassments and tensions of her later years were as great as before. She was going on with their work. Her life turned to the United Nations and a peaceful solution of the world's problems, America's problems, and the problems of every human.

She is busier than ever, having fewer around to help, and I know every letter is an additional burden, so I never write. She knows I love her, as a friend and as the world's friend. This book, with all its flaws and the wish that it were better, is dedicated to Eleanor Roosevelt.

I think they both held that the answer lay in progress and in leaders independent of politics. President Roosevelt stood by his ideals and never traded to the machine. In spite of hatred and lies, he proved it was not all-powerful, and by so proving he gave millions the courage to hold on.

I have seen her once since.

313

She came to the White House for some reason. One of the ushers called me, and said she was in the ushers' office. We shook hands. Nothing much was said. It was strange to have her waiting in an office on our corridor. When I went back to my own office I could hear the sound of my own steps in the hall.

It had been a noisy corridor, highway to the world's doings, with Anna's children running in and out of my office, John's baby climbing into my lap, and that great booming Roosevelt laugh sounding from the doctor's office down the hall.

The White House was an official building again.

It had been a happy home. A brave and cheerful pair had lived there while the world was dark.

CPSIA information can be obtained
at www.ICGtesting.com
Printed in the USA
BVHW040705140122
626152BV00005B/273